ADVANCES IN
GROUP PROCESSES

Volume 15 • 1998

ADVANCES IN GROUP PROCESSES

Series Editor: EDWARD J. LAWLER
Department of Organizational Behavior
Cornell University

Volume Editors: JOHN SKVORETZ
Department of Sociology
University of South Carolina

JACEK SZMATKA
Jagiellonian University
and University of South Carolina

VOLUME 15 • 1998

 JAI PRESS INC.

Stamford, Connecticut   *London, England*

ISBN: 0-7623-0362-X

ISSN: 0882-6145

Manufactured in the United States of America

CONTENTS

LIST OF CONTRIBUTORS

Joseph Berger

Department of Sociology
Stanford University

Alison Bianchi

Department of Sociology
Stanford University

R. Thomas Boone

Brandeis University and
Department of Psychology
Assumption College

Michael J.G. Cain

Political Science Department
University of Mississippi

M. Hamit Fisek

Department of Psychology
Bogazici University

Martha Foschi

Department of Anthropology and
    Sociology
University of British Columbia

Elise M. Fullmer

Department of Sociology
University of North Carolina, Charlotte

Stuart J. Hysom

Department of Sociology
Emory University

Michael W. Macy

Department of Sociology
Cornell University

Joanna Mazur

Department of Sociology
Jagiellonian University

Barbara F. Meeker

Sociology Department
University of Maryland

Paul T. Munroe   Department of Sociology
                                  Stanford University

Robert K. Shelly   Department of Anthropology and
                                      Sociology
                                  Ohio University

Steven D. Silver   Laboratory for Social Research
                                  Stanford University

Jacek Szmatka   Department of Sociology
                                  University of South Carolina

Geoffrey Tootell   Department of Sociology
                                  San Jose State University

Lisa Troyer   Department of Sociology
                                  University of Iowa

Murray Webster, Jr.   Department of Sociology
                                  University of North Carolina, Charlotte

SEXUAL ORIENTATION AND OCCUPATION AS STATUS

Murray Webster, Jr., Stuart J. Hysom, and
Elise M. Fullmer

ABSTRACT

Two vignette studies show that both occupation and sexual orientation function as
diffuse status characteristics as that term is used in theories of status generalization.
Volunteers at University of North Carolina, Charlotte, and San Francisco State University completed questionnaires measuring status generalization for two target individuals, men in study 1, women in study 2, differing by sexual orientation and
occupation. Results show *performance expectations* based on both occupation and
sexual orientation. We describe the value of studying status aspects of personal characteristics, and we identify topics and suggest methods for further investigation.

Personal characteristics can powerfully affect social structure and face-to-face
interaction. People notice some characteristics, such as gender, age, and skin color
and may infer others, such as occupation, wealth, education, and sexual orientation.

Advances in Group Processes, Volume 15, pages 1-21.
Copyright © 1998 by JAI Press Inc.
All rights of reproduction in any form reserved.
ISBN: 0-7623-0362-X

Those observations and inferences affect beliefs and behavior, and thus they structure interaction. Here we report two empirical studies of ways that two significant personal characteristics—occupation and sexual orientation—affect beliefs, behavior, and group structure. We use a theory of *status generalization processes* that describes how certain types of characteristics can organize interaction by producing, among other effects, power and prestige structures in small groups.

The group structuring processes of occupation are well known and we use occupation largely as a control variable. Less is understood about ways sexual orientation may affect fact-to-face interaction. Cathryn Johnson (1995), writing in this series, reviewed recent sexual orientation research that examines stereotypes, interpersonal bias, and institutional discrimination facing gay and lesbian individuals. She advanced an argument that sexual orientation is a *diffuse status characteristic*, as that term is used in theories of status generalization. The literature she reviewed supports that argument by showing that different states of sexual orientation (heterosexual, gay male, and lesbian) are differentially evaluated in contemporary American society.

We extend this line of work by reporting here the first independent empirical test of a claim that sexual orientation may act as a status characteristic. We also explore how orientation's effects interact with views on desirability of heterosexuality and with the other status characteristic, occupation. Not only are heterosexual and homosexual persons differentially evaluated, but also we show that differential expectations for competence attach to sexual orientation. Most of the competency expectation differences between gay and straight individuals would not be predicted by previous research on stereotyping on the basis of sexual orientation.

THE THEORY OF STATUS GENERALIZATION

Status generalization is a process that structures face-to-face interaction around *status characteristics* individuals bring to group situations. The effects occur in collective task focused interaction situations; that is, where individuals gather for the purpose of solving some problem.[1] Examples of situations within the theory's scope include committees, teams, and juries.

The process begins when individuals' status characteristics become *salient*. Characteristics generally become salient if they differentiate individuals, or if people already have reason to believe the characteristics are relevant to the group's task. For instance, when individuals in a group see gender or skin color differences, those characteristics become salient. Next, according to processes described in the theory, individuals form *performance expectation states* based on salient characteristics. Expectation states are anticipations of ability to perform whatever task is before the group. They have the same value as society's value of the status characteristics: high expectations form for individuals having the socially defined positive state of a status characteristic, and low expectations form for individuals having the negative state. Individuals with positively valued states of a characteristic thus are expected to perform better at whatever tasks the group may face. Performance expectations function as a theoretical construct. Though not directly observable, they have observable consequences on behavior and group structure. For instance, high performance expectations lead to conscious beliefs about competence and leadership, higher interaction rates, deference, agreement, and positive evaluations from others. These advantages and disadvantages, taken together, constitute the *power and prestige structure* of a group. (For fuller presentation with discussion of the theory, please see Berger, Norman, Balkwell, and Smith 1992; or Fisek, Berger, and Norman 1995; for evidence supporting the theory, see Berger, Fisek, Norman, and Zelditch 1977; Berger et al., 1992; or Webster and Foschi 1988).

SEXUAL ORIENTATION AND OCCUPATION AS DIFFUSE STATUS CHARACTERISTICS

To support an instantiational claim that something is a diffuse status characteristic, we must show it meets the explicit theoretical definition of that term.

> D is a diffuse status characteristic if and only if: (1) there are at least two states, differentially evaluated in the society; (2) for each state, there are *specific performance expectations*, such that people in one category are expected to be able to perform some task better than people in another category; and (3) there also are associated *general expectations*, such that people in one category are thought to have greater ability at "most tasks" (Wagner and Berger 1993, p. 28).

Thus gender is a status characteristic in our society because (1) there are social advantages and disadvantages associated with its states; (2) men are thought more competent at various specific skills and abilities, such as quantitative reasoning than are women; and (3) men are thought to be better at "most tasks" than are women.[2]

We believe both occupation and sexual orientation readily meet the definition of a diffuse status characteristic in the theory.

That occupation has differentially evaluated states (part 1 of the definition) is well documented by studies of occupational prestige (for instance, Hodge, Siegel, and Rossi 1964; Miller 1991, pp. 341-351; Nakao and Treas 1994; Treiman 1977). We know from other studies that competencies often are inferred from occupations as well (parts 2 and 3 of the definition). The theory of status generalization therefore offers an explanation for effects of occupation such as Strodtbeck, James, and Hawkins' (1957) observations that jurors with managerial jobs interacted more, exerted more influence over verdicts, and were more likely to be chosen foreperson than those with manual labor occupations. Similarly, it explains why higher-ranking military officers exerted more influence, even at nonmilitary group tasks in Torrance's (1954 [1965]) studies. (For other applications of the theory to occupations and other characteristics, see Berger, Wagner, and Zelditch 1985.)

Sexual orientation, though recently of applied interest, has not been studied analytically from a sociological perspective.[3] It is an intriguing characteristic. Whether announced or inferred, its obvious features—erotic choice and behavior—are not at issue in the majority of social situations. Someone who believes, correctly or incorrectly, he or she has met a gay (or straight) person often behaves differently in nonsexual situations, simply because of that fact.

We believe that part of the meaning of orientation is that it is a *diffuse status characteristic* in the United States, and perhaps in other societies. If orientation is a status characteristic, then status generalization theories provide a way to analyze some of its interaction effects. Whatever its other social significance, sexual orientation can produce many of the same interaction consequences as other status characteristics, such as occupation, gender, or skin color. We may be able to clarify Freud's (1935 [1957]) well-known statement that "Homosexuality assuredly is no advantage...." to specify *what sorts* of advantages and disadvantages it can produce. They are the power and prestige components of group interaction, produced by an underlying structure of specific and general performance expectation states created through status generalization.

Part 1 of the definition is well documented (Herek 1991; Johnson 1995; Plummer 1975; Preston and Stanley 1987). We focus on parts 2 and 3. Do people believe heterosexuals can do certain tasks and "most tasks" better than homosexuals?[4] Imagine a situation of two target individuals and an observer who is asked to make certain judgments about them. For a simple case, only two characteristics are known that distinguish the individuals: occupation and sexual orientation. A target may be described as possessing a particular state of orientation only, of occupation only, or of both orientation and occupation. When both characteristics are present, they may be evaluated either consistently or inconsistently; that is, high prestige occupation paired with either heterosexual or homosexual orientation.

When an observer is asked to report his or her relative performance expectations for two targets, the theory predicts the following:

Hypothesis 1.   If the only differentiating status information available is sexual orientation, an observer will form higher performance expectations for a heterosexual target individual than for a homosexual target individual.

The reasoning follows. By assumption 1 of the theory, differentiating status information will become salient. By assumption 2, unless orientation is known to be irrelevant to the situation, an observer will form performance expectations consistent with the social evaluation of the differentiating status characteristic. If status generalization occurs, by assumption 5, an observer will report higher performance expectations for a heterosexual target than for the homosexual.

(Explicit statement of the assumptions is available in Webster and Foschi 1988, chap. 1, and other sources.)

Similarly, where only occupation is known, the same assumptions yield:

Hypothesis 2. If the only differentiating status information available is occupation, an observer will form higher performance expectations for a target individual who is a computer analyst than for a target individual who is a dishwasher.

When both characteristics are present and evaluated consistently, assumption 4 of the theory predicts aggregation.[5] All salient status information gets used; none is ignored; thus:

Hypothesis 3. If a target individual's sexual orientation and occupation both are known and they are evaluated consistently, an observer will form higher performance expectations for the target with the highly evaluated states of the status characteristics than for the target with the lower evaluated states.

And the effect of two consistent characteristics exceeds either alone:

Hypothesis 4. If both sexual orientation and occupation are known and the states each target individual possesses are consistent, an observer will differentiate performance expectations for the targets more than if only one status element were salient.[6]

When targets' status characteristics are inconsistent, we again predict that both will function in status generalization, but this time they will counter each other.[7] How much status advantage does a gay man or lesbian with a high status occupation gain over another with a low status occupation? How much status advantage does a heterosexual gain over a homosexual, given that they hold the same occupation?

Hypothesis 5. If a first target individual has only the low state of a characteristic D1 and a second target has the low state of D1 and the high state of D2, an observer will form higher performance expectations for the second target than for the first.

To measure performance expectations, we adapted a questionnaire previously used to instantiate another status characteristic, physical attractiveness (Webster and Driskell 1983). That and a later study (Balkwell, Berger, Webster, Nelson-Kilger, and Cashen 1992) show questionnaire items are sensitive to specific and

Table 1.   Conditions of the Study and Scale Items

Condition	Sexual Orientation	Occupation
1. Orientation only	Person A: heterosexual Person B: homosexual	(no information)
2. Occupation only	(no information)	Person A: computer systems analyst Person B: dishwasher
3. Both, consistent	Person A: heterosexual Person B: homosexual	Person A: computer systems analyst Person B: dishwasher
4. Both, inconsistent	Person A: heterosexual Person B: homosexual	Person A: dishwasher Person B: computer systems analyst

1.   How intelligent do you believe Person A is, as compared to Person B?

A is much more intelligent (1)	A is some- what more intelligent (2)	A is slightly more intelligent (3)	A and B are exactly the same in intelligence (4)	B is slightly more intelligent (5)	B is somewhat more intelligent (6)	B is much more intelligent (7)

(Similar response choices for all items)

2.   ...do at situations in general....?

3.   ... compare in terms of things that you think count in this world, ...?

4.   ...reading ability....?

5.   ...grade point average (GPA)...?

6.   ...Army General Classification Test (AGCT) score ....? [study 1]; Scholastic Assessment Test (SAT)....? [study 2]

general expectations. We constructed booklets containing vignette descriptions of two target individuals, followed by expectation measures.

The design is shown at the top of Table 1. Condition 1 has only sexual orientation differentiating target individuals; this condition directly tests the instantiation claim for orientation. Condition 2 has only occupation. Because of much previous work, we anticipate that an instantiation claim for occupation will be confirmed. Condition 2 allows us assess the adequacy of our measures and to compare occupation's effects to those of orientation. Condition 3 has both characteristics, consistently (we presume) evaluated; condition 4 has inconsistent evaluations.

Items ask respondents to assess the relative competence of the two target individuals on a variety of specific and general skills, including reading ability, intelligence, high school grades, and "most things." Five items showing the highest factor loadings in an earlier study (Webster and Driskell 1983) were used, and we wrote one additional item for each of the two studies here, making a 6-item measure of performance expectations.[8] Seven-point anchored scales allowed respondents to report their relative inferences for the two target individuals. The center point, four, reflects exactly equal performance expectations for the targets; points one and seven represent much higher expectations for one target individual. The mean point checked on the six items forms our measure of the theoretical construct "expectation states."

TESTS OF THE HYPOTHESES

We conducted two empirical studies about nine months apart. In both, student volunteers in large lecture classes (biology, holistic health, political science, sociology, and social work) at the University of North Carolina at Charlotte (UNCC) and San Francisco State University (SFSU) completed questionnaires (study 1, n = 269; study 2, n = 549). We could not record how many of those contacted chose not to complete questionnaires, but it appeared that nearly all participated, lowering concern about selection bias.[9] Half the questionnaires in each condition presented the vignettes in reverse order to average any presentation order effects, and scores were transformed in coding to positions shown in Table 1.

Because expectation measure items were answered on a 7-point scale, with 4 as the midpoint, operational hypotheses become:
One characteristic:

Hypothesis 1. Mean expectation score in condition 1 < 4.0.

Hypothesis 2. Mean expectation score in condition 2 < 4.0.

Two consistent characteristics:

Hypothesis 3. Mean expectation score in condition 3 < 4.0.

Hypothesis 4. Mean expectation score in condition 3 < conditions 1, 2.

Two inconsistent characteristics:

Hypothesis 5. Mean expectation score in condition 4 > condition 1.

Failure of Hypothesis 1 might mean that orientation is not a status characteristic for these respondents, or that this questionnaire did not adequately measure expectations. We return to this issue below, in analyzing Study 1 data from SFSU. If Hypothesis 2 were not supported, we would suspect problems with our measure for this new situation. Hypothesis 3 predicts combining of these phenomenologically different characteristics, and Hypothesis 4 predicts the attenuation effect for consistently evaluated characteristics. Hypothesis 5 predicts combining of inconsistently-signed orientation and occupation. Hypothesis 5 would be disconfirmed

Table 2. Conditions, Number of Respondents, Performance
Expectations (Standard Errors), and Confidence Intervals, Male Targets

Condition and Status Information, (n)	Performance Expectations and (s.e.)	95% Confidence Interval
1. Orientation only (69)	3.82 (.077)	3.67-3.97
2. Occupation only (74)	3.08 (.124)	2.83-3.32
3. Orientation and occupation, consistent (61)	2.99 (.119)	2.75-3.22
4. Orientation and occupation, inconsistent (65)	4.92 (.113)	4.69-5.15

if, for instance, one of these characteristics were a "master status," so important that the other characteristic became irrelevant.[10]

FIRST STUDY: MALE TARGETS

As noted, respondents were 269 undergraduates enrolled at San Francisco State ($n = 102$) or University of North Carolina at Charlotte ($n = 167$). Vignettes described target individuals as men in the Army, a few years older than the respondent population. To manipulate sexual orientation (in conditions 1, 3, and 4) the vignette said "___ has had several intimate affairs, all of them with [women/men]. ____ considers himself a [heterosexual/homosexual]." To manipulate occupation (in conditions 2, 3 and 4), the vignette said "His occupation is [computer systems analyst/dishwasher]."

Following the vignettes were several questions asking whether respondents would prefer to associate with one or the other of the targets (desirability items), and asking for estimates of various abilities (performance expectation items). Table 2 shows mean expectation scale scores, by condition of the study.

Results in Table 2 confirm hypotheses 1, 2, 3 and 5 ($p < .05$). Initial interest attaches to Hypothesis 1, showing that sexual orientation indeed functions as a diffuse status characteristic; that is, it affects performance expectations. The effect, though significant, is small. Hypothesis 2 also is confirmed. The main value of this is to permit comparisons to orientation and to validate our measure, rather than to reconfirm occupation is a status characteristic in our society. Hypothesis 3 shows the predicted combining of orientation and occupation, despite their phenomenological dissimilarity.

Differences between conditions are in the direction predicted by Hypothesis 4, though only one is significant. A t-test on condition 1 > condition 3 shows $p < .01$; for condition 2 > condition 3, $p \approx .32$. Occupation has considerable weight when added to orientation, but any added effect of orientation with occupation fixed was not measurable.

Hypothesis 5, for inconsistent characteristics, is confirmed: condition 4 > condition 1, $p < .01$. There is, evidently, considerable status advantage for a gay man with a high status occupation, as compared to another with low status. Again, however, occupation has considerably more effect than orientation. A hypothesis comparable to Hypothesis 5 but varying orientation while holding occupation constant, would not be sustained.

Next we examine effects of these characteristics for different subgroups of respondents. Part 1 of the definition of a status characteristic requires that the categories have distinctly evaluated states. Initially, we presumed that part was not problematic for either characteristic, but that bears examining more closely.

Whether a characteristic is in fact status depends on time and place, and is changeable. *If* something is a status characteristic, then status generalization will occur. In any particular instance, it is important to know whether a particular respondent accepts social definitions making prestigious occupation or heterosexuality desirable. If some respondents reject that definition, occupation or sexual orientation may not be a status characteristic for them, and the theory would give no reason to predict differential performance expectations. Operationally, do respondents who negatively evaluate the homosexual state of target's orientation also form lower performance expectations for gay male targets than respondents who evaluate states of the characteristic as either neutral or positive? Similarly, does the desirability of an occupation affect its status organizing capacity?

Table 3. Conditions, Performance Expectations, (Standard Errors), and Number of Respondents by Positive and Negative Valences of Characteristics, Male Targets

Condition	Expectations for Target (s.e.), [n]	Expectations for Target (s.e.), [n]
1. Orientation only (target is homosexual)	heterosexual preferable 3.28 (.16) [18]	neutral or homosexual preferable 4.01 (.07) [54]
2. Occupation only (target is dishwasher)	computer scientist preferable 1.17 (.17) [2]	neutral or dishwasher preferable 3.13 (.12) [71]
3. Consistent orientation and occupation (target is homosexual dishwasher)	heterosexual computer scientist preferable 2.59 (.19) [19]	neutral or homosexual dishwasher preferable 3.17 (.14) [45]
4. Inconsistent orientation and occupation (target is homosexual computer scientist)	heterosexual dishwasher preferable 3.94 (.30) [9]	neutral or homosexual computer scientist preferable 5.09 (.11) [56]

We analyze performance expectation scores, controlling for answers to two desirability items in the questionnaire: who the respondent would prefer to talk with at a party, and who the respondent would rather have for a friend.[11]

Table 3 shows performance expectations assigned to the gay male target by respondents who "much prefer" or "slightly prefer" to associate with someone having the higher state of the characteristic, compared to those indifferent or preferring the lower state. Note that there is no unanimous preference for the heterosexual individual here. A considerable proportion of respondents in all conditions report indifference or a preference for the homosexual or the dishwasher.

Conditions 1 and 2 are most informative. With only orientation present in condition 1, respondents who see homosexuality negatively form expectations for the homosexual more than 4 standard errors below equality. Those seeing homosexuality as neutral or positive form virtually equal expectations for the two targets. This is the pattern we would expect if orientation is a status characteristic for the first group and not for the second group of respondents.

Condition 2, occupation, shows a similar pattern, though this time expectation formation occurs even among respondents who say they see being a dishwasher as neutral or positive. Those preferring the computer analyst form very low expectations for the dishwasher (1.17); those neutral or preferring the dishwasher still evidence displacement from equality (3.13), but it is much less. Occupation is so well established a status characteristic that performance expectations are associated with it even among those preferring to interact with a dishwasher rather than a computer analyst.

Briefly, we turn to sociological subgroups to explore the generality of status generalization based on sexual orientation. Table 4 shows data only from respondents at SFSU. Although SFSU and UNCC are similar in many ways—large public institutions drawing students from comparable socioeconomic status (SES) backgrounds in an urban setting and having similar entrance requirements—populations differ in geography and ethnic composition; perhaps also in cultural beliefs, attitudes, and religious influences.

Condition 1 (sexual orientation only) shows virtually no displacement from equality of the targets; at first, it might appear that sexual orientation is not a status

Table 4.   Conditions Number of Respondents, and Performance Expectations (Standard Errors), Male Targets, SFSU Subgroup

Condition (n)	Expectations (s.e.)
1 (29)	4.05 (.131)
2 (28)	3.33 (.259)[a]
3 (23)	2.80 (.200)[a]
4 (22)	5.25 (.188)

Note: [a]t-test of conditions 2 > 3, one-tail p = .14.

characteristic at SFSU. We believe such a conclusion would be incorrect, however. Failure of Hypothesis 1 could mean *either* that sexual orientation is not a status characteristic for those respondents *or* they do not report it, perhaps wishing to appear egalitarian.

Other cells of Table 4 can check this idea. If sexual orientation were *not* a status characteristic for this population, then it would be ignored in forming expectations; in the theory's terms, it would not be *salient*. In that case, the only salient characteristic in condition 3 would be occupation, and thus, we would expect expectations in condition 2 would equal those in condition 3. On the other hand, if orientation is a status characteristic but other concerns prevent respondents from reporting that fact when it is presented alone in the very simple condition 1, we might see its effects in the somewhat more complex condition 3. Sexual orientation should modify expectations produced by occupation, so condition 2 > 3. Table 4 shows that ordering, though small *n*s preclude significance ($p = .14$). Pending larger samples, we tentatively conclude sexual orientation is a status characteristic at San Francisco, but respondents may have been reluctant to report that to us.

Of other subgroups in our data (ethnicity,[12] age above and below the median of 24, major field of study), only gender shows an appreciable effect, with male respondents reporting stronger status generalization in condition 1 than female.[13] Mean response of women in condition 1 ($n = 43$) approximates equality of the targets (3.96); for men ($n = 27$), the score is 3.63; p (2-tailed) < .05). The effect is particular to sexual orientation; responses of men and women to occupation in condition 2 do not differ (females = 3.09; males = 3.02). Status generalization from occupation occurs similarly among women and men. Most of the status generalization from sexual orientation occurs among male respondents.

The weaker response of female respondents could be produced by either of two mechanisms, with differing interpretations for the social meaning of sexual orientation. First, only some of the women may recognize sexual orientation as a meaningful status characteristic; it may not become salient for others. By this mechanism, orientation is a status characteristic for some women but not for all, so the average effect in our data is small. A second mechanism is that the *strength* of this characteristic might be weaker for women than for men. By this mechanism, sexual orientation is just as likely to be salient for women as for men, but women do not weight it so highly as men do.

The smaller effect observed for female respondents might be produced either by (1) two subpopulations of women, some of whom treat orientation as salient and others who ignore it; or (2) a single population of women, all of whom notice the characteristic, but who treat it as having less importance than men do. If the first mechanism operated, it might be shown by greater variance of responses among women than among men; the second mechanism would not. In condition 1 of this study, for women $\sigma^2 = .34$; for men, $\sigma^2 = .45$.

This shows women are as likely as men to recognize the characteristic, but it is a less important status factor for women than for men.

SECOND STUDY: FEMALE TARGETS

Does sexual orientation carry comparable meanings for women and men; are gay men and lesbians similarly subject to status generalization by observers? Studies of attitudes and stereotyping (e.g, Herek 1994) show stronger prejudice toward men than women. On the other hand, Shilts (1993) reported more discrimination toward women, at least in the military. Occupation is, we believed, more likely to have comparable status effects for women as for men.

Besides a concern with including both genders in the study, there is theoretical reason to compare responses to women to the responses to men, at least for orientation. In an early review of attitudes towards sexual orientation, Herek (1984, p. 7) concluded that "heterosexuals tend to have more negative attitudes towards homosexuals of their own sex than of the opposite sex." Of course "attitudes" often refer to inferences other than ability, so it is not immediately clear whether we should expect that conclusion to apply to status generalization. However we did find weak generalization effects from women respondents to our male targets in study 1, so it is of interest to pursue comparison of expectations for female targets, by gender of respondents.

We constructed a second set of booklets, this time describing female targets who were otherwise comparable to the males in the first study. Targets were described as working for a large company, rather than the Army.[14] We also changed the specific characteristic from Air Force Qualification Test (AFQT) to Scholastic Assessment Test (SAT) as these targets were civilians. The respondent sample is larger (n = 549).

Four conditions, defined by orientation and occupation, were created as before. Table 5 reports overall expectation measures for this study. The Army General Classification Test (AGCT) item in Study 1 is replaced by SAT score for Study 2;

Table 5. Conditions, Number of Respondents, Performance Expectations (Standard Errors), and Confidence Intervals, Female Targets

Condition and Status Information, (n)	Expectations (s.e.)	95% Confidence Interval
1. Orientation only (150)	3.90 (.04)	3.82-3.99
2. Occupation only (132)	2.96 (.07)	2.82-3.09
3. Orientation and occupation, consistent (136)	2.99 (.07)	2.86-3.12
4. Orientation and occupation, inconsistent (131)	5.06 (.07)	4.93-5.20

other measures are the same. The same hypotheses may be derived as before. As in the first study, hypotheses 1, 2, 3, and 5 are supported ($p < .05$). That is, sexual orientation, occupation, and a consistent combination of orientation and occupation all produce predicted status generalization. High occupational status modifies the status disadvantage of being lesbian. As in the first study, Hypothesis 4 is not supported.

In condition 1, the second study may show a somewhat weaker effect of orientation alone. That is, the displacement of expectations below 4.0 is quite small in study 2. In fact, in study 2, the 95 percent confidence interval is only slightly below the 4.0 required to show status generalization (3.68 to 3.99). In the discussion section we consider potential interpretations of effect size.

Analyses by sociological subgroups show no differences in study 2. In particular, respondent gender does not affect status generalization in condition 1 (for males, 3.90; for females, 3.91). That finding contrasts with the first study, where female respondents showed less status generalization than did male respondents. Thus women showed a greater tendency to generalize on the basis of orientation when the targets are women. That is consistent with what Herek (1984) reported for attitudes. However we do not find a comparable stronger generalization by male respondents toward male targets. Male respondents in our two studies displayed about equal tendencies to generalize from sexual orientation whether the target is female or male.

Table 6 reports expectations by valence toward the characteristics in this study, comparable to Table 3 for the first study. These results show the same pat-

Table 6.   Conditions, Performance Expectations
(Standard Errors), Number of Respondents
by Positive and Negative Valences of Characteristics,
Female Targets

Condition	Expectations for Target (s.e.) [n]	Expectations for Target (s.e.) [n]
1. Orientation only (target is homosexual)	heterosexual preferable 3.82 (.05) [101]	neutral or homosexual preferable 4.11 (.05) [49]
2. Occupation only (target is dishwasher)	computer scientist preferable 2.50 (.09) [50]	neutral or dishwasher preferable 3.26 (.08) [82]
3. Consistent orientation and occupation (target is homosexual dishwasher)	heterosexual computer scientist preferable 2.90 (.08) [91]	neutral or homosexual dishwasher preferable 3.20 (.11) [45]
4. Inconsistent orientation and occupation (target is homosexual computer scientist)	heterosexual dishwasher preferable 4.94 (.09) [62]	neutral or homosexual computer scientist preferable 5.18 (.09) [69]

tern as for male targets. In condition 1, when homosexuality is evaluated negatively, respondents form corresponding low-performance expectations (> 3 s.e. from equality). Where homosexuality is neutral or positive, respondents actually form somewhat higher expectations for the homosexual target. In condition 2, whether or not respondents report evaluating the occupations, they form performance expectations from them, though expectations again are affected more among respondents who also report preferring to associate with the computer analyst.

DISCUSSION

We began this exploration with an interest in seeing whether current theories of status generalization processes could help understand some social meanings of occupation and sexual orientation. Both studies show that both characteristics produce performance expectations and carry status advantages and disadvantages for both women and men. When occupation and sexual orientation become salient to interactants, among other effects, status differences appear, affecting performance expectations for individuals. In this way, the two characteristics, quite different in most ways, have some similar interaction consequences.

The status significance for both characteristics is quite general. Effects appear in most sociologically meaningful subgroups of respondents, including geographic, age, and ethnicity differences.[15] Gender of respondent, however, does make a difference for orientation. Men were more likely to treat orientation as a status characteristic of men than women were; men and women were equally likely to treat orientation of women as a status characteristic. This result may be compared to those of Ridgeway, Johnson, and Diekema (1994), Smith-Lovin and Brody (1991), and Stewart (1988), who found that gender may be less significant a status characteristic for college-age women than it is for men; and to Johnson, Clay-Warner, and Funk (1996), who found that under some conditions, gender can be salient even in an all-female group. Our results parallel those of Herek (1994), who reported that male respondents held stronger negative attitudes toward, and stereotypes of, male homosexuals than did female respondents.

We do *not* claim status is the entire meaning of occupation or sexual orientation, just as it would be frivolous to say status is the entire meaning of skin color or gender. However status is *one* important element. In addition to emotions (such as fear, dislike, or envy), and cognitive prejudices that may appear when occupation and orientation differences become salient, status generalization effects may be expected.

For orientation, having a theory of how status operates, and knowing that orientation sometimes is status in our society, can sensitize observers to look for other consequences as well, and interpret them when they appear. For instance:

1. A juror identified as gay or lesbian probably will initiate less, have less influence over the verdict, and be less likely to be chosen foreperson than a comparable person not so identified (effects documented for occupations; Strodtbeck, James, and Hawkins 1957; Strodtbeck and Mann, 1956).
2. Managers in organizations, if they know (or infer) that an employee is gay or lesbian, may hold that employee to higher standards than others for equivalent evaluations, and will distribute rewards such as promotions and raises to them less readily than to other employees not so identified (documented for gender; Foschi, 1996; Jasso and Webster, 1997).[16]

Second, theoretical context provides guides for devising interventions to overcome undesirable consequences of occupational prestige and sexual orientation. Inferences that laborers cannot contribute much to a jury, and fears that gay officers might not be able to command effectively, can be addressed using techniques developed in other settings where it has been possible to overcome unwanted status generalization. One of Cohen's (1993) techniques, demonstrating competence of an individual having a status disadvantage, can be adapted to overcome generalization based on occupation, orientation, gender, or skin color.

Regarding orientation, the new finding of greatest theoretical significance is that performance expectations get created when it becomes salient. Performance expectations are the theoretical mechanism by which status generalization alters interaction patterns and group structure; individuals treat each other differently when they form ideas of relevant competencies and incompetencies. Whatever else sexual orientation may mean, it creates specific and general expectations for better performance by heterosexuals.

Performance expectations distinguish our approach from studies of stereotyping. While much research by psychologists has documented stereotypes regarding homosexuals, those focus on affect and personality traits, which are not the same as performance expectations. Whatever the stereotype of a homosexual may be, it probably does *not* include reading ability, high school marks, Army test scores, or SAT scores. We are not saying that stereotyping research focuses on the wrong factors, for stereotypes are important for understanding aspects of prejudice and violence. However, our approach differs from stereotyping research, and our findings do not simply replicate evidence of sexual stereotypes.

In both our studies, occupation produces considerable displacement from equality of expectations. The status difference between occupations here is considerable: NORC occupational prestige score differences are about 74 for computer systems analyst, and about 17 for dishwasher (Nakao and Treas, 1994). In comparison, sexual orientation displaced expectations less than occupation did, in some cases becoming invisible when combined with occupational differentiation. Several reasons for this are possible. Most important, as shown in Tables 3 and 6, status generalization for this characteristic depends on a respondent's valuing it negatively, and not all of them do. Those who view the characteristic negatively demonstrate considerable status generalization on that basis (displacements ~3 s.e). Occupation, more universally recognized as a status characteristic, produces differentiated performance expectations regardless of whether respondents would prefer to associate with the target individuals.

A theoretical explanation for the effect size difference between sexual orientation and occupation may be available in the theory of reward expectations (Berger, Fisek, Norman, and Wagner 1985). This theory describes processes by which actors develop expectations for the allocation of rewards in a process comparable to the status generalization process by which they develop performance expectations. It is possible to derive from this theory (theorem 5 in the paper) that a status characteristic associated with differentiated reward expectations (as, for instance, gender or occupation usually is) will produce greater effect on performance expectations than will another characteristic not linked to reward differences. If respondents in these studies expected differentiated pay levels to be associated with occupation, but held no such expectation for sexual orientation, theorem 5 from the theory of reward expectations would predict what we found; namely, that occupation would have more effect on performance expectations than would orientation.

At this point the explanation, while plausible, is untested because we do not know whether these respondents in fact hold differentiated reward expectations for occupations but not for gender. More importantly, the explanation is theoretically meaningful and testable.

We do know that respondents are concerned with self-presentation, as shown in the first study with SFSU respondents. Some may hesitate to tell us they form lower performance expectations for a gay target person than for a straight one. Perhaps the college climate discourages expressing any sort of differential evaluations based on status characteristics. Future research must anticipate that source of difficulty in data collection.[17]

A significant methodological concern for future studies is difficulty creating a realistic person for certain characteristics using vignettes. Occupational titles are widely understood and probably convey clear meaning; sexual orientation may not. When sexual orientation becomes salient in natural settings, it is accompanied by gestures, speech styles, and emotional responses; those were impossible to reproduce. The earlier research that served as a model for this study (Webster and Driskell 1983) manipulated physical attractiveness by presenting photographs of target individuals. If, instead of showing pictures, vignettes had stated "Person A is considered highly attractive," would respondents have attended adequately to the variable? Perhaps not; or at least not enough to measure with questionnaires.[18]

The best measure of performance expectations is behavioral, influence rejection in the standard laboratory experiment devised by Berger and associates (Berger et al., 1977, chap. 5). In this design, pairs (usually) of participants receive status and other information in phase 1 of the study, and then in phase 2 they interact with each other, resolving experimentally introduced disagreements. Disagreement interaction yields a statistic, $P(s)$, which has been shown to be a reliable measure of relative performance expectations for the participants.

Sexual orientation has not been studied experimentally, however, and little is known about appropriate techniques to create the characteristic believably in a laboratory setting. What is required, of course, is not so much to display characteristics of a real gay man or lesbian, but rather to create a person whom experimental respondents will *treat* as a homosexual. That may involve stereotypic appearance and gestures, hobbies, speech styles, postures, etc., using information from studies such as those by G. Berger, Rauzi, and Simkins (1987) and Herek (1994). Clearly several difficult operational questions will need to be addressed before it is possible to study orientation in the laboratory. However the benefits from using a standard experimental situation also are considerable, and make the project appealing. To begin, a laboratory experiment could produce clearer evidence of how status elements of orientation behave and how this characteristic combines with other status characteristics to form aggregate performance expectations.

Theoretical inquiry might help illuminate other aspects of sexual orientation and its effects on interaction. Johnson (1995) noted that, in many cases, people associate gender nonconformity with homosexuality; for instance, a gay man may also seem feminine. Activating gender along with orientation would explain cases of unusually strong interaction disadvantages sometimes present when both homosexuality and gender nonconformity are observed, and it could guide investigations into components of this status characteristic.

A second theoretical issue asks how sexual orientation acquired status value: why is this a *status* characteristic carrying invidious connotations and performance expectations instead of simply an unvalued nominal characteristic? Ridgeway's (1991; Ridgeway and Balkwell 1997) theory treats status acquisition, focusing on gender. While that theory probably will require some modification to apply to sexual orientation (see Webster and Hyson 1998), we believe the approach holds promise for this and many other status characteristics.

ACKNOWLEDGMENT

Some of these data were reported at seminars at the University of South Carolina and New York University, and at ASA, PSA, and Group Process meetings in the United States, and Poland. Joseph Berger, Cathryn Johnson, Kenneth Monteiro, and Henry Walker advised on theoretical and empirical design questions. Study 2 data collection were supported by Faculty Research grants to Webster and Fullmer; Kevin Childers was research assistant. We thank students and faculty at the University of North Carolina, Charlotte, and San Francisco State University for their assistance.

NOTES

1. Performance expectations involve only anticipations of task abilities. They omit emotions, sentiments, and other social responses that sometimes occur when status characteristics (including sexual orientation, gender, and skin color) become salient. The focus on task-relevant aspects of performance distinguishes our work from more global studies of stereotyping, a point we expand on below.

2. Those beliefs often are not true. What matters in making gender a status characteristic is that the beliefs are widely shared. Beliefs may be changing, so that differential performance expectations no longer attach to states of gender (see Smith-Lovin and Brody, 1991; also see Ridgeway et al. 1994, and Stewart 1988). If that occurs, gender will cease to be a status characteristic in our society.

3. Previously studied aspects of sexual orientation include prevalence and incidence (Laumann, Gagnon, Michael and Michaels, 1994, esp. pp. 283-290); social structures and norms (e.g., Blumstein and Schwartz 1985; Chauncey 1994; Cory 1951); life experiences of gay men and lesbians in our society (e.g., Bawer 1993; Monette 1992); etiology (e.g., Bell, Weinberg, and Hammersmith 1981; LeVay 1991a, b); and antecedents and content of views heterosexuals hold of lesbians and gay men (e.g., Herek 1994; Kite and Deaux 1986). Our approach, while consistent with many ideas from those other investigations, uses a theoretical perspective new to the study of sexual orientation. We focus only on group process effects of orientation: the performance expectations individuals may form when the characteristic becomes salient, and the potential of those expectations for affecting task-focused interaction and group structure.

4. A well-known U.S. Department of Defense (1982 [1994]) directive states:

Homosexuality is incompatible with military service. The presence in the military environment of persons who engage in homosexual conduct or who, by their statements, demonstrate a propensity to engage in homosexual conduct, seriously impairs the accomplishment of the military mission....

That includes considerations beyond our scope, such as discipline and trust. However "accomplishment of ...mission" clearly reveals concern for task performance.

5. We do not use assumption 3 of the theory in this research. That assumption applies to complex situations, with actors entering and leaving.

6. The combining function in assumption 4 incorporates an 'attenuation effect,' such that each additional unit of consistent status information has declining magnitude of effect on performance expectations. Thus the *displacement* of expectation scores from equality should be greater for two consistent characteristics (as Hypothesis 4 states), but not twice so great as for a single characteristic. Berger et al. (1992) present data from laboratory experiments that display the attenuation effect.

7. Whether two oppositely-signed characteristics perfectly cancel each other depends on their strength, perhaps roughly equivalent to characteristics' importance in a particular culture. Status generalization theories generally use a simplifying assumption that all status elements have the same potency. That assumption has not been modified to date because it has not prevented making some highly accurate predictions (see, for instance, Fisek et al. 1995).

8. Factor analysis shows the measure to be unidimensional (mean intercorrelation = .81 in study 1, and .82 in study 2).

9. We collated questionnaires before distribution; thus where respondents sat in classroom rows determined which condition they received. Respondents in adjacent seats received different questionnaires.

10. The idea of a master status, while appealing, is not predicted by theories of status generalization, and all evidence we know of shows that all salient status information is combined in forming performance expectation states (see Balkwell 1991).

11. Items correlate .80. These questions measure social desirability or evaluation of a characteristic, not performance connotations.

12. Asian respondents may generalize from sexual orientation slightly less than Caucasians. However results are confounded by school, for all but one of our Asian respondents were at SFSU. We know no comparable studies of Asian's attitudes. Herek (1994) reported stronger responses from African American respondents than Caucasians to an attitude scale on sexual orientation. Here, African Americans did not generalize more or less than Caucasians.

13. Whitley and Kite (1995) argue for some gender differences in attitudes toward homosexuality, and Herek and Glunt (1993) found men more negative than women towards homosexuality. Above we noted that gender differences in recognizing characteristics as *status* characteristics also have been reported.

14. When we presented study 1 at the 1995 ASA meetings, Lynn Smith-Lovin pointed out that we created *rule violators* as well as homosexuals, since acknowledging that fact has been prohibited in the military since 1993. (Affect Control Theory might study social identities created by combinations of occupation and sexual orientation with rule violation and conformity.) Consequently, we moved the job sites for study 2.

15. The effect appears cross-culturally. Since we completed Study 1, Stulhofer and Francetic (1996) translated our questionnaire into Croation and administered it to students at the University of Zagreb. In Croatian culture as well as our own, orientation evidently carries status connotations.

16. These effects can be produced solely by status generalization, independent of other processes such as envy of occupation, dislike of homosexuals, or prejudice.

17. Discrepancy between reported attitudes and behavior for race is widely recognized. See Webster and Driskell (1978) for status generalization; also see Schulman (1974).

18. Driskell and Muller (1988, 1990) and Balkwell et al. (1992) explore questionnaires as measures of expectations.

REFERENCES

Balkwell, J. 1991. "Status Characteristics and Social Interaction: An Assessment of Theoretical Variants." Pp. 135-176 in *Advances in Group Processes* Vol. 8, edited by E.J. Lawler, B. Markovsky, C.L. Ridgeway, and H.A Walker. Greenwich, CT: JAI Press.

Balkwell, J., J. Berger, M. Webster, M. Nelson-Kilger, and J. Cashen. 1992 'Processing Status Information: Some Tests of Competing Theoretical Arguments.' Pp. 1-20 in *Advances in Group Processes* Vol. 9, edited by E.J. Lawler, B. Markovsky, C.L. Ridgeway, and H.A. Walker. Greenwich, CT: JAI Press.

Bawer, B. 1993 *A Place at the Table: The Gay Individual in American Society.* New York: Poseidon Press.

Bell, A.P., M.S. Weinberg, and S.K. Hammersmith. 1981. *Sexual Preference: Its Development in Men and Women.* Bloomington, IN: Indiana University Press.

Berger, G., L. Hank, T. Rauzi, and L. Simkins. 1987. "Detection of Sexual Orientation by Heterosexuals and Homosexuals." *Journal of Homosexuality* 13: 83-100.

Berger, J., M.H. Fisek, R.Z. Norman, and M. Zelditch, Jr. 1977. *Status Characteristics and Social Interaction: An Expectation States Approach.* New York: Elsevier.

Berger, J., R.Z. Norman, J. Balkwell, and R.F. Smith. 1992. 'Status Inconsistency in Task Situations: A Test of Four Status Processing Principles. ' *American Sociological Review.* 57: 843-855.

Berger, J., D.G. Wagner, and M. Zelditch, Jr. 1985. "Introduction: Expectation States Theory: Review and Assessment." Pp. 1-72 in *Status, Rewards, and Influence: How Expectations Organize Behavior*, edited by J. Berger and M. Zelditch. San Francisco: Jossey-Bass.

Chauncey, G., 1994. *Gay New York: Gender, Urban Culture, and the Making of the Gay Male World.* New York: Basic Books.

Cohen, E.G., 1993. 'From Theory to Practice: The Development of an Applied Research Program.' Pp. 385-415 in *Theoretical Research Programs: Studies in the Growth of Theory*, edited by J. Berger and M. Zelditch, Jr. Stanford, CA: Stanford University Press.

Cohen, E.G., and L. Catanzarite. 1988. "Can Expectations for Competence be Altered in the Classroom?" Pp. 27-54 in *Status Generalization: New Theory and Research*, edited by M. Webster Jr. and M. Foschi. Stanford, CA: Stanford University Press.

Cory, D.W. (pseud.) 1951. *The Homosexual in America: A Subjective Approach*. New York: Greenberg.

Driskell, J.E., Jr. and N. Mullen. 1988. "Expectations and Actions." Pp. 399-412 in *Status Generalization: New Theory and Research*, edited by M. Webster, Jr. and M. Foschi. Stanford, CA: Stanford University Press.

Driskell, J.E. Jr., and B. Mullen. 1990. "Status, Expectations, and Behavior: A Meta-analytic Review and Test of the Theory." *Personality and Social Psychology Bulletin* 16: 541-553.

Fisek, M.H., J. Berger, and R.Z. Norman. 1991. "Participation in Heterogeneous and Homogeneous Groups: A Theoretical Integration.' *American Journal of Sociology* 97: 114-142.

Fisek, M.H., J. Berger, and R.Z. Norman. 1995. "Evaluations and the Formation of Expectations." *American Journal of Sociology* 101: 721-746.

Foschi, M. 1996. "Double Standards in the Evaluation of Men and Women." *Social Psychology Quarterly*, 59: 237-254.

Freud, S. 1935 [1957]. "Letter to a Mother." P. 195 in *The Life and Works of Sigmund Freud*, Vol. 3, edited by E. Jones. New York: Basic Books.

Herek, G.M., 1984. "Beyond 'Homophobia:' A Social Psychological Perspective on Attitudes toward Lesbians and Gay Men." Pp. 1-21 in *Bashers, Baiters, and Bigots: Homophobia in American Society*, edited by J. DeCecco. New York: Haworth

Herek, G.M. 1991. "Stigma, Prejudice, and Violence against Lesbians and Gay Men: Correlates and Gender Differences." Pp. 60-80 in *Homo Sexuality: Research Implications for Public Policy*, edited by J. Gonsiorek and J. Weinrich. Newbury Park, CA: Sage.

Herek, G.M. 1994. "Assessing Heterosexuals' Attitudes toward Lesbians and Gay Men." Pp. 206-228 in *Lesbian and Gay Psychology*, edited by B. Greene and G.M. Herek. Thousand Oaks, CA: Sage.

Herek, G.M., and E.K. Glunt. 1993. "Interpersonal Contact and Heterosexuals' Attitudes toward Gay Men: Results from a National Survey." *The Journal of Sex Research* 30: 239-244.

Hodge, R.M., P.M. Siegel, and P.H. Rossi. 1964. "Occupational Prestige in the United States, 1925-1963." *American Journal of Sociology*, 70: 286-302.

Jasso, G., and M. Webster, Jr. 1997. "Double Standards in Just Earnings for Male and Female Workers." *Social Psychology Quarterly* 60: 66-78.

Johnson, C. 1995. "Sexual Orientation as a Diffuse Status Characteristic: Implications for Small Group Interaction." Pp. 115-137 in *Advances in Group Processes*, Vol. 12, edited by B. Markovsky, M. Lovaglia, and K. Heimer. Greenwich, CT: JAI Press.

Johnson, C., J. Clay-Warner, and S.J. Funk. 1996. "Effects of Authority Structures and Gender on Interaction in Same-sex Task Groups." *Social Psychology Quarterly* 59: 221-236.

Kite, M.E., and K. Deaux. 1986. "Attitudes Toward Homosexuality: Assessment and Behavioral Consequences," *Basic and Applied Social Psychology* 7: 137-162.

Laumann, E.O., J.H. Gagnon, R.T. Michael, and S. Michaels. 1994. *The Social Organization of Sexuality: Sexual Practices in the United States*. Chicago: University of Chicago Press.

LeVay, S. 1991a. "News and Comment: Is Homosexuality Biological?" *Science* 253: 253, 257-259.

———. 1991b. "A Difference in Hypothalamic Structure between Heterosexual and Homosexual men." *Science* 253: 1034-1037.

Miller, D.C. 1991. *Handbook of Research Design and Social Measurement* (5th ed.). Beverly Hills, CA: Sage.

Monette, P. 1992. *Becoming a Man: Half a Life Story*. San Diego: Harcourt, Brace.

Nakao, K., and J. Treas. 1994. "Updating Occupational Prestige and Socioeconomic Scores: How the New Measures Measure Up." Pp. 1-72 in *Sociological Methodology*, Vol. 24, edited by P.V. Marsden. Cambridge, MA: Blackwell.

Plummer, K. 1975. *Sexual Stigma: An Interactionist Approach.* London: Routledge & Kegan Paul.

Preston, K., and K. Stanley. 1987. "'What's the Worst Thing...?' Gender Directed Insults." *Sex Roles* 17: 209-219.

Ridgeway, C.L. 1991. "The Social Construction of Status Value: Gender and other Nominal Characteristics," *Social Forces* 70: 367-386.

Ridgeway, C.L., and J. Balkwell. 1997. "Group Processes and the Diffusion of Status Beliefs." *Social Psychology Quarterly* 60: 14-31.

Ridgeway, C.L., C. Johnson, and D. Diekema. 1994 "External Status, Legitimacy, and Compliance in Male and Female Groups." *Social Forces* 72: 1051-1077.

Schulman, G.I. 1974. "Race, Sex, and Violence: A Laboratory Test of the Sexual Threat of the Black Male Hypothesis." *American Journal of Sociology* 79: 1260-1277.

Shilts, R. 1993. *Conduct Unbecoming: Lesbians and Gays in the U.S. Military—Vietnam to the Persian Gulf.* New York: St. Martin's Press.

Smith-Lovin, L., and C. Brody. 1991. "Interruptions in Group Discussions: The Effects of Gender and Group Composition," *American Sociological Review* 54: 424-435.

Stewart, P. 1988. "Women and Men in Groups: A Status Characteristics Approach to Interaction." Pp. 69-85 in *Status Generalization: New Theory and Research*, edited by M. Webster, Jr. and M. Foschi. Stanford, CA: Stanford University Press.

Strodtbeck, F.L., R.M. James, and C. Hawkins. 1957. "Social Status in Jury Deliberations." *Sociometry* 19: 3-11.

Strodtbeck, F.L. and R.D. Mann. 1956. "Sex Role Differentiation in Jury Deliberations." *American Sociological Review* 22: 713-719.

Stulhofer, A., and H. Francetic. 1996. "Sexual Orientation as a Diffuse Status Characteristic: A Bi-Cultural Comparison." *Sociological Review* (Zagreb) 205-214. (In Croatian with an English abstract)

Torrance, E.P. 1954 [1965]. "Some Consequences of Power Differences on Decision Making in Permanent and Temporary Three-man Groups." *Research Studies*, State University of Washington. Reprinted in A. P. Hare, E. F. Borgatta, and R. F. Bales (eds.), *Small Groups*, pp. 600-609. New York: Knopf.

Treiman, D.J., 1977. *Occupational Prestige in Comparative Perspective*. New York: Academic Press.

United States Department of Defense. 1982 [1994]. "Directive No. 1332.14, Enlisted Administrative Separations," (28 January) 1-9—1-13. Cited in D.F. Burrell, "The Debate on Homosexuals in the Military," pp. 17-31 in W.J. Scott and S. Carson Stanley (eds.) *Gays and Lesbians in the Military: Issues, Concerns, and Contrasts*. Hawthorne, NY: Aldine de Gruyter.

Wagner, D.G., and J. Berger. 1993. "Status Characteristics Theory: The Growth of a Program." Pp. 23-63 in *Theoretical Research Programs: Studies in the Growth of Theory*, edited by J. Berger and M. Zelditch, Jr. Stanford, CA: Stanford University Press.

Webster, M. Jr, and S. J. Hysom. 1998. "Creating Status Characteristics." *American Sociological Review* 63.

Webster, M., Jr., and J.E. Driskell. 1983. "Beauty as Status." *American Journal of Sociology* 89: 140-165.

Webster, M., Jr., and M. Foschi (eds.). 1988. *Status Generalization: New Theory and Research.* Stanford, CA: Stanford University Press.

Webster, M. Jr., and J. E. Driskell. 1978. "Status Generalization: A Review and Some New Data." *American Sociological Review* 43(2) (April): 220-236.

Whitley, B.E., Jr., and M.E. Kite. 1995. "Sex Differences in Attitudes toward Homosexuality: A Comment on Oliver and Hyde (1993)." *Psychological Bulletin* 117(1): 146-154.

SENTIMENT AND TASK PERFORMANCE EXPECTATIONS

M. Hamit Fişek and Joseph Berger

ABSTRACT

This paper presents a discussion of how the effect of interpersonal sentiments on status behaviors can be conceptualized within the framework of expectation states theory (Berger, Fisek, Norman, and Zelditch 1977). Two alternative approaches to the problem, sentiment as mediator of expectations, and sentiment as constituent of expectations, are identified. The two approaches are compared in terms of substantive theoretical considerations, available empirical evidence, and metatheoretical principles. A model for each approach is developed within the mathematical framework of the theory of status characteristics and expectation states, and tested against data from experiments conducted by Driskell and Webster (1997) and Lovaglia (1997). It is concluded that it is not possible to conclude the superiority of one approach over the other given the available empirical evidence and current levels of theoretical development.

Advances in Group Processes, Volume 15, pages 23-39.
ISBN: 0-7623-0362-X

INTRODUCTION

This paper is motivated by two recent papers, "Status, Emotion, and Structural Power" by Michael J. Lovaglia (1997) and "Status and Sentiment in Task Groups" by James E. Driskell Jr. and Murray Webster Jr. (1997). Both papers clearly show that subjects' states of affect, manipulated in a number of different ways in the laboratory, help determine the status behaviors emitted by the subjects. More precisely, both papers show that, controlling for task performance expectations, subjects who have positive sentiment (i.e., liking) for their working partners reject less influence from their partners compared to those who have negative sentiment (i.e., disliking), in a highly controlled experimental situation.

Both papers approach this phenomenon from the point of view of expectation states theory (Berger et al. 1977), as in the earlier work of Shelly, (1993) and pose the question of how sentiment and/or affect (see Ridgeway [1994] for a discussion of the distinction of the two concepts; for the purposes of this paper we do not distinguish between the two and use "sentiment" to refer to both) should be integrated into this particular theoretical framework. Our aim in this paper is to build on the considerable contribution of these papers, to explicate further the problem they pose, and to discuss the methodology of approaching the problem.

Background: The Theory of Expectation States

The theory of expectation states describes and explains how individuals in task-oriented groups form task-performance expectations for themselves and the other individuals in the group, how these expectations form the power and prestige order in the group, and how, in turn, the power and prestige order determines the individuals' status behaviors. The theory has grown over a long period of time by means of extensions, elaborations, and integrations of the various branches of the theory. One particular branch, the theory of status characteristics, differs from the others as it has a mathematical formulation, and thus has served as the focal point of integration of the various branches of the theory. Following Driskell and Webster we will use a simple diagram to describe the general features of expectation states theory.

The central principle of the theory is that expectations determine behavior, and that behavior also determines expectations. In this feedback cycle *expectations* is the fundamental theoretical concept, and the formation of expectations is the basic process. The entities which go into the formation of expectations are status elements. Some of these, as shown in box A in Figure 1, are external to the task situation: Diffuse and specific status characteristics (one of which may be the instrumental characteristic), categorical cues which indicate such characteristics, valued roles, and evaluations from sources (evaluators) who are not interactants in the task situation. It is these external status elements which determine the initial

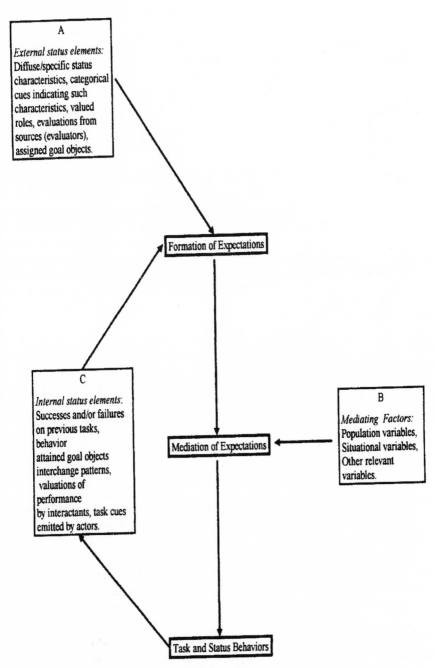

Figure 1. Expectation States Theory

expectations within a group, as symbolized by the arrow from box A to the "Formation of Expectations".

Expectations determine status behaviors, however, expectations are not the only determinants of status behaviors, and other factors mediate, transform, filter, or moderate the effect of expectations on behavior. The same pattern of expectations, or the same power and prestige order, may result in different status behaviors depending on situational factors: for example given the same power and prestige order, the greater the level of task orientation in the situation, the lower the rates of rejecting influence. Similarly the older the actors in the situation the higher the rates of rejecting influence for a given power and prestige order. Box B in Figure 1 shows the mediating factors, and the arrow from the box to "Mediation of Expectations" represents their action on expectations.

Thus it is not just expectations but *mediated* expectations which determine task and status behaviors. Furthermore status behaviors also generate other status elements within the task group, as symbolized by the arrow from "Task and Status Behaviors" to Box C. These internally generated status elements, as given in Box C, are previous successes and/or failures on tasks in the same situation, behavior interchange patterns (BIPs) which develop among the actors in the situation, evaluations of performance communicated by the actors to each other, and task cues which interacting individuals emit. These elements also enter the formation of aggregated expectations, as indicated by the arrow from Box C to the "Formation of Expectations." The resulting aggregate expectations may now modify the power and prestige order and result in a new pattern of status behaviors. Thus, expectation states theory has a dynamic concept of the power and prestige order, which may change and evolve as expectations are mediated by situational factors to determine behavior which, in turn, generates status elements which modify expectations in continuous cycles.

The specific form of the basic expectation assumption defines a function for predicting the rate at which a subject will reject influence in the standardized experimental situation associated with expectation states theory as below.

$$P(S) = m + q(e_p - e_o)$$

Thus the actor's rate of rejecting influence depends on his or her expectation advantage, the difference between the actor's self expectations, and his or her expectations for the other actor, and two parameters, m and q. The original thinking about these parameters was that m captured the special features of the subject population, and q those of the particular experimental manipulations. Thus m which gives the rate of rejecting influence for peers (when the expectation advantage is zero, the predicted rate is simply m) and was expected to be a function of age and gender, older groups having higher values of m than younger groups, and similarly male subjects having higher rates than females. Similarly q, which determines how much effect a unit of expectation advantage has (that is specifies how much a subject is affected by status differences) was expected to be a function of experimental procedures: For example, in an experiment with team scoring for performance q was expected to be higher than in an experiment with individual scoring for performance; subjects in a team scoring situation, being more dependent on their partners, were expected to pay more attention to expectation differences (Berger et al. 1977).

Later thinking has tended to see both parameters m and q as capturing both subject population and situational effects. Thus age need not only affect m, the rate at which peers reject influence, but also q, which determines how much effect expectations have: It is perfectly reasonable that younger subjects be more sensitive to expectation differences. Similarly team versus individual scoring of performance need not affect only q, but can conceivably affect m as well: There can be different characteristic rates for interaction between peers given the different types of scoring (Fişek, Norman, and Nelson-Kilger 1992). In a meta-analysis of 24 experiments done in the standardized experimental situation, Fişek, and his associates (1992) have shown that age, indeed, has a significant effect on m, older groups having higher m values than younger groups; but that gender has no effect on m. On the other hand a situational feature, the ratio of disagreement trials to the total number of trials also has a significant effect on m such that the higher this ratio, the higher the value of m. No situational effect, among the few considered, has a significant effect on q, but gender does: Females have a higher q value than males, showing greater effect of expectations. However, a study of a different set of seven experiments (Fişek, Berger, and Norman 1995) has shown no effect of gender on q either.

Thus in the context of expectation states theory, status behaviors are not only determined by expectations, but a whole host of other factors, both situational and individual, which can *mediate* how expectations influence behavior.

The Problem

The question which Driskell and Webster explicitly, and Lovaglia implicitly poses is whether *sentiment* is best conceptualized as a status element which enters into the formation of aggregated expectation states, that is, as a constitutive component of expectation states, or if it should be thought of as a factor which mediates the effect of expectations on behavior.

This problem will be addressed in more general terms: Given that status behaviors can be affected by a multitude of factors, and that it is desirable to integrate their effects into expectation states theory, especially if it is desired to construct models which can predict behavior at the individual level, then how should one decide whether a given factor should be conceptualized as entering into the formation of expectations or as filtering and mediating their effects?

THE BASIC CONSIDERATIONS

In order to decide whether a factor is to be integrated with expectation states theory, we believe that three different kinds of issues have to be considered if the decision is to be made with reasonable confidence. These are:

1. substantive theoretical considerations;
2. empirical evidence; and
3. metatheoretical considerations.

We believe that none of these categories takes precedence over the others, and each needs to be separately evaluated, however any one type of consideration, when contradictory information from the other types is not forthcoming, may decide the issue by itself.

If it is not possible to discriminate between these two approaches on the basis of these considerations, then the burden of proof should be on showing, or at least formulating a reasonable rationale for a factor entering into the formation of expectations, rather than the other way around, if parsimonious theoretical formulations are to be preferred. The conception of a factor as a constituent of expectations places it squarely in the core of expectation states theory, but the conception of the same factor as a mediator places it on, as it were, the periphery, leaving the core formulation as a simpler formulation. In fact, the mediation approach places sentiment in the *specific model* which is constructed to apply the general model of status characteristics and expectation states to particular concrete situations.

Thus if it is not possible to construct a superior rationale for either approach, then the principle of parsimony suggests that the mediator approach be adopted at least on a provisional basis, until further evidence or theoretical development accumulates.

We will now take up each of the three categories of issues in turn.

Substantive Theoretical Issues

Substantive theory may sometimes, but certainly not always, indicate whether a factor should be considered one which enters into the formation of aggregated expectation states or one which mediates the effect of expectation states on status behaviors.

For example, we have mentioned above that in the original formulation, age and sex of subjects and the way team performance is scored, among other factors, were left out of the formation of expectations to be considered mediating factors. Age and sex are both status characteristics, and if they are salient in the situation they will enter into the formation of expectations as status elements, if they are not salient, than expectation states theory says that they should not affect expectations. The kind of age and sex effects expected in this context is that older individuals and males have higher influence rejection rates among status equals than younger individuals and females respectively. That is a male interacting with a status equal other will have a higher rate of rejecting influence compared to a female interacting with a status equal other; an older actor interacting with a status equal other will have a higher rate of rejecting influence compared to a younger actor interacting with a status equal other. These effects cannot be explained in terms of expectation differences, as the conditions under which the effects are expected to occur are assumed to be ones where there are no expectation differences.

In terms of team versus individual scoring of group performance, the argument has to be a little different—it is that it is very difficult, if not impossible, to link the method of group performance scoring with the process of expectation formation.

A good illustration of how substantive theoretical considerations may clearly decide the case comes from the Camilleri and Berger (1967) experiment. In this study the effect of different degrees of responsibility for group decisions on the rate of rejection of influence was investigated in the standardized experimental situation. The subjects were manipulated into a number of different expectation states with respect to their partners in the usual manner of expectation states experiments, however, for each expectation state three different experimental conditions were created: In one condition the subject had equal responsibility over the group decision, in the other two the subject was either the "decision maker," having full responsibility for the group decision, or the "advisor," having no responsibility for the group decision. The rates of rejection of influence of decision makers and advisors were dramatically different from each other and the equal responsibility subject for each different expectation state.

It would be quite simple to formulate the distribution of responsibility as entering into the formation of expectations. The current conceptual armory of expectation states theory includes the concept of "valued role," and "decision maker" and "advisor" can clearly be considered instances of this concept, and thus enter the formation of expectations. Obviously decision maker is the more highly valued of the two roles, therefore their salience would increase the expectations for the decision maker and decrease those for the advisor. However, controlling for expectations, the rate of rejection of influence of decision makers are lower than those of equal responsibility subjects, who in turn have lower rates than advisors. Thus such a conceptualization leads to results inconsistent with the central assertion of expectation states theory—that power and prestige positions and therefore power and prestige behaviors are direct functions of expectations. Therefore, the conclusion has to be that the effect observed is not an expectations effect, but one of mediation of expectations.

In the case of sentiment, it seems to us that substantive theoretical considerations have little to tell us about how sentiment should be conceptualized. The two statements:

Holding all differentiation in terms of status elements constant, actors who have positive sentiment for the other actor will develop higher expectations, and actors who have negative sentiment for the other actor will develop lower expectations, compared to an actor who is neutral about the other actor.

and

Holding expectation advantages constant, actors who have positive sentiment for the other actor will emit fewer high status behaviors, and actors who have negative sentiment for the other actor will emit more high status behaviors, compared to an actor who is neutral about the other actor.

Are equally reasonable from the substantive theory point of view, and little can be said for or against either one on substantive theoretical grounds.

Empirical Evidence

One would think that empirical evidence would be the most straightforward way of deciding whether a factor is a determinant or mediator of expectations, however that is not the case. The reason is that "expectation states" is a theoretical construct, a product of the theoretician's mind and it is not assumed that it necessarily exists in the subject's mind. This idea has been one of the guiding principles of the expectation states program and has dictated the design of empirical studies. The typical experiment creates the conditions for the formation of expectations and then observes the behavioral consequences, without any attempt to actually access expectation states in any way. This makes it difficult to tell whether a factor which was manipulated during the creation of the experimental conditions and had an effect on the outcome behaviors, entered into the formation of expectations or mediated them. This is the case with the Lovaglia experiments, it is clear that sentiment or affect states are changing outcome behaviors, but it is not clear if this is because they are entering in the process of formation of expectations or if they are mediating the way in which expectations determine behavior.

However, it is possible to design experiments which can differentiate between the two alternatives, as witness the Driskell and Webster (1997) study. Driskell and Webster create two experimental conditions in which the only factor manipulated are sentiment states with the result that behavior in the two conditions are not significantly different: The inference is that differentiated sentiment did not lead to differentiated expectations. They then create two experimental conditions for high-low and low-high expectations to demonstrate that status manipulations do indeed result in different levels of rejection of influence, implying differentiated expectations. Finally they take the low-high status manipulation and create two further experimental conditions by manipulating positive and negative sentiment states. The result is that the different sentiment states do lead to different rates of rejection of influence. Given differentiated expectations sentiment states do have an effect on behavior. The clear implication is that sentiment is a mediator of expectations.

Some evidence for sentiment as constituent of expectations also exists: Shelly (1996) reports that questionnaire data shows that liked persons are more highly evaluated on both performance and nonperformance items as compared to disliked persons. Since evaluations do lead to expectations (Berger and Conner 1974) this result implies that sentiment becomes a constituent of expectations.

Thus while empirical evidence will not allow us to make a definite case for either approach, it is the case that Driskell and Webster's experimental results are more in the nature of direct evidence and that our conclusion is that empirical evidence slightly favors the mediation conceptualization.

Empirical evidence, when available, is obviously an excellent basis for deciding between the two alternative ways in which new factors may be incorporated into expectation states theory, however such empirical evidence is not easy to collect and calls for complex experimental designs involving serious inferential leaps.

Metatheoretical Considerations

We have already introduced the first of the metatheoretical considerations which apply to our problem—parsimony. Occam's razor is a metatheoretical principle shared by all scientific disciplines, and is certainly also a very practical consideration—we want to deal with as simple theoretical formulations as possible.

The second consideration is the "usefulness" of a theoretical integration. Both metatheoretical and practical considerations dictate that a piece of theoretical development be useful in the sense of generating new predictions which could not be generated before, and/or increasing the scope of the theory.

Thus the questions which should be asked about alternative ways of incorporating a new factor into expectation states theory, are the following: Which alternative leads to the simpler theoretical formulation? Which alternative provides greater increase in scope or new predictions, and is generally more useful?

We will take up the second question first: Obviously the integration of sentiment states with expectation states theory by either approach constitutes an important extension of the scope of the theory. However, it seems that the sentiment as constituent approach can lead to further extensions of scope. If sentiments lead to expectations consistent with those sentiments, the theory can be extended to deal with status characteristics where there are differential evaluations in terms of honor, esteem, and respect which lead to differential sentiments which are not in line with generalized expectations associated with the status characteristics. Thus the theory will be able to deal with characteristics such as Japanese-American and Jewish-American, which cannot be satisfactorily handled at the present time. Similarly the theory could be extended to cover characteristics which have differential evaluations in terms of honor, esteem, and respect, but have no generalized expectations associated with them. Thus from the point of view of usefulness, the constituent approach appears to have an edge over the mediator approach.

The simplicity of the two approaches can best be assessed by constructing models integrating sentiment into expectation states theory as a constituent element or as a mediating factor. We offer here an exercise of constructing simple models for both approaches and comparing them.

SIMPLE MODELS FOR SENTIMENT AND EXPECTATIONS

A "Sentiment as Mediator" Model

Let us consider the specific form of the basic expectation assumption:

$$P(S) = m + q (e_p - e_o)$$

In terms of the mathematical formulation, the assertion that sentiment is a mediator of expectations translates into the statement that the parameters m and q are functions of sentiment state. Let us say we have a variable a, sentiment state, which is coded as 1, 0, −1 to represent positive, neutral, and negative states of sentiment. This is the simplest possible conceptualization of sentiment as a variable and corresponds to the currently available experimental manipulations. We can now say,

$$m = f(a) \quad and \quad q = g(a).$$

However, we know from the Driskell and Webster study that sentiment makes no difference for status equals. Therefore m is not effected by sentiment state and the first of these equations can be eliminated.

What specific forms should the function, $g(a)$, have? We again invoke the principle of simplicity and assume as a first approximation that is a simple linear function. Our theoretical statement is that:

the amount by which a unit of expectations changes the rate of power and prestige behaviors is a linear function of sentiment state, that is

$$q = q_0 + q_a a$$

More specifically, q is the amount by which the influence rejection rate changes for one unit of expectation advantage, and we are saying that this quantity is a function of sentiment state, q_0 being the amount for the neutral sentiment state, with this amount increasing by q_a if the subject is in a positive sentiment state and decreasing by the same amount if the subject is in a negative sentiment state. This equation can be substituted in the original $P(S)$ function to obtain the overall prediction function for the rate of rejecting influence.

$$P(S) = m + (q_0 + q_a a)(e_p - e_o)$$

Simplifying the equation and rearranging terms we have

$$P(S) = m_0 + q_0(e_p - e_o) + q_a[a(e_p - e_o)]$$

However this function will not quite work as it stands because it makes the effect of sentiment state dependent on the sign of the expectation advantage, but we want the effect of sentiment state to be independent of expectation state. Regardless of whether an actor has positive or negative expectation advantage with respect to another, positive sentiment will decrease and negative sentiment increase the rate of rejecting influence. Therefore we modify the function by taking the absolute value of the expectation advantage in the last term of the function to obtain

$$P(S) = m_0 + q_0(e_p - e_o) + q_a[a + |e_p - e_o|]$$

We now have a prediction function with three parameters, m, q_0 and q_a. Since this is a linear function, least squares estimates for these parameters can be simply obtained by doing a regression of $P(S)$ on $(e_p - e_o)$ and the product of the absolute value of $(e_p - e_o)$ and a.

A "Sentiment as Constituent" Model

The construction of a "constituent" model for sentiment is not as straightforward as constructing the "mediator" model. In order to enter the formation of expectations sentiment states must generate status elements, and the principle of parsimony requires that before creating new elements in the theoretical system we should consider using elements which already exist. Of those the most likely candidate to capture the effect of sentiment states is the BIP, that is the Behavior Interchange Pattern. A behavior interchange pattern is a stable and consistent pattern of behavior involving two actors such that it signifies a power and prestige differentiation between the actors. We conceptualize the actor who has the higher power and prestige position as possessing the positive part or component of the behavior interchange pattern, $b(+)$, and the other actor as possessing the negative part or component, $b(-)$. When a BIP becomes salient, it activates *status typifications* such as leader- follower, initiator-reactor, $B(+)$ - $B(-)$ to which it is relevant, and these status typifications provide connections to task outcomes and thus become bases of expectations.

Table 1. Goodness-of-fit Statistics for the Driskell and Webster Data

Condition: Affect State, Task Expectations	Observed P(S)	The Mediator Model $m = .633$ $q_c = .173$ $q_a = .253$ Predicted P(S)	Difference	The Constituent Model $m = .635$ $q = .215$ Predicted P(S)	Difference	N
None, High-Low	0.708	0.696	0.012	0.714	−0.006	20
None, Low-High	0.553	0.569	−0.016	0.556	−0.003	19
Positive, None	0.631	0.633	−0.002	0.635	−0.004	21
Negative None	0.61	0.633	−0.023	0.635	−0.025	21
Positive, Low-High	0.491	0.477	0.014	0.492	−0.001	17
Negative, Low-High	0.676	0.662	0.014	0.635	0.041	17

$$\chi^2 = 2.197 \qquad\qquad \chi^2 = 3.713$$
$$df = 3 \qquad\qquad\qquad df = 4$$
$$p = .533 \qquad\qquad\quad p = .446$$
$$R^2 = .990 \qquad\qquad\; R^2 = .984$$

The BIP is a concept developed for open interaction situations, but it can be made to apply to the highly controlled experimental situation of expectation states theory with a little stretching: An actor who has positive sentiment for the other, reduces his or her rate of rejecting influence, that is comes to behave more deferentially, the actor cannot observe what the other actor is doing however it is not unreasonable to assume that he or she assumes the other to behave in a complementary way. After all, if you change your mind to agree with another person, you do not expect that person to turn around and adopt your original position. Thus it can be said that a BIP becomes salient from the actor's point of view (let us note that all expectation states theory is formulated from a single actor's point of view). A similar argument applies to the actor who has negative sentiment for the other. Remembering the Driskell and Webster result that sentiment does not change the behavior of status equals we formulate the following assumption.

Table 2.   Goodness-of-fit Statistics for the Lovaglia Data

Condition: Affect State, Task Expectations	Observed P(S)	The Mediator Model $m = .503$ $q_c = .116$ $q_a = .076$ Predicted P(S)	Difference	The Constituent Model $m = .503$ $q = .354$ Predicted P(S)	Difference	N
Positive, High-Low	.59	.553	.037	.503	.087	10
Negative, High-Low	.70	.738	−038	.738	−.038	10
Positive, Low-High	.23	.268	−.038	.268	−.038	10
Negative, Low-High	.49	.453	.037	.503	−.013	10

$$\chi^2 = 5.178 \qquad\qquad \chi^2 = 9.156$$
$$df = 1 \qquad\qquad df = 2$$
$$p = .023 \qquad\qquad p = .0103$$
$$R^2 = .947 \qquad\qquad R^2 = .905$$

Given that there is status differentiation between p and o, and that p has a sentiment state with respect to o, then a BIP between p and o will become salient in the situation, such that p will possess the negative component of the BIP if the sentiment state is positive, and the positive component of the BIP if the sentiment state is negative.

Given this assumption the standard machinery of the mathematical formulation of the theory of status characteristics and expectation states will generate predictions for situations where different sentiment states exist.

The Comparison of the Mediator and Constituent Models

To compare these two models the first thing to be done is to examine their goodness-of-fit to the available data. We have already described the Driskell and Webster data and we can start out by looking at the fit of these two models to this data set.

We obtain the parameter estimates for the mediator model by doing regression analysis on the data. The obtained prediction function is given below.

$$P(S) = .633 + .173 (e_p - e_o) + .253 a \mid e_p - e_o \mid$$

Regression analysis, as well as providing parameter estimates, also gives measures of goodness-of-fit of the model to the data. However, in this case we do not want to use the regression statistics to evaluate goodness-of-fit because of the very small sample size—we have estimated three parameters from six data points. Therefore we do another test for goodness-of-fit; given the predictions of the above function, following Balkwell (1991) we do the chi-square test. The results are given in Table 1.

The results of the chi-square test need little comment, the fit of this model to the Driskell and Webster data is obviously very good. We next examine the fit of the constituent model to the same set of data. We do not present the details of how the predictions of the model are obtained since it is a straightforward application of the standard status characteristics and expectation states model with the addition of BIPs to represent sentiment states. The results are also given in Table 1.

The fit of the constituent model to this set of data is also very good—it certainly is not possible to reject the model. However comparing the relative fits of the models it is clear that the mediator model fits better, even if marginally. All statistics are in favor of the mediator model,[1] and visual comparison of the models' predictions to the observed data points shows that while both models fit five of the six conditions equally well, in the sixth condition, the low-high expectations and negative sentiment condition, the constituent model does clearly worse than the mediator model.

We next look at the data from the Lovaglia study. Lovaglia carried out a two-factor experiment crossing expectation states and sentiment states in the standardized experimental situation of the expectation states tradition. Expectation states were manipulated by a diffuse status characteristic, education: The subjects who were undergraduates were led to believe that they were working together with either a graduate student or a high school student.[2] Sentiment states were manipulated through gift exchange: The subjects were asked to give a gift to their partners, to generate positive sentiment the partner responded handsomely, and to create negative sentiment the partner did not reciprocate. The results of the study and the fit of the two models are given in Table 2.

This time neither model fits well. Both models can be rejected at the .05 level of confidence; given the poor fits of both models, there is little point to comparing them.

It is an interesting question why both models fit the Driskell and Webster data so well, and the Lovaglia data so poorly. It may be the case that the differences between the two studies in the manipulation of sentiment states are the causes of this disparity. As we noted, Driskell and Webster manipulated affect states by giving the subjects an opinion values survey and telling them that they agreed or disagreed with each other to produce liking or disliking respectively. Lovaglia used a different technique, subjects were encouraged to exchange gifts—to produce positive affect the subjects who gave a gift of a rose to partner, received a rose from partner. To produce negative affect, the subject who gave a rose to partner received a message which said "No gift, I did not come here to make friends, I came here to make money." Driskell and Webster may be manipulating more stable sentiments, where Lovaglia is manipulating emotional reactions, that is affect states (cf. Ridgeway 1994). It may be the case that our approach of not distinguishing between sentiment and affect is not adequate to the task, and that in the context of expectation states theory, it is necessary to distinguish between the two. An intuitively reasonable explanation of the discrepancy of the data from the model predictions could be that "affect" or emotional arousal has more effect on subjects who have low-high expectations compared to subjects who have high-low expectations.

Another possible explanation is that the positive and negative manipulations in the Lovaglia study are not symmetric—the negative manipulation may be stronger than the positive. This difference may also possibly explain the difference in the fits of the models.

Given that the mediator model fits the Driskell and Webster data marginally better than the constituent model, also given that the mediator model, although it includes one extra empirical parameter, is very simple and straightforward while the constituent model is a little "forced," it seems reasonable to conclude that considerations of simplicity (and of course good fit) favor the mediator model, even if slightly. This does not, of course, mean that a better constituent model cannot be constructed.

CONCLUDING REMARKS

We have started out with the question of whether affect states should be conceptualized as determinants or mediators of task performance expectations. We have generalized the question to all factors which affect task and status behaviors and which are not part of expectation states theory at this point, and presented criteria for deciding on this issue. We have also applied these criteria to affect.

In terms of substantive theoretical considerations we have said that the constituent and mediator conceptualizations are basically equivalent.

In terms of empirical evidence, we have said that there is evidence for both models, although, the Driskell and Webster data which indicates the mediator conceptualization is more direct to the point.

In terms of metatheoretical considerations, we have demonstrated that the mediator conceptualization leads to a simpler model which also fits the available data slightly better than a model derived from the constituent conceptualization. But we have also argued that a constituent formulation maybe more useful in extending the scope of the theory.

The obvious conclusion has to be that, given the current state of theoretical development and empirical evidence, it is not possible to decide between the two approaches. These evaluations are of course subject to change over time as more data is collected, and more theoretical work is carried out on models. We hope this discussion will also be useful for theoretical work on the integration of other factors into the expectation states framework.

ACKNOWLEDGMENT

An earlier version of this paper was presented at the First International Conference on Theory and Research in Group Processes, Jagiellonian University, Cracow, Poland, June 18-21, 1996. M. Hamit Fişek's work on this project has been supported by the Turkish Academy of Sciences and the Boğaziçi University Research Fund (project #94B0751). Joseph Berger's work has been supported by the Hoover Institution at Stanford University.

NOTES

1.   The R^2's reported are reduction in chi-square from fitting the uniform distribution to the data.

2.   The subjects were told their partners grade point averages (GPAs), a high value for the graduate student and a low value for the high school student; they were also given a short test similar to the task and reported scores in line with the status discrimination. These manipulations were carried out because in an earlier study the education characteristic did not have an effect by itself. However these manipulations raise questions about how the situation should be graphed. Should GPA be represented as a second diffuse status characteristic and the test ability as a specific characteristics, or should they be treated as cues which activate the education characteristic? In the case of the mediator model, since the study involves one single level of expectation values, it makes no difference how the situation is graphed. However, in the case of the constituent model, since sentiment enters into the formation of expectations, it does make a difference. Thus the mediator model seems to have an "artifactual" advantage over the constituent model. Since our purpose is fundamentally methodological, and we wish to compare the two models without any such biases, we decided to go with the representation which gives the best fit for the constituent model. That is, the single diffuse status characteristic representation, and not the two diffuse, one specific characteristic representation which may be the substantively more correct representation.

REFERENCES

Balkwell, J.W. 1991. "From Expectations to Behavior: An Improved Postulate for Expectation States Theory." *American Sociological Review* 56: 355-369.

Berger, J., and T.L. Conner. 1974. "Performance Expectations and Behavior in Small Groups: A Revised Formulation." Pp. 85-110 in *Expectation States Theory: A Theoretical Research Program,* edited by J. Berger, T.L. Conner and M.H. Fişek. Cambridge, MA: Winthrop.

Berger, J., M.H. Fişek, R.Z. Norman and M. Zelditch. 1977. *Status Characteristics and Social Interaction.* New York: Elsevier.

Camilleri, S.F., and J. Berger. 1967. "Decision-Making and Social Influence: A Model and an Experimental Test." *Sociometry* 30: 365-378.

Driskell, J.E., Jr., and Webster, Jr. (1977). "Status and Sentiment in Task Groups." Pp. 179-200 in *Status, Network, and Structure: Theory Development in Group Processes,* edited by J. Szmatka, J. Skvoretz, and J. Berger. Stanford, CA: Stanford University Press.

Fişek, M..H., J. Berger, and R..Z. Norman. 1995. "Evaluations and the Formation of Expectations." *American Journal of Sociology* 101: 721-746.

Fişek, M.H., R.Z. Norman, and M. Nelson-Kilger. 1992. "Status Characteristics and Expectation States Theory: A Priori Model Parameters and Test." *Journal of Mathematical Sociology* 16: 285-303.

Lovaglia, M.J. (1997). "Status, Emotion, and Structural Power." Pp. 159-178 in *Status, Network, and Structure: Theory Development in Group Processes,* edited by J. Szmatka, J. Skvoretz, and J. Berger. Stanford, CA: Stanford University Press.

Ridgeway, C.L. 1994. "Affect." Pp. 205-230 in *Group Processes,* edited by M. Foschi and E. J. Lawler. Chicago, IL: Nelson-Hall Publishers.

Shelly, R.K. 1993. "How Sentiments Organize Interaction." Pp. 113-132 in *Advances in Group Processes,* vol. 10, edited by E.J. Lawler, B. Markovsky, K. Heimer, and J.O'Brien. Greenwhich, CT: JAI Press.

Shelly, R.K. 1996. "Status Value in Non-Status Situations." Paper presented at the "First International Conference on Theory and Research in Group Processes," Jagiellonian University, Cracow, Poland, June 18-21.

SOME DEVELOPMENTS IN
EXPECTATION STATES THEORY:
GRADUATED EXPECTATIONS?

Robert K. Shelly

ABSTRACT

Expectation states organize interpersonal behavior in a variety of social settings, including task groups, classrooms, and business firms. Expectation states result from information processing engaged in by actors as they encounter one another, perform tasks together, or observe behavior of others. Expectation states theory asserts expectations for performance are based on information about relative abilities, membership in particular social groups, or demonstrated skills at tasks. This paper examines whether different levels of status characteristics are reflected in graduated expectations. Data examined in this paper measure expectations that actors hold based on the status characteristics of others. These status characteristics reflect varying degrees of task relevance and task competence. Data show that expectations are differentiated if task competence meets a minimal standard, that degree of task relevance is reflected in expectations, and that a step-like function may describe graded expectations.

Advances in Group Processes, Volume 15, pages 41-57.
Copyright © 1998 by JAI Press Inc.
All rights of reproduction in any form reserved.
ISBN: 0-7623-0362-X

Expectations for performance of self and others organize behavior in a variety of social settings. For instance, who is influenced by whom in laboratory task groups, in classroom settings, and research and development groups in business is highly correlated with expectations actors have for one another in the situation. These expectations reflect information processing outcomes of knowledge about status characteristics actors bring to the social situation.

Status characteristics are culturally derived beliefs about who is likely to do better at tasks or who has more skill. Cultural beliefs which refer to general categories of actors and situations are called *diffuse* characteristics. Cultural beliefs which refer to particular situations and skills and abilities of actors are called *specific* characteristics. In addition, status characteristics may be based on category membership, such as race or gender, or on fine gradations of position on continuous variates, such as income or occupational prestige.

Expectations are theoretical constructs in that they are not directly observable; we observe their consequences. Such constructs provide conceptual tools which serve as the basis for theories and models of social processes (Berger, Cohen, Snell, and Zelditch 1962). In this case, expectations help explain how phenomena actors observe in a social setting lead to regularized behavior in the same or similar settings. For instance, education as reflected in such features of speech as diction, vocabulary, and grammar allow actors to "place" others in a social hierarchy based on very brief encounters. This placement has consequences for actors in who gets to contribute to a group task, who is likely to influence whom, and whose contributions are likely to be seen by others as valuable.

Expectations are generally thought to have state-like properties. Actors assign self and others to high or low expectation states based on how self and others are perceived with respect to a received standard or in relation to others in the social setting. For instance, an actor who displays high levels of education by employing proper grammar, a complex vocabulary, and good diction would be assigned a "high" state in comparison to some abstract standard. Such an actor would also be in a high state relative to an actor who uses poor grammar, simple vocabulary, and poor diction.

Expectation states are translated into behavior when actors offer others chances to contribute to tasks, accept or reject influence, or praise others based on the relative standing of each other. Actors in situations where others are in the same state show "equality" behavior, that is, they influence each other equally often, talk about the same amount, and show equal levels of approval for each others' contributions. Actors in situations where self and other are in different states differentiate their behavior. In such situations, one actor will talk more, be more influential, and receive more praise for his or her contributions.

STATUS CHARACTERISTICS

Status characteristics are social attributes actors possess. Cultural beliefs about social inequalities are attached to these attributes. Status characteristics are often linked to socially-valued task outcomes. For instance, perceiving that an actor has a high level of education is often associated with beliefs that the actor has better ideas, thinks more clearly about task solutions, or may know more answers to trivia questions. Knowledge of status characteristics and the associated beliefs that are labeled *expectation states* organize behavior in a variety of social settings (Wagner and Berger 1993).

Diffuse status characteristics organize interaction through a *burden of proof* process. In this process, actors are presumed to process information *as if* the following chain of events describes the phenomenon. An actor perceives status information about self and other(s) in a social setting. This status information is sufficient to rank order those present in a hierarchy. The members of the group then are asked to accomplish some valued task which has success and failure as possible outcomes. The burden of proof process links the status hierarchy to task outcomes unless it is specifically dissociated from the task. Expectations for performance are formed and translated into behavior by persons in the setting.

A rank order of education may be the basis for the formation of expectation states if it is the only basis of discrimination between individuals in a social situation. Highly educated individuals would be expected to do well on any task confronting a group if others were less well educated. This would be the case even if persons in the situation confronted a task for which the well educated had no knowledge or training.

Peter Blau (1977, 1994) introduced a distinction between categorical status structures and graduated status structures which has provided an impetus for theoretical developments in the study of expectation formation. It provided background for Ridgeway's (1991) development of an explanation for how social categories acquire status value. Recent work by Foddy and Smithson (1996) has attempted to take advantage of the concept of graduated status structures.

Research has shown that the categorical differences represented by gender, race, and physical attractiveness are diffuse status characteristics in American society. Similar results have been reported for the characteristics of educational attainment and occupation, though experiments have usually focused only on two states, high and low, of each characteristic (see Wagner and Berger [1993] for a review of this work). The graph-theoretic model of expectation formation developed by Berger, Fisek, Norman, and Zelditch (1977) represents this expectation process as:

$$\text{Diffuse Status Characteristic} \rightarrow \text{GES} \rightarrow \text{Specific Expectations} \qquad (1)$$

where GES is the Generalized Expectation State.

Specific status characteristics are skills and abilities possessed by an actor that are directly relevant to a task. The link between status characteristics and expectation states is directly established in this case because of the link between task outcomes and status information. For instance, education could be a specific status characteristic in a situation where actors are asked to perform an academic task such as writing a paragraph or creating a slogan to describe a group activity. The graph-theoretic model suggests the following path structure for specific expectations:

$$\text{Specific status characteristic} \rightarrow \text{Specific expectations.} \qquad (2)$$

For both cases, the link from specific expectations to behavior is added to the graph to complete the information→expectation→behavior link posited in expectation states theory and is used to derive predictions about behavior in experimental and real-world settings. Experimental tests of this conceptualization have generally focused on two actor, two state situations. One actor is told he or she has a high or low level of the skill needed for the task, and the other actor is given information that is complementary.

Two important issues are raised by these recent developments in the study of status orders. The first—do instantiations of categorical and graduated expectations differ from one another—has received very little attention. Foddy and Smithson (1996) suggest that such a distinction is conceptually and empirically useful. The second—how expectations are formed as distinct from how they are translated into behavior—has received a bit more attention. Balkwell, Berger, Webster, Nelson-Kilger, and Cashen (1992) examine this issue and show that actors form expectations that are reflected in choices in a social dilemma based on comparisons between two others. Webster and Driskell (1983) have shown that expectations are formed based on categorical classifications of attractiveness. These expectations may be measured in ways that are distinct from studies that employ translations into behavior.

In order to address these two issues it is necessary to sort out the effects of diffuse and specific characteristics, the role of categorical and graduated status orders, and the effects of norms that define standards for deciding that one actor is in the high state and another actor is in the low state of a status characteristic. Foschi (1989; Foschi, Lai, and Sigerson 1994; Foschi, Sigerson, and Lembesis 1995) has found actors employ task-intrinsic standards in forming beliefs about future behavior of self and other. Such standards constitute a yardstick to determine whether or not an actor possesses or does not possess an ability, skill, or status that entails forming an expectation of being able to perform a task. These standards may be contrasted with the relational standard adopted by most researchers in expectation states theory which says actors simply need to know whether they are better than, the same as, or worse than others in the situation in order to form expectations for future performance.

An important implication of the work on task-based standards versus relative standards is that under some conditions it may be important to know that one has met or surpassed a standard in order to form expectations, but under other conditions knowing one's relative position in the group may be sufficient to establish expectation advantages or disadvantages. Identifying conditions under which such processes operate is the focus of the research reported here.

Two issues are important to this project. First, differences in differentiation implied in diffuse and specific status characteristics suggests a rank order of importance of status information for a specific task situation. The theoretical development of information processing provided by expectation states theory suggests diffuse status characteristics have less impact on the formation of expectations than does information provided by specific status characteristics (Berger, Fisek, Norman, and Zelditch 1977, p.118-119).

An interesting, unexplored question is whether or not it is possible to differentiate the degree of task relevance within a set of specific status characteristics. For instance, abstract quantitative reasoning skills are a specific status characteristic which has varying degrees of relevance for particular tasks. In an engineering task, such skills may be highly relevant, but in a task involving developing budget summaries, such skills may be less relevant than concrete computational skills.

Research by Balkwell et al. (1992) provides some support for the hypothesized differences between diffuse and specific characteristics. Research examining degree of task relevance has not examined this question, but it seems reasonable to presume that the information processing steps needed to link specific performances to expectations for future performance are fewer in number than those needed to link diffuse or specific characteristics to expectations for future performance. For instance, in (2) above, the path from status characteristic to expectation is only one step, but the length or strength of that path may vary with the situational relevance of the status information.

Second, normative standards play a part in the formation of expectations. Normative patterns for possession of skills and abilities provide information in assessing whether or not actors form expectations for success or failure in a particular setting. This issue has been explored in recent work by Foddy and Smithson (1996) and by Foschi and her associates (Foschi, Warriner, and Hart 1985; Foschi and Freeman, 1991; Foschi, Lai and Sigerson, 1994; Foschi, 1996). Standards may be imposed by experimenters, employers, or other situational authorities (Foschi et al., 1985). They may also be activated by subjects and measured directly (Foschi 1996) or indirectly (Foschi, Lai, and Sigerson, 1994; Foschi, Sigerson, and Lembesis 1995).

Two hypotheses are examined in the research reported here. The first considers whether diffuse or specific status characteristics lead to the formation of different types of expectation states. This hypothesis asserts actors in expectation states studies form expectations for future performance based on how closely linked status information is to task outcome. The strongest expectations for future performance should be based on situational performance measured on a specific status characteristic, followed by expectations based on specific status characteristics based on knowledge about particular skills or abilities of actors, with expectations based on diffuse status characteristics weakest. A corollary for this hypothesis asserts that different levels of differentiation of characteristics affect the extent to which subjects hold different levels of expectations for future task performance. In particular, actors should form expectations for future performance that are more differentiated if status characteristics are more differentiated.

The second hypothesis asserts that actors form expectations for others by comparing status characteristics of actors to one another or to standards available in the situation. These standards may be task specific or normative and may be activated by internal information processing by the actor or by external imposition by experimenters or other authority figures. In the particular study reported here, cultural knowledge is presumed to activate the standard. These hypotheses are examined in a research context designed to focus specifically on the formation of expectations as the dependent variable of interest.

METHODS

Most expectation states studies employ a standard experimental setting in which actors are first made aware of status information about themselves and others in the setting. Actors then engage in some type of cooperative task in the second part of these studies. Feedback in the cooperative task situation is managed by the experimenter so that resolutions of disagreements about who is right about the task can be used as a measure of expectations of the actors. Status information supplied to the actors in the first part of the study affects the formation of expectations translated into behavior in the second part of the study. Foddy and Smithson (1996) describe such a study in detail.

Other techniques have been used to study the formation of expectations and their translation into behavior. In one instance, Webster and Sobieszek (1974) developed an experiment to examine how actors choose referent others. In this study actors chose who to accept evaluations from about their own performances. Status positions of evaluators were varied in the situation. Another technique presents subjects with a vignette or series of vignettes and asks them to make choices between alternative behaviors. Balkwell et al. (1992) used this technique to determine whether expectation states could be measured independently of behavior. Subjects were asked to choose an adviser from two persons who had high or low states of various status characteristics. Some characteristics were diffuse while others were specific.

Foschi (Foschi, Lai, and Sigerson, 1994; Foschi, Sigerson and Lembesis, 1995) has used an "in-basket" technique to study effects of task-based standards and possession of diffuse status characteristics on choices made by subjects. In these studies, subjects are presented with a description of a social situation containing status information about two actors. Student subjects were asked to make decisions about whom to hire for an important intern opportunity. Status information was varied around normative standards for the job candidates. The stimulus individuals were presented as either male or female to activate a diffuse characteristic in the situation. The dependent measure was which candidate was chosen by the subject for the job opportunity.

In both studies, choices between two socially meaningful alternatives and questions about perceived competence and suitability for a task were employed to test hypotheses about formation of expectations. The advantage of these techniques is that they approximate the influence experiment design by equating higher probability of one type of behavior with possession of high states of a characteristic. Similarly, higher probability of a different outcome is expected with the low state of a status characteristic. Combinations of diffuse and specific characteristics can be used to predict different choice outcomes as well.

The vignette studies, in-basket technique, and influence experiments have provided only limited opportunities to test hypotheses about expectations formed by actors about who will perform at what level in future task situations. Expectation states theory implies actors who form diffuse expectations expect subjects of those expectations to perform well or poorly, regardless of the situation. It also implies actors who form specific expectations expect subjects to do well on tasks in the present situation, but not necessarily in others.[1] Finally, the theory implies that actors who form performance expectations expect that only future performances of the same task type are likely to reflect expectation states.

The study reported here employs a technique that asked subjects to report expectations about one actor in comparison to another actor portrayed in a vignette. The vignettes employed in this study are variations of those employed by Balkwell et al. (1992). These vignettes were first developed by Margolin (1985).

Subjects are presented with a scenario involving a common classroom situation confronted by many college students. The description of the situation asks the student subject to imagine arriving early for a test to find two other students already in the room. The subject is presented as not knowing how to do a type of problem on the upcoming test. Conflicting advice is given by the two others. Each of the two others is characterized by different status characteristics. Subjects are asked to decide whose advice to take. The situation meets minimal scope conditions of an expectation states study in that an evaluative environment exists and a valued task is the focus of activity. However, there is no collective orientation in this research situation.

Subjects in the Balkwell et al. (1992) and Margolin (1985) studies are told the two others possess varied states on several status characteristics. Some of these states are high while others are low. The status characteristics are varied over diffuse, specific, and performance characteristics. The choices made by subjects support expectation states theory in that advisors with high status are chosen more often than advisors with low status. Choosing an advisor from others with mixed status on a variety of characteristics follows combination rules derived from expectation states theory for formation of expectations based on conflicting status information (Berger, Norman, Balkwell, and Smith 1992).

The present study varies the procedure by presenting one attribute for each vignette and asking subjects to report their beliefs about which of the two others is likely to perform better in the future in the situation or is likely to do better in other situations. Questions were asked about a variety of performances in the specific situation and in more general situations beyond the classroom context. In particular, the subject was asked whether she or he thought the high status actor would be likely to do better in the class, be a better overall student, secure a better job after graduation, be more intelligent, be more competent, be a better problem solver, and whether she or he was likely to receive an "A" grade on the next test. The questions about securing a better job after graduation, being more intelligent, and being more competent was chosen to assess beliefs about diffuse status characteristics. The questions about being a better overall student, likelihood of receiving an "A" grade on the next test, and being better at solving problems were chosen to assess beliefs about specific status characteristics.

Questions asked subjects to compare the high status person to the low status person and respond on a five-point scale. This scale had as its low value n (one) the verbal description that the two stimulus persons in the vignette were about the same on the topic described in the question. The high value (five) employed the verbal descriptor that the high status person was a great deal better than the low status person. No verbal descriptors were given for the intermediate scale values of two through four. This approach to asking questions about expectations was chosen because it offered respondents a clear choice about whether the high status actor was the same as or better than the low status actor. It also has the advantage of reflecting the upper half of a nine-point scale in a compact space. A similar strategy, with differently worded questions, was employed by Webster and Driskell (1983).

Different vignettes were presented to each subject in a packet. Each vignette informed the subject that the two persons described in the situation were the same age and sex in order to try to reduce effects of these diffuse status characteristics. Three different versions of each vignette were employed in the study. Each subject received one form of each vignette. One vignette asked the subject to respond to a situation in which the subjects varied on their high school class rank. In one version, the high status person was presented as from the upper third of his or her high school class. The low status person was presented as in the lower third of his or her class in this vignette. Other versions of this vignette identified the high status person as from the upper ten percent of the class and the low status person as from the lower half of the class.[2]

A second vignette asked subjects to respond to a stimulus situation in which the subject knew the approximate score of the two stimulus others on a standardized test of mathematical ability employed by the university in its admission process. This situation is one in which a specific status characteristic varies for actors in the situation. The high status person was presented as having scored at the fifty-fifth, seventy-fifth, or eighty-fifth percentile on this test, depending on the form given to a particular subject. The low status person was presented as having scored at the complementary percentile rank—the forty-fifth, twenty-fifth, or fifteenth percentile respectively.[3]

The third vignette asked subjects to respond to a situation in which they knew how the stimulus actors had performed on previous tests in the class. This vignette presented a situation in which actors form expectations for a specific status characteristic based directly on performances in the situation. In the first vignette, the high status person was described as having received one "A" grade on the previous test in the class. The low status person was described as having received a "C" grade on the previous test in this case. In the second vignette, the high status person was described as having received three "A" grades on the previous tests while the low status person had received three "C" grades. In the third vignette, the high status person was described as having received five "A" grades on previous tests while the low status person had received five "C" grades.

Subjects received a packet containing a set of vignettes, including one from each set described above.

Specific hypotheses for the data in this study are:

Hypothesis 1. Respondents form differentiated expectations for all conditions of the design. They expect the high status actor to be better in the class, be a better student, get a better job, be more intelligent, be more competent, be a better problem solver, and to do better on the next test. Subjects should form expectations for performance that are unitary for the diffuse characteristic and differentiated for specific characteristics.

Hypothesis 1. Subjects should form more differentiated expectations if the relative difference between the high and low actors is greater. The high status actor should be expected to do better if she or he has a higher class rank than if she or he has a lower class rank. The potential advisor portrayed in the ninetieth percentile should be evaluated more highly than the potential advisor in the sixty-sixth percentile. High status potential advisors with prior test scores of three "A" grades should be perceived as more capable than those with one "A" grade, and less capable than those with five "A" grades on prior tests.

Table 3.   Mean Expectation Scores for the
Performance Based Specific Characteristic Prior Test Grade

Stem	Test One "A"	Test Three "A"	Test Five "A"
Better in class	3.513	4.540	4.561
	$n = 76$	$n = 74$	$n = 114$
Better student	2.368	2.743	3.026
	$n = 76$	$n = 74$	$n = 114$
Better job	2.079	2.446	2.658
	$n = 76$	$n = 74$	$n = 114$
More intelligent	2.250	2.808	2.939
	$n = 76$	$n = 74$	$n = 114$
More competent	2.276	2.743	2.833
	$n = 76$	$n = 74$	$n = 114$
Better problem solver	2.816	3.446	3.553
	$n = 76$	$n = 74$	$n = 114$
Expect on next test	3.408	4.392	4.482
	$n = 76$	$n = 74$	$n = 114$

8.402 for the two-item scale based on prior test performance in the class, and 13.780 for the five-item scale based on prior test performance. Variances were homogeneous for all of the scales except the two item scale based on prior test performance.

One-way analysis of variance was performed for the expectation scales for each status characteristic to determine whether mean scores differed by level of manipulated status difference. Table 4 contains the mean value for each scale for each condition of each status characteristic. Tests were performed to determine whether these means differ by level of status difference portrayed in the vignettes, a key issue in assessing Hypothesis 2.

Overall, the data offer mixed support for Hypothesis 2. Subjects differentiate expectations based on the status information presented to them. Scores were compared to a hypothetical value for each scale based on the null hypothesis of equality of belief about potential advisors. T values ranged from 29.99 to 60.11 with d.f. $= 263$. Significance levels are below .005 for one-tail tests. This result is consistent with the outcome for each scale question evaluated independently.

Subjects develop expectations about the future performance of others based on the information presented in the vignette. High school class rank and performance on a standardized test of ability create similar patterns of belief with a unitary scale structure that is distinct from the equality point. Expectations based on performance on a specific status characteristic are elaborately differentiated compared to those based on either high school class rank or standardized test score. This result is supported by the scale analysis that showed two subscales of expectation for the specific performance based expectations, but only one for diffuse and specific characteristics.

Table 4. Expectation Scale Score Means by Condition of the Status Characteristic High School Rank and Standardized Test

Status Characteristic	Mean Scale Score	s.d.
High School Rank		
66 percentile	22.540 (n = 76)	6.323
90 percentile	22.540 (n = 74)	5.970
90 percentile	23.551 (n = 114)	6.522
Standardized Test		
55 percentile	17.474* (n = 114)	5.583
75 percentile	20.474 (n = 76)	5.795
85 percentile	21.770 (n = 74)	5.994
Prior Test (Two Item Scale)		
One "A" grade	6.921* (n = 76)	1.802
Three "A" grades	8.932 (n = 74)	1.398
Five "A" grades	9.044 (n = 114)	1.215
Prior Test (Five Item Scale)		
One "A" grade	11.790* (n = 76)	4.113
Three "A" grades	13.986 (n = 74)	4.715
Five "A" grades	15.009 (n = 114)	4.780

Note: *This mean is significantly different from others in this set of comparisons.

Subjects perceive the high status other in the same way for high school class rank regardless of the relative position of that person in their class. Differences in the level of difference for the diffuse status characteristic do not appear to produce differences in the formation of expectations consistent with Hypothesis 2.

Results for performance-based expectations lead to a different conclusion. Those who have demonstrated ability by multiple successes are seen as more likely to have similar success in the future. Mean scale scores of 6.921 for Scale 1 and 11.790 for Scale 2 are significantly different from 8.932 and 13.986, respectively. Scores of 8.932 and 9.044 for Scale 1 and 13.986 and 15.009 for Scale 2 are not different from one another.

Thus, there is an overall effect consistent with Hypothesis 2 for two of the three status manipulations in the vignettes. The one exception occurs for the diffuse status characteristic. Respondents do not differentiate between levels of this characteristic. Respondents formed expectations that vary by level of difference in status for actors described with specific status characteristics whether this information was historical or based on situational performances.

Respondents formed expectations for the high status actor in the vignette employing the standardized test score consistent with Hypothesis 2. The effects of differences in status identified in the data based on the standardized test manipulation show differences between levels, but only between those persons identified as below or above the university standard. Expectations for those at or above the university standard are not differentiated by respondents. Mean scale scores for those below the University standard are 17.474 versus scale scores of 20.474 for those at the standard and 21.770 for those above the standard.

CONCLUDING REMARKS

The question pursued in this study is whether expectations as measured when subjects respond to stimuli constructed to portray differences in status characteristics satisfy the conceptualization of expectation states as discrete dispositions. I also attempt to determine whether expectations are cognitively simple or complex. Two hypotheses about such beliefs were tested with data from subjects who responded to a series of vignettes. The research design is a between-subjects design for different levels of each status characteristic. The belief elements asked about specific expectations for two actors who were contrasted with each other in the context of a class where the respondent needed advice about how to do a type of problem in an upcoming mathematics test.

First, it is clear that respondents in this situation form differentiated beliefs about the future performances of the two stimulus actors. For all comparisons, the high-status actor is expected to perform better than the low-status actor. This result is consistent across all differences in status attributes and for all questions asked in the research instrument.

When the data are analyzed to determine if type and level of status characteristic make a difference in expectation formation, three effects are important to note. First, the status characteristic remotest from the situation seems to lead to the least differentiation of expectations across levels of the characteristic. Subjects do not see being the high-status actor differently whether this person is portrayed as in the top third or top tenth of their high school class. Relational differences in status information are sufficient for the development of differential performance expectations by actors when diffuse status is salient.

Second, the results for the specific status manipulation in this data suggest that normative, or task-specific standards, are sufficient for the development of expectations. This manipulation was designed to test whether degree of difference was important, as well as, whether being above or below a normative standard had an effect. The relative difference between status characteristics of advisors does not appear to be an important differentiating feature for subjects in this study.

Third, results for the specific characteristic based on performance show a strong effect for differences between two levels of performance. Expectations in this situation appears to have a step-function quality. Going from the lowest level of differentiation to one above it produces significant differences in expectations about future performance, but going from the intermediate value to a superior value does not have a significant effect. Levels of success appear to lead to differentiated expectations for the task-relevant standardized test and performance-based differences. This result raises an important unexplored issue for expectation states theory: What is the just noticeable difference in levels of status characteristics that leads to the formation of performance expectations? This issue has not been explored, but has particular implications in stratification systems with multiple levels in a social hierarchy and is certainly deserving of attention.

A more parsimonious explanation for the results reported here is based on the formulation of expectation advantage first advanced by Berger et al. (1977). Actors who have status information about any comparison, whether it is one in which one actor is advantaged or one in which both are equal, form performanance expectations based on the clarity of status information, not the magnitude of differences between actors. It is not necessary to posit that individual actors form performance expectations from fine distinctions in status information. It is sufficient, in this interpretation, that actors be rank ordered on a status dimension.[5]

To summarize, subjects respond to vignettes in a manner consistent with conceptualizations of the theoretical construct of expectation state. These responses are complex in that differences in expectations vary across types of status characteristics and across levels within types of characteristics. Status information provided to subjects organizes expectations for future behavior, and thus constitutes the first step in the expectation-behavior link. What is unclear and in need of further investigation is just how differences in status lead to differences in expectations. Under one interpretation of the results reported here, graduated status characteristics lead to the formation of graded expectations. An alternative explanation that differences observed in the data support the simpler idea that any difference is reflected in expectation. These results suggest that it is investigations of whether differences in diffuse and specific characteristics lead to differences in expectations that may be measured in behavioral settings. The question of the extent to which expectations are unitary or multidimensional constructs also remains. These data suggest the answer may depend on the nature of the characteristic that is salient in the situation. Diffuse status characteristics appear to lead to the formation of unitary expectations, while specific expectations based on performance at the specific task result in differentiated expectations.

ACKNOWLEDGMENTS

This is a revised version of a paper read at the First International Conference on Theory an Group Processes held at Jagellonian University, Krakow, Poland, June, 1996. Martha Fos chi and Murray Webster Jr. read and provided an important critiques of an earlier version c this paper. I am very grateful for their contributions to this research. The incisive comment of an anonymous reviewer are also gratefully acknowledged.

NOTES

1.   There is evidence to support a claim that expectations associated with specific characteristic carry over from one situation to another similar to the effects of a diffuse characteristic in a situatic where it is the only basis of discrimination between actors (Wagner and Berger 1982).

2.   Only two versions of the status manipulation were employed for high school class rank. The decision to limit the variation on this status characteristic was made so as to make maximum use of th available subject pool. The wording of the vignette was varied slightly to determine if presenting statu information using different wordings had any effect on responses to these questions. No effect was sig nificant across forms for this variation.

3.   The university average score for incoming freshmen on this test is approximately the seventy fifth percentile (Michael Williford, Ohio University's Director of Institutional Research, personal com munication). This value approximates an institutional norm and may be said to constitute a task-spe cific standard in this case. The data are widely disseminated in newspaper stories and by word of mout so that incoming students are well aware of the averages for scores and class rank.

4.   Webster and Driskell (1983) perform a factor analysis for the items they employed to asses whether appearance is a diffuse status characteristic. They report a one-factor solution in their analysi for a diffuse status characteristic.

5.   This interpretation of results was suggested by a reviewer. I am grateful for the suggestion an have incorporated it into the discussion to highlight the issue of how expectations are formed given var ious sorts of status information in a social situation.

REFERENCES

Balkwell, J., J. Berger, M. Webster Jr., M. Nelson-Kilger, and J. Cashen. 1992. "Processing Statu Information: Some Tests of Competing Theoretical Arguments." Pp. 1-20 in Advances i Group Processes, Vol. 9, edited by E. Lawler, B. Markovsky, C. Ridgeway, and H. Walke Greenwich, CT: JAI Press.

Berger, J., B.P. Cohen, J.L. Snell, and M. Zelditch Jr. 1962. *Types of Formalization in Small Grou_ Research*. Boston, MA. Houghton, Mifflin.

Berger, J., M.H. Fisek, R. Norman, and M. Zelditch Jr. 1977. *Status Characteristics and Social Inter action: An Expectation-States Approach*. New York: Elsevier.

Berger, J., R.Z. Norman, J. Balkwell, and R.F. Smith. 1992. "Status Inconsistency in Task Situations A Test of Four Status Processing Principles." *American Sociological Review* 56: 843-855.

Blau, P. 1977. *Inequality and Heterogeneity*. New York: The Free Press.

_____. 1994. *Structural Contexts of Opportunity*. Chicago, IL: The University of Chicago Press.

Foddy, M., and M. Smithson. 1996. "Relative Ability, Paths of Relevance, and Influence in Task-ori ented Groups." *Social Psychology Quarterly* 59: 140-153.

Foschi, M. 1989. "Status Characteristics, Standards, and Attributions." Pp. 58-72 in *Sociological Theories in Progress,* edited by J. Berger, M. Zelditch Jr., and B. Anderson. Newbury Park, CA: Sage.

———. 1996. "Double Standards in the Evaluation of Men and Women." *Social Psychology Quarterly.* 59: 237-254.

Foschi, M., and S. Freeman. 1991. "Inferior Performance, Standards, and Influence in Same-sex dyads." Canadian Journal of Behavioural Science 23: 99-113.

Foschi, M., L. Lai, and K. Sigerson. 1994. "Gender and Double Standards in the Assessment of Job Applicants." *Social Psychology Quarterly* 57: 326-339.

Foschi, M., K. Sigerson, and M. Lembesis. 1995. "Assessing Job Applicants: The Relative Effects of Gender, Academic Record, and Decision-type." *Small Group Research* 26: 328-352.

Foschi, M., G. K. Warriner, and S. D. Hart. 1985. "Standards, Expectations, and Interpersonal Influence." *Social Psychology Quarterly* 48: 108-117.

Margolin, L. 1985. A Criticism of the Theory of Status Characteristics: How Applicable is This Theory to Actual Group Experience? Doctoral Dissertation. Department of Sociology, University of Nebraska.

Ridgeway, C. 1991. "The Social Construction of Status Value: Gender and other Nominal Characteristics." Social Forces 70: 367-386.

Wagner, D., and J. Berger. 1993. "Status Characteristics Theory: The Growth of a Program." Pp. 25-63 in *Theoretical Research Programs: Studies in the Growth of Theory,* edited by J. Berger and M. Zelditch Jr. Stanford, CA. Stanford University Press.

———. 1982. "Paths of Relevance and the Induction of Status-task Expectancies: A Research Note." *Social Forces* 61: 575-586.

Webster, M., Jr., and B. Sobieszek. 1974. *Sources of Self Evaluation: A Formal Theory of Significant Others and Social Influence.* New York: John Wiley.

Webster, M., Jr., and J. Driskell. 1983. "Beauty as Status." *American Journal of Sociology* 89: 140-165.

DOUBLE STANDARDS:
TYPES, CONDITIONS, AND CONSEQUENCES

Martha Foschi

ABSTRACT

This paper examines theory and research on double standards—the practice of using different requirements for the inference of possession of an attribute, depending on who the actors being assessed are. The paper focuses on the use of double standards for competence and begins with a review of the conditions under which status characteristics (e.g., gender, ethnicity, socioeconomic class) become a basis for such practice. The central hypotheses advanced in this area state that individuals defined as lower-status actors will tend to be assessed by a stricter standard than those seen as higher-status actors and that, as a result, the same level of performance by both will be more likely to elicit an inference of ability in the latter than in the former. Extensions of these propositions to include other bases for competence double standards (e.g., actors' personality characteristics, allocated rewards, sentiments of either like or dislike among actors) are also proposed. Next, double standards in the inference of other types of valued attributes (e.g., beauty, morality, mental health) are discussed, and the relationship between these practices and competence double standards is examined. For all these types of double standards, research evidence is

Advances in Group Processes, Volume 15, pages 59-80.
ISBN: 0-7623-0362-X

reviewed and areas for further investigation are suggested. The paper concludes with a discussion of the use of "reverse double standards for competence"—that is, the practice of applying more lenient standards to lower-status actors—and of some of the conditions under which it occurs.

INTRODUCTION

When people interact in groups they often—intentionally or not—give information about each other on a wide range of traits that they might possess, such as competence, honesty, and assertiveness. It is also common for participants in such interactions to generalize from limited evidence about those traits to their more permanent assignment to the actors involved. For example, on the basis of two intelligent comments made by a person during a group discussion, another group member concludes that the person is intelligent. This paper concerns some aspects of this process. The focus is on the role that standards—or norms specifying minimum evidence requirements—play in those inferences.

The issue of central interest is that the *same* available evidence is often assessed through a *different* standard, and that in many occasions, this difference is a function of who the actors in question are. Thus, the same act may be interpreted as either an indication of assertiveness or of aggressiveness, depending on whether the performer is a man or a woman, or the same mark on an exam may be seen as either conclusive or inconclusive evidence of competence, depending on the student's skin color. Under what conditions do these different inferences occur? What are the traits involved? What are the consequences of the application of such double standards? These are some of the questions addressed in this paper.

THE INFERENCE OF COMPETENCE: THEORETICAL BACKGROUND

Since it is useful to organize the discussion in terms of the *types of traits* that are being inferred, I begin by discussing the inference of competence. I define "competence" broadly to refer to the ability to do well on a task judged to be valuable. Thus, competence may range from the ability necessary to solve geometrical puzzles to the set of skills required to fulfill a professional position. The assessment of task competence is of central importance in person perception: it often anchors and defines how other judgements about individuals are made, and has long-term consequences for their interactions, such as the distribution of opportunities to perform and the assignment of organizational rewards. Because of this centrality, the assessment of competence is also the focus of the present paper.

Expectation states theory (Berger, Fisek, Norman, and Zelditch 1977; Berger, Wagner, and Zelditch 1985; Wagner and Berger 1993; Webster and Foschi 1988) provides a solid, comprehensive account of the processes through which people assign levels of competence to each other in task groups. The theory has a long-standing tradition, and empirical findings provide strong support for its predictions. In this paper I formulate and develop ideas within the context of this theory. A core concept in the expectation states program is that of a "status characteristic," defined as any valued attribute implying task competence. Such characteristics consist of at least two states (e.g., either high or low level of mechanical ability, either limited or extensive formal education), one of which is evaluated more positively than the other. These attributes are also defined as ranging from specific to diffuse, depending on their perceived applicability. A specific characteristic is associated with well-defined performance expectations; a diffuse characteristic carries, in addition, predictions about performance on a wide, indeterminate variety of tasks. In many societies, gender, ethnicity, and socioeconomic class constitute diffuse status characteristics for large numbers of individuals. Thus, women, for example, are often expected not only to be inferior to men in various specific skills, but also to be inferior in general competence (see Wagner and Berger 1997 for a review of expectation states research on gender).

Another central concept is that of "performance expectations." The theory specifies how members of a task group form such expectations for each other. These are predictions about the likely quality of their performances on the task at hand, and reflect levels of perceived competence. Expectation states are said to develop for "self"—the focal actor—relative to each other member of the group. Expectations may be based on either the group members' status characteristics or on their actual performances on the task, or on both. The assumed relationship between status characteristics and the task is also a factor. For example, the performance expectations developed by the members of a mixed-sex group will vary depending on whether the task is perceived to be "masculine," "feminine," or of no gender linkage. The theory focuses on the expectations that are formed by group members who are both task oriented (i.e., motivated to do the task well) and collectively oriented (i.e., prepared to take each other's ideas into account toward the solution of a joint task). Performance expectations, in turn, have a strong effect in determining the nature of the interaction that takes place: these expectations affect the distribution of action opportunities among group members, the rate at which they accept such opportunities, the type of evaluations they receive, and the amount of influence they exert. These four factors, comprising what is known as the *power and prestige order of the group*, contribute in turn to the self-maintenance of the initial expectations.

It is useful to view the theory as consisting of two main branches, each investigating a different basis for the formation of expectations. Thus one of these branches (evaluations and expectations theory) is concerned with the role of performance evaluations, while the other (status characteristics theory) focuses on the role of status attributes. Of particular interest here is the work, formulated within the first of these branches, that examines the expectations developed by group members on the basis of the performance evaluations they receive from a source outside the group. A "source" is defined as a person or set of persons who is (are) accepted by a group member as more capable of evaluating performances than is the group member himself or herself. Research within this branch has examined properties of both the source and the evaluations, and has tested for the effects of these variables on expectations. Thus the source may or may not be knowledgeable, or it may be of higher, equal, or lower status relative to a given group member. The evaluations, on the other hand, may be either many or a few, or they may be either consistent or inconsistent with each other (Webster and Sobieszek 1974; Crundall and Foddy 1981).

Working within this branch and focusing on the evaluations received, I have proposed that the standards for ability and for lack of ability used by the source (and accepted by group members) constitute another important factor affecting expectations. For example, a score of 14 correct answers out of 20 is sufficient demonstration of ability if the standard is 12 or more, but that same score becomes unconvincing evidence of skill if the standard is 17 or more. Thus standards act as filters mediating the relationship between evaluations and expectations (Foschi and Foschi 1979). Standards may be classified as either strict or lenient (or high or low, respectively), depending on the level and number of the requirements imposed. A strict standard for *ability* requires more evidence of competence than does a lenient standard. Conversely, a strict standard for *lack of ability* tolerates less evidence of incompetence than does a lenient standard. In the above example, the standard of 12 or more correct is a more lenient ability standard than that of 17 or more correct. Furthermore, 17 or more correct in several comparable tests of the same ability is a stricter standard than 17 or more correct in a single test of that ability. When evaluations meet a given standard, strong or conclusive expectations are formed. On the other hand, when evaluations fall outside that standard, expectations are weak or inconclusive (Foschi and Foddy 1988; Foschi, Warriner, and Hart 1985). The strength of the expectations, in turn, is reflected in the power and prestige order of the group that develops. Several hypotheses on performance evaluations, standards, and level of exerted influence have been tested empirically, with results showing clear support (Foschi et al. 1985; Foschi and Freeman 1991). (There is also work formulated outside the expectation states tradition and investigating related ideas; see Miller and Prentice 1996 for a review).

STATUS-BASED DOUBLE STANDARDS FOR COMPETENCE

Theoretical Formulations

Foschi and Foddy (1988) have proposed a conceptualization of double standards for competence that links them to status differences. This conceptualization, in turn, is the basis for two theories (Foddy and Smithson 1989; Foschi 1989) on status characteristics and multiple standards. Both theories combine elements from the two main branches of the expectation states program and constitute refinements and extensions of aspects of that program; my own model also incorporates ideas from attribution research on the causal interpretation of success and failure by performers from different social categories. Although the two theories use different formalizations, they make compatible predictions.

The following summarizes the core of the ideas I propose in Foschi (1989). The theory is formulated for a situation where self works on a joint task with a partner or "other"—the same basic unit of analysis that is investigated in most of expectation states theory. The propositions are stated from self's point of view and apply to any status characteristics—specific or diffuse, individually as well as in combination with others. Scope conditions are as follows. Self values the task and is motivated both to do well at it and to arrive at accurate assessments of the two performers' competence. The situation of central interest is one in which the two persons differ with respect to a status characteristic but perform at the same level (either equally well or equally poorly). The performance evaluations originate in a source outside the group and are considered by self to be objective (i.e., unbiased). There are, however, no previously set and agreed upon standards by which to infer ability (or lack thereof) from those evaluations. Furthermore, self himself or herself treats the characteristic as having status value,[1] and has no other grounds (apart from status and performance evaluation) on which to base assessments of the two persons' relative levels of competence. Under these conditions, are the equal performances sufficient to equalize the two actors in perceived ability, or does the status difference still have an effect in the inferences that are made? In Foschi (1989) I have proposed that the latter will be the case—a result of the activation and application of different, status-based standards to the two persons. In other words, those who are considered to be of lower status will have their performances scrutinized and then assessed by a stricter standard than those who are of higher status; the latter, on the other hand, will be given the benefit of the doubt and will be treated with a more lenient standard than the former.[2] I have also proposed a similar situation for the inference of lack of ability—in that case, the higher the status, the more convincing the demonstration of incompetence will have to be.

These ideas can be easily extended to situations where the attribute in question has more than two states, for example, three levels of socioeconomic class or four levels of ethnic background. In each of these cases, if a different standard is activated for each level of the characteristic, the standard is then a "multiple" one.[3] Foschi (1989) also incorporates relevance between status and the task at hand as an additional variable. Thus, the task may be seen as either (1) masculine, (2) feminine, (3) explicitly dissociated from gender, or (4) not explicitly defined in relation to gender. More lenient standards for the male than for the female performer are predicted for (1).[4] This is also the prediction for (4), where gender and task become related through status generalization—a process by which a status attribute becomes relevant to the task at hand unless there is specific information to the contrary. In such a case, the double standards will be less pronounced than when the task is masculine, but they will manifest themselves nevertheless. No double standards benefiting the male performer are predicted for (2) or (3). Finally, another extension includes situations in which self is not engaged in a collaborative task with a partner, but is instead a nonperforming evaluator of two (or more) performers (Foschi 1989).

Once a double standard is activated and used, it affects the extent to which ability is inferred—in much the same way as when standards are provided by an outside source. The application of a more lenient standard to the higher-status person ensures that more ability is assigned to him or her than to the lower-status person with the same record, regardless of level of performance. Thus double standards contribute to the maintenance of the initial, status-based assignment of competence. The practice is both subtle (as it involves neither devaluing nor overvaluing a performance in an overt manner) and not necessarily conscious (as an actor does not have to formulate such standards explicitly in order to use them). Because even those who are aware of applying double standards often consider them to be of dubious legitimacy, the practice is seldom explicitly communicated to the performers. Moreover, double standards for competence may take on many forms— from different requirements on a test measuring the ability in question (e.g., the standard may be set as a minimum of 70% correct answers for one group and a minimum of 80% correct answers for another) to different requirements regarding qualities not directly related or even unrelated to the task (e.g., requiring a confident demeanor and/or a cooperative style for one group but not for another) (Carli 1990; Foschi and Foddy 1988; Ridgeway 1982). Sometimes the practice takes the form of applying a universalistic standard to one group and a particularistic standard to another. By allowing for special circumstances, the latter is more lenient than the former. Lorber (1984, Chapter 1) presents an insightful description of situations whereby women are held to universalistic standards while exceptions are permitted to men.

Foschi (1989) is an elaboration of the graph-theoretic formulation of status characteristic theory, and utilizes graphs and paths of relevance as its key concepts. Foddy and Smithson (1989), on the other hand, propose an alternative account of double standards that is formalized through fuzzy sets. The use of different formalizations is the major difference between the two models—both treat double standards as an order-preserving mechanism whereby the lower-status actor has to show more evidence of ability (or less evidence of lack of ability). A feature of special interest in the Foddy and Smithson formulation is that the concept of "double standard" is extended to include the rules whereby status and performance are combined. That is, it is not only that performance requirements will be stricter for the lower-status actor. In addition, the rules for combining performance and status information may give less weight to this actor's successes and more weight to his or her failures, than to the corresponding performances by the higher-status actor.

Outside the expectation states framework, the work by Biernat and associates on stereotypes and the shifting standards model is clearly of interest here (Biernat 1995; Biernat and Kobrynowicz 1997; Biernat and Manis 1994). The core idea in their work is also that standards change as a function of who is being evaluated. Although evaluatees are described in terms of social categories rather than status characteristics, these authors treat the two concepts as having considerable overlap (and, for the most part, use examples of social categories that coincide with the examples of status characteristics used in the expectation states tradition). However, Biernat and colleagues also propose that different conditions result in either a more lenient or a stricter standard for devalued groups, and discuss attributes other than competence. For these reasons, their work is relevant to more than one section of this paper and is therefore discussed at various places below.

Empirical Evidence and Assessment

Double standards for competence that benefit the higher-status performer are common in a variety of everyday task settings, ranging from informal discussion groups to the formal evaluation of job performance in work organizations. Several authors have offered *accounts and descriptions* of this practice; although the expression "double standards" is not always explicitly used, it is clear that authors are referring to different requirements for different types of actors. In the vast majority of cases the status attribute that activates the double standard is gender. Examples may be found in Eichler (1977, 1980), Epstein (1970a, Chapter 5; 1981, Chapter 1), and Hochschild (1974); see Foschi (1992) for a review of this literature.

Over the last several years, considerable *research evidence* on this practice has accumulated. This evidence may be classified as direct or indirect. I define "direct evidence" as that resulting from work specifically designed to test hypotheses on status and double standards; "indirect evidence" comes from research that, although not designed for those purposes, nevertheless investigates this practice. The following discussion concerns only the former.[5]

To my knowledge, all but one of the studies providing direct evidence originate in tests of the theoretical formulations outlined above. The exception is the work by Yogev and Shapira (1987) examining credentials for employment—a variable closely related to attributed competence. The authors propose the existence of a double standard for credentialism for members of two ethnic groups in Israel and report survey data supporting their claim: they found educational requirements for employment to be differentiated by level and type of education which, in turn, differed by ethnic group.

Several experiments test hypotheses derived from the two expectation states models. A study reported in Foddy and Graham (1987) employed a variant of the standardized setting commonly used to assess the effects of expectations on influence rejection (Webster and Sobieszek 1974, Appendix 1). Subjects participated in either same-sex or opposite-sex dyads, and performed a visual perception task described to them as either masculine, feminine, or of no known sex linkage. Next they received prearranged scores indicating that self was either definitely superior or definitely inferior to the partner; following this, standards for ability and for lack of ability were elicited. The results on ability standards set for oneself in the opposite-sex groups are of particular interest here. As predicted, the authors found that for the masculine task, (a) women set a stricter standard for themselves than did men, and (b) this effect was larger when the woman had a lower rather than a higher score than her partner. Compared to men, women also set a stricter standard for themselves in the neutral task, although here the effects were stronger when women had outperformed their partner. Also as predicted, no double standard was evident when the task was described as feminine.

The two experiments I report in Foschi (1996) also used a variant of the standardized setting of expectation states research. Subjects participated in opposite-sex dyads and were assigned at random to either control or experimental conditions. The perceptual task was defined to participants as one on which men usually do better than women. In the first experiment, the focus was on standards for ability set for either self or the partner. In the experimental conditions, prearranged scores showed ordinary performances by both persons, although in half of these conditions self's scores were slightly better than the partner's, while the scores were reversed in the other half. (I chose an ordinary level of performance on the assumption that double standards would be more likely to occur at that level, that is, when outcomes do not provide a clear indication of ability.) Subjects then set ability standards for the performer with the higher score—either self or other. As predicted, the female performer was, overall, held to a higher standard than her male counterpart. The gap between standards was wider when the target person was the partner rather than self.

The second experiment examined the effects of accountability on double standards. This variable is defined as the extent to which an actor expects having to justify his or her assessments of group members—in this case, including choice of standards. As anticipated, there was a significant difference between the standards set for the male and the female partner when accountability was low, but this difference was no longer significant when accountability was increased to a medium level. These results suggest that, for these subjects, the legitimacy of using gender as an indication of competence was somewhat limited. This is not surprising, given the major changes that have occurred in this respect in the United States and Canada in recent years. It is also worth noting that, as proposed, in all three of these expectation states experiments employing variants of the standardized setting (Foddy and Graham 1987; Foschi 1996), measures of competence in self and partner were consistent with measures of standards—that is, the higher the ability requirements imposed on an actor, the less ability inferred in him or her relative to the partner and the less influence the actor is able to exert.

Another expectation states experiment in this area is the one reported in Foschi, Lai, and Sigerson (1994). The study tests hypotheses about the use of double standards when self is a nonperforming assessor of two performers (rather than being both a performer and an assessor, as in the self-and-other context of the studies discussed above). This new design involves the examination of files of applicants for engineering jobs, and recreates several features of a hiring decision. Variables included both sex of performer and sex of assessor, as follows. Subjects were male and female undergraduates who believed they were members of a university-wide committee making recommendations on the selection of applicants. The critical choice to be made by each person was between a male and a female applicant with average but slightly different academic records. Both applicants were said to be semi-finalists in the competition for the position. A key assumption in this design links beliefs to decisions: the higher the ability an applicant is perceived to have, the higher his or her chances of receiving a hiring recommendation. Moreover, subjects were not asked directly about their standards but instead revealed them through their recommendations. In one experimental condition the man held the better record, while in the other the situation was reversed. Results from male subjects indicate that when the male candidate was the better performer, he was chosen more often, and considered more competent and suitable for the job, than when the female candidate was in that position. Female subjects, on the other hand, did not exhibit such a double standard. This corresponds with the authors' hypothesis that men and women would differ in the extent to which they treated gender as a cue to competence and, as a result, in the extent to which they would activate different standards.

A variant of this design was employed in Foschi, Sigerson, and Lembesis (1995) to explore conditions of activation of double standards for competence as well as rewards. In this study each subject made decisions about one candidate at a time— rather than about a pair. The candidate, again said to be a semi-finalist for a position, was either a man or a woman with qualifications that were either average or outstanding. As anticipated, no double standards were found when decisions about competence had to be made in the absence of a direct comparison. Instead, double standards emerged when subjects had the possibility of activating comparisons between the candidate and other performers, namely when they had to make reward allocations (i.e., suggest a salary figure). Furthermore, the double standard favored the male performer when level of performance was average but was reversed to benefit the female performer when that level was outstanding. As proposed in that article, the woman with the outstanding qualifications may have been seen as better than, rather than equal to, the comparable man. It is also possible that subjects felt it was legitimate to redress past gender inequalities as long as the female candidate was exceptional. I discuss this issue later in this paper.

The topic investigated by Biernat and associates in their shifting standards model is similar to the one addressed by the expectation states work on double standards—namely, whether variations in judgment requirements occur when

evaluating individuals from different social groups. The models from the two traditions, however, differ in several respects. One important contribution of the work
on shifting standards is to ask whether the extent of the variation depends on the
type of scale used—namely, objective or subjective. Biernat and colleagues had
proposed that stereotypes would affect the standards applied if respondents were
asked to set them on subjective scales, but not if the scales were objective. That is,
subjective scales would enable different values to be assessed as indicating the
same level of an attribute (e.g., in the case of height, a man measuring 6 feet 2
inches and a woman measuring 5 feet 9 inches could both be considered to be tall)
but objective scales (e.g. a scale that would define "tallness" as a specific range of
values expressed in feet and inches) would not. Because they invite the use of different standards, subjective assessments do not reveal evidence of stereotyping
(e.g., that men are often judged to be taller than women) as much as objective
assessments do. Biernat and Manis (1994) examine inferences of competence and
report four studies investigating academic and verbal abilities in relation to gender,
and verbal and athletic abilities in relation to skin color. In all cases the predictions
about stereotypes, type of scale, and shifting standards were supported. (See also,
Biernat, Manis, and Nelson [1991] discussed later in this paper for double standards in the inference of other traits.)

More recently, Biernat and Kobrynowicz (1997) have compared the shifting
standards and the expectation states models, and have proposed that they have different domains, namely, that they apply to inferences about different *levels* of ability. Thus, these authors argue, if two clearly different questions are asked, one
about conclusive demonstration of competence and the other about minimum ability, the expectation states models address the former whereas the shifting standards model applies to the latter. Biernat and Kobrynowicz (1997) propose that,
for the inference of minimum ability, decisions are made separately for lower- and
higher-status groups, and standards are set to merely reflect the expectations held
for each. Since the expectation is of a lower level of performance for devalued
groups, the standard is more lenient for them. This is exemplified by statements
such as "the performance is good for a woman." The expectation states models, on
the other hand, concern decisions about documenting ability and involve comparisons across, rather than within, groups. The same successful performance has different informational value depending on the performer's status, as the probability
of the event is seen as varying with that factor. Standards for ability reflect these
differences and are therefore set to be stricter for the lower-status performer.

Biernat and Kobrynowicz (1997) report two studies designed to assess where
evaluatees differed in either sex or skin color. In line with predictions, entry
requirements (minimum performance standards) were lower for women than for
men, and for blacks than for whites. For each of these social categories, however,
the reverse occurred for ability inference, also as predicted. It is worth noting that
in the expectation states studies where questions about standards were explicitly
asked (Foddy and Graham 1987; Foschi 1996), these questions were indeed

phrased in terms of scores required to conclude that a person "definitely has (or does not have) ability." Moreover, the competitive evaluation context created in Foschi et al. (1994, 1995) required that subjects made more than a mere inference about the candidates' minimum levels of ability. In other words, empirical results from tests of the expectation states models are consistent with the argument about different levels of ability presented by Biernat and colleagues.

In sum, research findings on status and standards for competence show substantial support for the prediction that, when an inference about definite possession of ability is to be made, lower-status individuals will be held to a stricter standard for competence than their higher-status counterparts. The research also identifies several conditions for the operation of this practice, notably a low level of accountability and a salient status difference between two performers. The work includes survey as well as experimental evidence, and the latter originates in studies using two different types of settings: laboratory contexts where subjects set ability standards for a visual perception task, and situations recreating features of the assessment of job applicants. Moreover, standards were assessed directly in some of the studies and indirectly in others. This variety strengthens the findings.

In my view, the results also suggest three areas where it would be useful to carry out research in the future, as follows.

1.   Although the hypotheses from the models discussed above are formulated in abstract terms using either the concept of "status characteristic" or that of "social category," most of the evidence gathered so far involves gender (a few studies investigate skin color). For a wider empirical basis, it would be important to operationalize those concepts differently in future studies. This would not only establish that the process is not specific to any particular attribute but would also enable researchers to compare the degree to which various attributes activate double standards.

2.   The empirical work carried out so far focuses on double standards for ability. However, two of the theoretical proposals (Foddy and Smithson 1989; Foschi 1989) include both types of double standards—for ability as well as for lack of ability. In other words, the exclusion of lower-status members through different requirements can occur at two levels. For example, if the higher-status actor's performance is *successful*, he or she is given the benefit of the doubt and treated with a more lenient standard for ability. On the other hand, if that person's performance is *unsuccessful*, a reluctance to assign incompetence to him or her results in a more lenient standard for lack of ability (i.e., a standard that tolerates more evidence of poor results). In many competitive evaluation contexts (e.g., the assessment of job applicants, the selection of candidates for admission to graduate school, juried competitions in the performing arts, and mandatory promotion reviews in the workplace), two important decisions occur: one involves excluding those evaluatees "not in the running," and the other, selecting from the "short list." The former decision implies activating standards for lack of ability while the latter entails the

use of ability standards. Propositions about the use of both types of double standards await empirical testing. Results from such tests would contribute to a more comprehensive understanding of this practice.

3.   Both Foddy and Smithson (1989) and Foschi (1989) include relevance between status and task as a variable in their models. In expectation states theory terms, relevance refers to the anticipated relationship between those two factors; namely, the extent to which a person views status level as a predictor of either success or failure at a task. The concept of "relevance" is therefore very similar to that of statistical association (in a person's mind). Thus a task is masculine if, overall, men are expected to perform it better than women, and feminine if the reverse is anticipated. Moreover, a task may be more or less masculine (or feminine) depending on the strength of this association. For example, the expectation could be either that 90 percent of men will perform the task better than women, or that only 60 percent will do so. One should also consider that views about such statistical associations may be shared with others in a given social system to various degrees—that is, consensus could range from high to low. (On the creation and spread of status beliefs, see Ridgeway and Balkwell 1997). In turn, both of these factors, strength of association and level of consensus, would affect the legitimacy that self confers to the use of double standards (see Ridgeway and Berger 1986, and Ridgeway and Walker 1995 for analyses of the role of legitimation processes in the formation of expectations). Developing theoretical links of this type between double standards for competence and other branches of expectation states research promises to yield fruitful results.

DOUBLE STANDARDS FOR COMPETENCE: OTHER BASES

A growing literature, both within and outside expectation states theory, indicates that factors other than status have an effect on inferences of competence. Three extensions of the theory that incorporate such factors are of special interest here, namely those extensions concerning (a) the allocation of rewards, (b) the assignment of personality and moral characteristics, and (c) the existence of prior affective linkages among group members. Let us consider each in relation to the activation of double standards.

(a)   The relationships between status, performance, and the allocation of rewards have been of interest to expectation states researchers from the earlier statements of the theory (Berger, Fisek, Norman, and Wagner 1985; Berger, Zelditch, Anderson and Cohen 1972). Several experiments provide empirical evidence of these relationships, as follows. Cook (1975) created conditions of either equity or inequity between perceived ability and assigned rewards, and investigated the effects of these conditions on performance expectations; Parcel and Cook (1977) examined the extent to which actors allocated rewards in a manner consistent with status. The *reverse* process has also been examined, and that is the situation that is of special interest in this section. Thus, Harrod (1980) and Stewart and Moore (1992) studied whether perceptions of competence resulted from knowledge of the pay allocated to self and other by a party outside the group. The two actors were paid either the same or different amounts; in both cases, the authors found support for the hypothesis that rewards would generate congruent performance expectations.

One could then ask if rewards would also generate different standards for competence. This is precisely the question posed by Freeman (1995) in developing an extension of Foschi (1989). To explore that question, Freeman designed an experiment where differences in the rewards received by self and partner were either consistent or inconsistent with differences in their performance outcomes (scores). Subjects were subsequently asked to set standards for themselves, for both ability and lack of ability. Results indicate that rewards were indeed used as a basis for ability standards: those subjects who received lower rewards than their partner set stricter standards for themselves than those subjects who received higher rewards, and this occurred regardless of level of performance. Freeman also found that rewards had a stronger effect on those standards than did performance outcomes. On the other hand, performance outcomes but not rewards showed a significant effect on standards for lack of ability, and there was a significant interaction between the two factors. The strictest standard for lack of ability was set by those receiving lower scores but higher rewards; the most lenient, by those in the higher scores–lower rewards condition. I examine this topic further later in this section.

(b) Other extensions of the core ideas of expectation states theory include the introduction of the concepts of "personality characteristic" and "moral characteristic," and the development of hypotheses about their effects in task groups (Berger 1988; Driskell 1982; Johnston 1988; Webster 1982). Examples of the former type of characteristic are qualities such as "friendly," "shy to strangers," and "hostile to authority," while the latter may be exemplified by traits such as "honest," "trustworthy," and "devious." Both types imply broadly-defined attributions of what is perceived to be a person's true nature or character, but moral characteristics also include judgments of what is right and what is wrong. Neither characteristic implies, by itself, levels of competence. Nevertheless, in situations where an inference about competence must be made and no other information is available, they can be used for such purpose. Hypotheses about this relationship and the conditions under which it occurs have been proposed for personality characteristics in Driskell (1982) and moral characteristics in Webster (1982). Driskell (1982) also reports supporting experimental evidence. To my knowledge, no tests have yet been conducted on the effects of moral characteristics on performance expectations. If personality and moral attributes result in inferences of competence, the next logical step would be to extend the research to investigate whether they activate different standards for competence as well.

(c) There is now also considerable evidence of the role that interpersonal affect processes play in the formation of performance expectations. Under the term "affect" I include both emotions and sentiments; this area of investigation is also often referred to as "socioemotional" behavior, in contrast to the more "task-related" aspects of group interaction. Emotions are generally defined as transitory, short-lived feelings, whereas sentiments are seen as more stable attitudes. Sentiments as well as emotions may vary in intensity. The work carried out so far in this area from the expectation states tradition shows a rich variety of topics. Thus, researchers have investigated how status affects the expression of socioemotional behavior (Ridgeway and Johnson 1990), the mechanisms and the extent to which emotions and sentiments affect performance expectations (Shelly 1993), and the relative effects of status and emotion on those expectations (Berger 1988; Johnston 1988; Lovaglia and Houser 1996; Shelly 1993; Shelly and Webster 1997). It would also be worthwhile to explore whether or not it is through the activation of "affect states" that personality and moral characteristics elicit judgments of competence.

Since affect processes have been found to play a key part in the formation of performance expectations, I propose that they should also have such an effect on standards for ability and lack of ability. In Foschi (1997) I present an extension of Foschi (1989) and compare status-based to affect-based double standards. This extension focuses on sentiments of like and dislike. Sentiments, by themselves, imply neither competence nor incompetence. However, I propose that, the same as with personality and moral characteristics, an assessor will use them as a basis for such inferences when (i) they differentiate the two actors, (ii) no other bases for judging competence are available, and (iii) the actors perform at the same level.

As discussed earlier, the use of double standards involves neither devaluating nor overevaluating a performance in an explicit way. The performance, instead, can simply be deemed either to be "not good enough" or to surpass standards. For this reason, it may not only be the case that double standards can be activated by affect states but that this practice may even be a *common* inclusion/exclusion mechanism in those task situations where assessors have clear affective linkages (either positive or negative) to the performers. In other words, different standards may be preferred over the direct expression of biases because they conceal sentiments of like and dislike (and thus the motivation to favor some and to hinder others) in situations, such as task contexts, where the influence of those sentiments would not be appropriate. In this way, that influence can nevertheless take place. The empirical test of this proposition would be of considerable theoretical and applied interest.

In Foschi (1997) I propose that status has a stronger impact than affect on the activation of double standards, on the assumption that status generates predictions about the quality of performances whereas affect does not. I also propose that, for a thorough understanding of the combined effects of these two factors, it would be useful to operationalize status (both specific and diffuse) and affect in a variety of ways. This should also include examining the effects of different levels of relevance between status and task, as well as of different motivations underlying the affect states. More generally, it would be important to investigate the relative effects of all three factors discussed in this section, as well as to examine how each of them interacts with status—as some of the work discussed in this section has begun to do.

DOUBLE STANDARDS IN THE INFERENCE OF OTHER ATTRIBUTES

Although the focus of this paper is on double standards for competence, it is important to note that the practice is not limited to that domain but is, in fact, frequently observed with respect to a variety of other attributes. An example would be the situation where the same evidence of criminal behavior results in either a verdict of guilt or of innocence, depending on the accused person's gender or skin color. In general terms, a double (or multiple) standard is the practice of applying different requirements to different categories of people for the inference of a specified level of an attribute. There are numerous accounts and descriptions of this larger family of double standards, as well as considerable research evidence for some of them. Since these other manifestations of the practice are not the focus of this paper, I only include a brief overview of this work.

The most commonly discussed and researched double standard is the one consisting of different codes of sexual behavior for the inference of marriage desirability, sexual morality, and personality traits in men and women (Eichler 1980; Hynie and Lydon 1995). The two codes allow for a wider range and frequency of sexual experience from men than from women. It should be noted, however, that there is now some evidence that this double standard is no longer accepted by many in the United States and Canada (see, for example, Jacoby and Williams 1985; O'Sullivan 1995). Other frequently examined double standards include work on: (i) the physical signs of aging in men and women and the resulting different inferences about a person's attractiveness and overall worth (Bell 1970; Deutsch, Zalenski, and Clark 1986; Nuccio 1989; Sontag 1972); (ii) the assessment of the same behavior by both sexes through different definitions of mental health (Maslin and Davis 1975; Tudor, Tudor, and Gove 1979); and (iii) similar qualifications, differences in political affiliation and country of origin, and contrasting views about a person's suitability for either legal immigrant or refugee status (Whitaker 1987).

Given that experimental research provides the strongest inferences about a relationship between variables, it is important to point out that some of the evidence on these other types of double standards is indeed either experimental or quasi-experimental. Thus, several of the studies mentioned earlier belong in that group (Deutsch et al. 1986; Hynie and Lydon 1995; Jacoby and Williams 1985; O'Sullivan 1995; Maslin and Davis 1975). Examples of other such studies and the topics they investigate are as follows: skin color and the extent to which a person is deemed to deserve financial assistance from the state (Sniderman, Piazza, Tetlock, Kendrick 1991); gender, qualifications, and decisions about either just earnings (Jasso and Webster 1997) or recommended salary (Foschi et al. 1995); gender, quality and appropriateness of role behavior, and whether causal attributions are personal or situational (Galper and Luck 1980); and gender and judgments of height, weight, age, and income (Biernat et al. 1991).

Even a brief review such as the present one shows that the basis for these other types of double standards is usually a diffuse status characteristic—most often gender—as it was also the case for competence double standards. Here again, the standard imposed is stricter for the person who holds lower status.

My particular interest in these other double standards lies in their possible relationship to the inference of competence. The review in this section reveals that the qualities inferred are indeed often closely associated with competence: personal worth, mental health, income, salary, just earnings, suitability for legal admission into a country. How do double standards operate when there is such a close connection between attributes? Does the practice simply extend from one domain to the other? If so, how much does the spread depend on the factor activating the initial double standard? For example, the work conducted so far identifies gender as a factor particularly apt to activate a multiplicity of double standards. Thus, it could be that treating men and women with different requirements for personal worth facilitates the use of a double standard for competence. A similar process may also operate in the other direction and link, for instance, double standards for competence with those for rewards. In addition, it would be worthwhile to explore such extensions when the association between the attributes is not as close (as for example, between morality and competence). Addressing these questions would be an important step toward increasing our knowledge of this practice.

"REVERSE" DOUBLE STANDARDS AND CONCLUSIONS

In this article I examine theory and research on the practice of applying different standards in the inference of competence, depending on who the performers are. Most of the research conducted so far on this practice concerns status differences as its basis. Thus, several experiments provide evidence of stricter standards for women than for men in situations where both had performed at the same level. I also discuss extensions of these ideas that include other, nonstatus bases for double standards. For example, I propose that actors' personality characteristics, allocated rewards, and sentiments of like and dislike, can similarly activate different standards for ability. Finally, I examine how the use of double standards is not limited to the inference of competence, as I discuss evidence of their operation in the inference of other attributes, such as beauty, morality, and overall personal worth.

The review presented in this paper thus reveals double standards as an important mechanism through which actors, depending on their ranking on socially valued attributes, either benefit or are hindered in the assignment of other such attributes. The practice is subtle and not necessarily conscious, but nevertheless effective in contributing to the maintenance of the status quo in a wide variety of social interaction domains.

It is not surprising then that "reverse" double standards have been advocated by some as an instrument for change. This has been particularly the case about inferences of competence in task settings on the basis of gender and skin color in the United States and Canada over the last two decades. The practice, however, can seldom escape having a patronizing component—that is, an implication that the lower-status person cannot meet universalistic standards and therefore has to be judged by different, more lenient rules (for a description of this practice, see for example Biernat and Kobrynowicz 1997; Blalock 1979; Epstein 1970b, 1991). In turn, applying more lenient standards to the lower-status person often results in the inference of a lower level of ability in that person and therefore, in the *maintenance* rather than the change of the status quo.

Apart from the consequences of such reverse double standards, it is important to understand under what conditions they occur. Some of the research described above provides useful leads in this respect. Thus the following conditions, identified by that work as required for the activation of stricter standards for the lower status actor, also contribute to the understanding of the reverse practice: (i) the assessor is motivated to arrive at accurate assessments of the performers' competence; (ii) the performers differ with respect to a status characteristic and this difference is salient to the assessor; (iii) the characteristic carries status value for the assessor; (iv) the performances are of the same level but provide inconclusive evidence of either ability or lack of ability (that is, are neither outstanding nor extremely poor); and (v) the assessor anticipates a low level of accountability for his or her appraisals.

If any one of these conditions is not met, one would expect that the gap in standards would close. This is, for example, exactly what I found in Foschi (1996) when level of accountability was increased—as discussed earlier in this paper. Similarly, the results reported in Foschi et al. (1995) support the inclusion of the condition that a salient status difference must exist between the performers. But what about *reversing* the double standard? There are many indications that in both the United States and Canada, the number of people who accept that gender is a cue to competence has decreased. This may also be the case, although the decrease may not have been as pronounced, for skin color. In other words, fewer assessors in these societies would now meet the third condition listed above, if the characteristic in question is either of these attributes.[6] These assessors would tend to treat both performers with the same standard, and some may even use reverse double standards. They may do so because of their own motivation to redress past discrimination, because of pressures of political correctness, or because they are mandated to meet quotas. It is also possible that assessors may think that equal, outstanding performances by, for example, a man and a woman, are not really equal but in fact demonstrate the woman's superiority, given the difficulties that she likely had to overcome in order to produce such a performance. In other words, the assessors would be compensating for those difficulties. Results from Foschi et al. (1995) indicate that an outstanding performance may be required for such a reversal (in that case, in standards for rewards) to occur.

Another condition for reverse double standards has been proposed by Biernat and Kobrynowicz (1997). As I discuss earlier, these authors argue that the nature of the decision may affect the direction of the double standard—stricter for devalued groups if the issue is to infer definite ability (in line with the first of the conditions listed above), but more lenient for those groups if only minimum ability is to be appraised. More generally, the work by these authors suggests two factors that would be worthwhile investigating in this area, either as scope conditions or as additional independent variables: the importance of the decision to be made, and the costs to the assessor for being wrong.

As this review shows, several of the conditions under which double standards for competence occur have been identified, and considerable knowledge has now accumulated in this area. There is, however, much that has yet to be learned, particularly about nonstatus bases for this practice, and about how it relates to double standards in the inference of other valued attributes. In my opinion, it would be of special interest to design studies to systematically investigate the two types of competence double standards—either stricter or more lenient for the lower-status person. To that effect, it would be mportant to experimentally manipulate some of the factors described in this section. For example, participants could be assigned at random to conditions of either pressure or no pressure to give politically correct responses, or of either presence or absence of quotas for the hiring of women candidates. In this respect, designs that simulate hiring and promotion decisions, such as the designs used in Biernat and Kobrynowicz (1997) and in Foschi et al. (1994, 1995), provide experimental contexts that are not only highly engaging for the participants but also offer the possibility of studying a wide variety of factors in the use of double standards.

ACKNOWLEDGMENT

This paper was prepared with the financial assistance of Research Grant #410-97-0101 from the Social Sciences and Humanities Research Council of Canada. I gratefully acknowledge this support. I also thank Vanessa Lapointe and Martin Meissner for helpful comments on an earlier version.

NOTES

1.   I distinguish between an attribute having status value (1) in a social system and (2) for an individual. Thus, gender may be a status characteristic in a given society but not for a particular individual

within it, or gender may be such a characteristic for an individual but not for the society to which he or she belongs. Both conditions are required in this formulation.

2. Notice that the application of a double standard is different from the use of biased evaluations. The latter occur in situations where there are no objective means of evaluating an outcome and one or more characteristics of the actor become the evaluation criterion (a). This process is illustrated in Goldberg's (1968) well-known study where, regarding various fields, respondents were found to make different evaluations of the same professional essay depending on whether they believed the author to be a man or a woman. Double standards, on the other hand, occur when two or more performers differ with respect to at least one socially valued attribute but an objective evaluation of their performances has shown these to be of equal level. A different standard applied to each of these performances results in different inferences about how much ability each person has.

3. Although throughout this paper I present ideas that apply equally to double and multiple standards, my examples are about dichotomized attributes. Therefore, I mostly use the expression "double standards."

4. I use the singular form "double standard" to refer to either (i) the different requirements used by one person when assessing two specific actors or (ii) the average requirement applied to two actors by several asessors. However, I use the plural "double standards" if I wish to emphasize that a double standard of *different magnitude* is being used in each case, either by each of several assessors or by the same assessor across various circumstances and/or actors.

5. A review of the indirect evidence for the case of gender, originating in expectation states theory, appears in Foschi (1997). Two recent experiments that also belong in this group are reported in Shackelford, Wood, and Worchel (1997). In all cases, the studies provide substantial evidence that different requirements for competence are set for women and for men.

6. The number of empirical cases to which a theory applies and its explanatory power are two separate issues. Thus, a theory may provide a good explanation of a few empirical situations, or a poor explanation of many. A theory does not, of course, have to explain only currently occurring situations; the abstractly-defined class of phenomena to which it applies may not exist under present circumstances. Furthermore, in the specific case of expectation states theory, it is worth noting that its scope is not limited to any particular society and therefore that its validity is independent of the particular attributes that constitute a status characteristic in any given society. The theory makes predictions that are conditional on, among other factors, an attribute being a status characteristic in the social system under consideration.

REFERENCES

Bell, I. P. 1970. "The Double Standard." *Trans-action* 8: 75-80.

Berger, J. 1988. "Directions in Expectation States Research." Pp. 450-474 and 522-528 in *Status Generalization: New Theory and Research*, edited by M. Webster Jr. and M. Foschi. Stanford, CA: Stanford University Press.

Berger, J., M.H. Fisek, R.Z. Norman, and D.G. Wagner. 1985. "Formation of Reward Expectations in Status Situations." Pp. 215-261 in *Status, Rewards and Influence: How Expectations Organize Behavior,* edited by Joseph Berger and Morris Zelditch Jr. San Francisco, CA: Jossey-Bass.

Berger, J., M.H. Fisek, R.Z. Norman, and M. Zelditch Jr. 1977. *Status Characteristics and Social Interaction: An Expectation States Approach*. New York: Elsevier.

Berger, J., D.G. Wagner, and M. Zelditch Jr. 1985. "Introduction: Expectation States Theory—Review and Assessment." Pp. 1-72 in *Status, Rewards and Influence: How Expectations Organize Behavior,* edited by J. Berger and M. Zelditch Jr. San Francisco, CA: Jossey-Bass.

Berger, J., M. Zelditch Jr., B. Anderson, and B.P. Cohen. 1972. "Structural Aspects of Distributive Justice: A Status-Value Formulation." Pp. 119-146 in *Sociological Theories in Progress*, Vol. 2, edited by J. Berger, M. Zelditch Jr., and B. Anderson. Boston, MA: Houghton Mifflin.

Biernat, M. 1995. "The Shifting Standards Model: Implications of Stereotype Accuracy for Social
    Judgment." Pp. 87-114 in *Stereotype Accuracy: Toward Appreciating Group Differences,*
    edited by Y. Lee, L.J. Jussim, and C.R. McCauley. Washington, DC: American Psychological
    Association.
Biernat, M., and D. Kobrynowicz. 1997. "Gender- and Race-Based Standards for Competence: Lower
    Minimum Standards but Higher Ability Standards for Devalued Groups." *Journal of Personal-
    ity and Social Psychology* 72: 544-557.
Biernat, M., and M. Manis. 1994. "Shifting Standards and Stereotype-Based Judgments." *Journal of
    Personality and Social Psychology* 66: 5-20.
Biernat, M., M. Manis, and T.E. Nelson. 1991. "Stereotypes and Standards of Judgment." *Journal of
    Personality and Social Psychology* 60: 485-499.
Blalock, H.M. 1979. *Black-White Relations in the 1980's: Toward a Long-Term Policy.* New York:
    Praeger.
Carli, L.L. 1990. "Gender, Language, and Influence." *Journal of Personality and Social Psychology*
    59: 941-951.
Cook, K.S. 1975. "Expectations, Evaluations and Equity." *American Sociological Review* 40: 372-388.
Crundall, I., and M. Foddy. 1981. "Vicarious Exposure to a Task as a Basis of Evaluative Competence."
    Social Psychology Quarterly 44: 331-338.
Deutsch, F.M., C.M. Zalenski, and M.E. Clark. 1986. "Is There a Double Standard of Aging?" *Journal
    of Applied Social Psychology* 16: 771-785.
Driskell, J.E. Jr. 1982. "Personal Characteristics and Performance Expectations." *Social Psychology
    Quarterly* 45: 229-237.
Eichler, M. 1977. "The Double Standard as an Indicator of Sex-Status Differentials." *Atlantis:* 3: 1-21.
———. 1980. *The Double Standard: A Feminist Critique of Feminist Social Science.* London: Croom
    Helm.
Epstein, C.F.. 1970a. *Woman's Place: Options and Limits in Professional Careers.* Berkeley, CA: Uni-
    versity of California Press.
———. 1970b. "Encountering the Male Establishment: Sex-Status Limits on Women's Careers in the
    Professions." *American Journal of Sociology* 75: 965-82.
———. 1981. *Women in Law.* New York: Basic Books.
———. 1991. "Constraints on Excellence: Structural and Cultural Barriers to the Recognition and
    emonstration of Achievement." Pp. 239-258, 317-318, and 336-337 in *The Outer Circle:
    Women in the Scientific Community,* edited by H. Zuckerman, J.R. Cole, and J.T. Bruer. New
    York: W.W. Norton.
Foddy, M., and H. Graham. 1987. "Sex and Double Standards in the Inference of Ability." Paper pre-
    sented at the Annual Meeting of the Canadian Psychological Association, Vancouver, British
    Columbia.
Foddy, M., and M. Smithson. 1989. "Fuzzy Sets and Double Standards: Modeling the Process of Abil-
    ity Inference." Pp. 73-99 in *Sociological Theories in Progress: New Formulations,* edited by J.
    Berger, M. Zelditch Jr., and B. Anderson. Newbury Park, CA: Sage.
Foschi, M. 1989. "Status Characteristics, Standards, and Attributions." Pp. 58-72 in *Sociological The-
    ories in Progress: New Formulations,* edited by J. Berger, M. Zelditch Jr., and B. Anderson.
    Newbury Park, CA: Sage.
———. 1992. "Gender and Double Standards for Competence." Pp. 181-207 in *Gender, Interaction,
    and Inequality,* edited by C.L. Ridgeway. New York: Springer-Verlag.
———. 1996. "Double Standards in the Evaluation of Men and Women." *Social Psychology Quarterly*
    59: 237-254.
———. 1997. "Status, Affect, and Multiple Standards for Competence." Pp. 201-221 in *Status, Net-
    work, and Structure: Theory Development in Group Processes,* edited by J. Szmatka, J.
    Skvoretz, and J. Berger. Stanford, CA: Stanford University Press.

Foschi, M., and M. Foddy. 1988. "Standards, Performances, and the Formation of Self-Other Expectations." Pp. 248-260 and 501-503 in *Status Generalization: New Theory and Research*, edited by M. Webster Jr. and M. Foschi. Stanford, CA: Stanford University Press.

Foschi, M., and R. Foschi. 1979. "A Bayesian Model for Performance Expectations: Extension and Simulation." *Social Psychology Quarterly* 42: 232-241.

Foschi, M., and S. Freeman. 1991. "Inferior Performance, Standards, and Influence in Same-Sex Dyads." *Canadian Journal of Behavioural Science* 23: 99-113.

Foschi, M., L. Lai, and K. Sigerson. 1994. "Gender and Double Standards in the Assessment of Job Applicants." *Social Psychology Quarterly* 57: 326-339.

Foschi, M., K. Sigerson, and M. Lembesis. 1995. "Assessing Job Applicants: The Relative Effects of Gender, Academic Record, and Decision Type." *Small Group Research* 26: 328-352.

Foschi, M., G.K. Warriner, and S.D. Hart. 1985. "Standards, Expectations, and Interpersonal Influence." *Social Psychology Quarterly* 48: 108-117.

Freeman, S.K. 1995. "Double Standards and Pay: The Relationship Between Standards for Performance and Rewards." Ph.D. Dissertation, Department of Sociology, Stanford University.

Galper, R.E., and D. Luck. 1980. "Gender, Evaluation, and Causal Attribution: The Double Standard Is Alive and Well." *Sex Roles* 6: 273-283.

Goldberg, P. 1968. "Are Women Prejudiced Against Women?" *Trans-action* 5: 28-30.

Harrod, W.J. 1980. "Expectations from Unequal Rewards." *Social Psychology Quarterly* 43: 126-130.

Hochschild, A. 1974. "Making It: Marginality and Obstacles to Minority Consciousness." Pp. 194-199 in *Women and Success: The Anatomy of Achievement*, edited by R.B. Kundsin. New York: William Morrow.

Hynie, M., and J.E. Lydon. 1995. "Women's Perceptions of Female Contraceptive Behavior: Experimental Evidence of the Sexual Double Standard." *Psychology of Women Quarterly* 19: 563-581.

Jacoby, A.P., and J.D. Williams. 1985. "Effects of Premarital Sexual Standards and Behavior on Dating and Marriage Desirability." *Journal of Marriage and the Family* 47: 1059-1065.

Jasso, G., and M. Webster Jr. 1997. "Double Standards in Just Earnings for Male and Female Workers." *Social Psychology Quarterly* 60: 66-78.

Johnston, J.R. 1988. "The Structure of Ex-Spousal Relations: An Exercise in Theoretical Integration and Application." Pp. 309-326 and 509-510 in *Status Generalization: New Theory and Research*, edited by M. Webster Jr. and M. Foschi. Stanford, CA: Stanford University Press.

Lorber, J. 1984. *Women Physicians: Career, Status, and Power.* New York: Tavistock.

Lovaglia, M.J., and J.A. Houser. 1996. "Emotional Reactions and Status in Groups." *American Sociological Review* 61: 867-883.

Maslin, A., and J.L. Davis. 1975. "Sex-Role Stereotyping as a Factor in Mental Health Standards Among Counselors-in-Training." *Journal of Counseling Psychology* 22: 87-91.

Miller, D.T., and D.A. Prentice. 1996. "The Construction of Social Norms and Standards." Pp. 799-829 in *Social Psychology: Handbook of Basic Principles*, edited by E.T. Higgins and A. W. Kruglanski. New York: The Guilford Press.

Nuccio, K.E. 1989. "The Double Standard of Aging and Older Women's Employment." *Journal of Women and Aging* 1: 317-338.

O'Sullivan, L.F. 1995. "Less Is More: The Effects of Sexual Experience on Judgments of Men's and Women's Personality Characteristics and Relationship Desirability." *Sex Roles* 33: 159-181.

Parcel, T.L., and K.S. Cook. 1977. "Status Characteristics, Reward Allocation, and Equity." *Sociometry* 40: 311-324.

Ridgeway, C.L. 1982. "Status in Groups: The Importance of Motivation." *American Sociological Review* 47: 76-88.

Ridgeway, C.L., and J.W. Balkwell. 1997. "Group Processes and the Difussion of Status Beliefs." *Social Psychology Quarterly* 60: 14-31.

Ridgeway, C.L., and J. Berger. 1986. "Expectations, Legitimation, and Dominance Behavior in Task Groups." *American Sociological Review* 51: 603-617.

Ridgeway, C.L., and C. Johnson. 1990. "What Is the Relationship Between Socioemotional Behavior and Status in Task Groups?" *American Journal of Sociology* 95: 1189-1212.

Ridgeway, C.L., and H.A. Walker. 1995. "Status Structures." Pp. 281-310 in *SociologicalPerspectives in Social Psychology,* edited by K.S. Cook, G.A. Fine, and J.S. House. Boston, MA: Allyn and Bacon.

Shackelford, S., W. Wood, and S. Worchel. 1997. "Behavioral Styles and the Influence of Women in Mixed-Sex Groups." *Social Psychology Quarterly* 59: 284-293.

Shelly, R.K. 1993. "How Sentiments Organize Interaction." *Advances in Group Processes* 10: 113-132.

Shelly, R.K., and M. Webster Jr. 1997. "How Formal Status, Liking, and Ability Status Structure Interaction: Three Theoretical Principles and a Test." *Sociological Perspectives* 40: 81-107.

Sniderman, P.M., T. Piazza, P.E. Tetlock, and A. Kendrick. 1991. "The New Racism." *American Journal of Political Science* 35: 423-447.

Sontag, S. 1972 (September 23). "The Double Standard of Aging." *Saturday Review*: 29-38.

Stewart, P.A., and J.C. Moore Jr. 1992. "Wage Disparities and Performance Expectations." *Social Psychology Quarterly* 55: 78-85.

Tudor, W., J. Tudor, and W.R. Gove. 1979. "The Effect of Sex Role Differences on the Societal Reaction to Mental Retardation." *Social Forces* 57: 871-886.

Wagner, D.G., and J. Berger. 1993. "Status Characteristics Theory: The Growth of a Program." Pp. 23-63 and 454-463 in *Theoretical Research Programs: Studies in the Growth of Theory,* edited by J. Berger and M. Zelditch Jr. Stanford, CA: Stanford University Press.

———. 1997. "Gender and Interpersonal Task Behaviors: Status Expectation Accounts." *Sociological Perspectives* 40: 1-32.

Webster, M., Jr. 1982. "Moral Characteristics and Status Generalization." Research proposal funded by the National Science Foundation.

Webster, M., Jr., and M. Foschi. 1988. "Overview of Status Generalization." Pp. 1-20 and 477-478 in *Status Generalization: New Theory and Research*, edited by M. Webster Jr. and M. Foschi. Stanford, CA: Stanford University Press.

Webster, M., Jr., and B. Sobieszek. 1974. *Sources of Self-Evaluation: A Formal Theory of Significant Others and Social Influence.* New York: John Wiley.

Whitaker, R. 1987. *Double Standard: The Secret History of Canadian Immigration.* Toronto: Lester & Orpen Dennys.

Yogev, A., and R. Shapira. 1987. "Ethnicity, Meritocracy and Credentialism in Israel: Elaborating the Credential Society Thesis." *Research in Social Stratification and Mobility* 6: 187-212.

NEED AS A BASIS OF
REWARD ALLOCATION

Barbara F. Meeker

ABSTRACT

Need, along with equality and equity, has been proposed by numerous theorists as one of the fundamental allocation or distributive justice rules in interpersonal exchange. This paper examines several bodies of literature to see what conditions have been proposed as being causes or consequences of the existence of need-based allocation as a legitimate rule for reward allocation.

INTRODUCTION

Are there conditions under which people will allocate to others on the basis of those others' needs? If so, what are those conditions? and, what are the consequences of acting on need as an allocation rule? Need has been listed by both philosophers and social scientists as one of several legitimate allocation or distributive justice rules, along with equality, equity, and occasionally others.

Advances in Group Processes, Volume 15, pages 81-102.
Copyright © 1998 by JAI Press Inc.
All rights of reproduction in any form reserved.
ISBN: 0-7623-0362-X

However, it has been less often examined than the others. My intention in this paper is to examine need as an allocation principle. First, I develop a working definition of need and of need-based allocation. Then I review several bodies of literature representing research programs that address questions of the conditions under which "need" may be a legitimate principle of reward allocation and the consequences of implementing a need based allocation principle. Finally, I present several theoretical principles that seem justified on the basis of the literature reviewed.

ALLOCATION THEORIES, NEED, AND LEGITIMACY

Allocation theories are also known as theories of distributive justice, fairness, and equity. Theories of allocation appear in many branches of social theory and research, including political philosophy, law, organization and management research, studies of personal relationships, and exchange theory.

A variety of distribution or allocation rules may be invoked as *just* or *fair.* Equity or proportionality (allocation based on input or contribution), equality, and need are three of the most commonly mentioned (Deutsch 1985), along with reciprocity (Gouldner 1960). A recent review of social exchange (Molm and Cook 1995) notes that although the writers important in development of social exchange theory (including Homans 1961 [1974]; Blau 1964; and Thibaut and Kelley 1959) all included norms of distributive justice or fair exchange in their formulations, "The issue of the relative strength of structural sources of power versus norms constraining power use is still unresolved" (p. 227). Another recent discussion (Hegtvedt and Markovsky 1995) similarly observes that although many researchers agree that multiple rules exist, few models address the development of different justice principles. However, it is my argument that actually quite a bit is known about conditions surrounding the use of need as a principle of distributive justice.

A dictionary definition of need is as follows: "need: n [ME ned, from OE nied, akin to OHG 'not' distress, need]."

1. necessary duty, obligation
2. a. a lack of something requisite, desirable, or useful
    b. a physiological or psychological requirement for the well-being of an organism
3. a. condition requiring supply or relief
4. lack of the means of subsistence, poverty (Webster's Ninth New Collegiate Dictionary, 1985) other synonyms: essential, necessity, requirement; destitution, distress, indigence.

The first meaning (necessary duty) is not what is usually meant in the literature on allocation although it certainly is one of the common uses (as in "I need to finish this paper this week"). All the other meanings are consistent with the uses in the social psychological research literature, although individual studies are not always consistent about which of these meanings is intended.

Need, thus defined, has dimensions involving both a *lack* or absence of something, and the alleviation of *suffering*; a need specifies an item or action in the absence of which there will be distress (note the origin of the word in a word meaning 'distress') and in the presence of which suffering or distress will be relieved. There is also an element of *causality*, involving both the logical concepts of *sufficiency* (the provision of the item will be effective in changing the outcome from one of suffering to one of no or less suffering), and *necessity* (without the item, the sufferer may cease to exist, or the task or obligation will be unfulfilled). The word need also in some cases refers specifically to economic lack, as shown in the synonyms of poverty, indigence, and destitution.

A *need-based allocation* (or distribution) is an *act that is intended to relieve a need on the part of another, without immediate reciprocity from that other.* I will use the terms allocation and distribution equivalently; both refer to the transfer of something of positive value from one person or party to another. Transfers of items or actions of negative value (e.g., punishments) are not included, since literature on the allocation of punishments topics has seldom considered "need". This definition does limit the acts so defined to those that consciously or intentionally, rather than accidentally, relieve a need.

Defining need-based allocation as action that reduces the suffering of another without immediate reciprocity from the recipient does not require us to include "altruism" in the definition, because the actor may well be rewarded, but by some other person or event, or at some other time. It does allow us to distinguish need-based allocation from determination of value in reciprocal exchanges (as in I lack apples and you lack oranges, so a trade of oranges for apples will benefit us both). We can assume that *some* motivation for making need-based allocation is indeed reciprocal exchange, for example, in an exchange of assistance for gratitude. However, I will be pursuing information about *other* sources of need-based allocations. That is, the need-based allocations in which I am interested are, in the short run at least, asymmetric. Additional sources of motivation for need-based allocations may include: intrinsic rewards from the act of "helping" other than those provided by the recipient; rewards from actors other than the recipient; delayed rewards from the recipient or others; and most especially the existence of allocation norms.

An *allocation norm* (or distributive justice norm) is a *normative statement that in some specific situation allocations should be based on a specific principle such as need.* Allocation norms specify both what are legitimate claims of need and whether need should be a factor in allocations. For example, although it may be normative for parents to meet needs of their children, or teachers to respond to the needs of their students, the child who claims to *need* an extra candy bar, or the student who claims to *need* a B in a professor's course will probably not be treated to an allocation based on their self-proclaimed need.

The idea that need-based allocations are normative brings us to the question of how and when actions may be defined as normative or legitimate. An action is legitimate if persons in the situation believe that it is *right* or *proper*. If persons in a situation believe that an action is legitimate, they will engage in it without external coercion and without requiring extensive persuasion. An especially useful set of current theories of legitimacy in sociology are those developed by Dornbusch and Scott (1975) and Zelditch and Walker (1984); see also Walker and Zelditch (1993); Walker, Thomas and Zelditch (1986); Walker, Rogers and Zelditch (1988) and a review by Ridgeway and Walker (1995).

Legitimacy, in this view, stems from two sources; *propriety*, which is the belief by an individual in the rightness or morality of an action; and *validity*, the recognition (regardless of what one's own opinion is of the rightness of an action) that it will be enforced by other group members and/or by leaders or authorities outside the group. According to these theories, propriety and validity are theoretically distinct states, which influence each other.

I have grouped the research literatures I will review into psychological and sociological approaches. The "psychological" approaches focus on individual motivation, and include: Multiple distribution rule theorists; equity theorists; research on helping behavior; and the "just world" research program. The "sociological" approaches focus on group structure and processes, and include: Reward expectation theory; attitudes toward economic inequality and entitlement; exchange network approaches; research on task interdependence; and research on justice norms within specific social settings. The psychological literature focuses mostly on sources of propriety, that is, the reasons that individuals come to accept need-based allocation as right or appropriate from their own individual perspectives. On the other hand, literature from sociology, political science, economics and philosophy is more often addressed to questions of validity, that is, reasons a collective may develop need-based allocation norms.

PSYCHOLOGICAL APPROACHES TO NEED

Multiple Distribution Norms

It is research and theory in this category that has most explicitly considered "need" as a separate allocation principle. These researchers agree that it is most useful to postulate that there are several distributive justice norms or principles. (Examples include: Deutsch 1975, 1985; Lamm and Schwinger 1980; Leventhal 1976; Leventhal, Karuza, and Fry 1980; Leventhal, Weiss, and Buttrick 1973; Mikula 1980; Schwinger 1980; Tornblom and Foa 1983; Wagstaff 1994; Wagstaff, Huggins, and Perfect 1991). The challenge with this approach is to identify the different principles, and then to investigate both their causes and their consequences.

The authors who recognize more than one principle of distributive justice tend to draw on philosophers for some of their theoretical discussion (especially Rawls 1971; also, for example, Galston 1980). Merit-based (equitable), equal, and need-based are among the commonly mentioned principles of distribution that may be "just."

Several variations of need-based distributive justice norms have been proposed. These include: social responsibility (Berkowitz and Daniels 1963), which is a norm that people should help others who are dependent on them, even if there is no immediate prospect of reciprocity; humanitarian norms (Schwartz 1975), which prescribe that one should respond to the needs of strangers; and allocation based on relative need (e.g., Deutsch 1985; Schwinger 1980; Elliott and Meeker 1986; Meeker and Elliott 1995). Most researchers in this tradition now believe that choices among allocation principles in most settings involve compromises rather than strict adoption of one and rejection of all others (see for example, Griffith 1989).

Deutsch (1975, 1985) has proposed that the type of distributive justice principle implemented in a social setting will both be caused by and produce compatible task and socioemotional processes:

> In cooperative relations in which productivity is a primary goal, equity rather than equality or need will be the dominant principle of distributive justice.
>
> In cooperative relations in which the fostering or maintenance of enjoyable social relations is the common goal, equality will be the dominant principle of distributive justice.
>
> In cooperative relations in which the fostering of personal development and personal welfare is the common goal, need will be the dominant principle of distributive justice. (Deutsch 1985, p. 38)

He also suggests that "Need and equality as distributive values are closely linked and sometimes not distinguished" (p. 43), except that "caring" or need-based systems may involve unequal dependency. In general, he sees the solidarity (equality) and caring (need-based) orientations as emotional rather than task oriented and in Parsons' (1951) terms, particularistic, affective, and not achievement oriented.

Theories within this approach such as Deutsch's (1985) use a psychological cognitive consistency explanation. That is, it is assumed that individuals will be more likely to accept an allocation principle that is consistent with other ideas and feelings they have about the setting, themselves, and the other people in it. This produces a "functional" argument that relationships are more stable if group situations in which there are strong positive emotional bonds are also those in which distributions are based on need and in which task performance is downplayed and invidious distinctions among group members are minimized. However, some researchers point out that need-based allocations may enhance group task performance by enabling all group members to contribute to the task (e.g., Schwinger

1980, Mikula 1980). Also, being recognized as needy may lead to humiliation for the needy person. Thus, there may be both task-related and negative emotional consequences of need-based allocations.

Evidence that people under some conditions will allocate consistently with another's need even when other allocation schemes such as equity or equality are salient is provided by Deutsch (1975, 1985) and by Elliott and Meeker (1984; 1986, Meeker and Elliott 1987, 1995). The Elliott and Meeker research uses a vignette format in which a subject is asked to imagine him/her self the supervisor of a group of student research assistants, whose task is to conduct telephone interviews for a survey research organization. Various features of the group and the individuals are described. Then the subject is told it is up to "you, as the project supervisor" to divide up $1,000 among the five research assistants "according to whatever distribution seems to be most fitting." The subject then writes in an amount for each of the five hypothetical research assistants.

In the vignettes, individual level of task output is manipulated by listing the different number of phone calls for each research assistant. In two of these studies (Elliott and Meeker 1986; Meeker and Elliott 1995) level of need was manipulated by a description of the research assistants' answers to a question on the employment application which asked how important was "personal financial need" in taking the job. The results showed that dollar allocations were greater for targets described as high output, but also for targets described as having high need. One variation described differences in group morale (high morale versus low morale) and another described differences in task outcome (successful task completion versus failure to complete the task). Both morale and task outcome had complex interactions with allocations, but there was no evidence that need was a more common basis for allocations under high morale than under low morale.

Elliott and Meeker's results show that allocation based on need can occur. However, they seem to contradict many of Deutsch's (1975) assumptions: The vignette described a work setting, not a family or "caring" setting; need was not the basis of allocation more frequently when there were positive emotional relationships among the recipients; the subjects clearly cared about work productivity at the same time they cared about need; and perhaps most interesting, need was a factor that created invidious comparisons among individuals rather than being associated with egalitarianism. In fact, allocation based on need seemed quite unlike the warm, cuddly, nontask oriented atmosphere posited by Deutsch (1975, 1985) as compatible with its invocation as a norm of distributive justice.

Equity Theorists

Equity theory (e.g. Walster, Bersheid, and Walster 1976; see also other papers in the same volume, edited by Berkowitz and Walster 1976; see also Utne and Kidd 1980) also has its roots in cognitive dissonance theory. This tradition assumes that all judgments of *fairness* or *equity* are based on a perceived balance between valued inputs and valued outcomes. The ratio of inputs to outcomes is compared for two members of a dyad. Inequitable ratios are assumed to create dissonance. Consequences of failure to achieve equity include emotional distress and actions to restore balance, to redefine the values of inputs and outcomes, or to leave the situation. The challenge for researchers using this framework is to locate appropriate inputs and outcomes, and to develop mathematical formulas by which these can be combined into a single measure of equity.

Equity theory would require us to treat need as a type of input, and little research in this tradition assesses its independent role. However, several programs of research within this tradition do deal with reactions to suffering, more specifically with how an individual reacts to having caused harm to another, (e.g. Austin, Walster and Utne 1976), to deserved versus undeserved suffering, to exploitative relationships, and to differences between impersonal and intimate relationships (see Walster, Bersheid and Walster, 1976). Results of such research show that subjects are more likely to act to alleviate harm they have caused to another when the harm is small enough, and the ameliorative actions available are easy enough, to make the alleviation a success. In contrast, harm that has turned out to be greater than can readily be reversed tends to produce no action, redefinition of the harm or dislike of the victim (Austin, Walster, and Utne 1976). The idea that one reaction to the emotional distress created by observing undeserved (hence inequitable) suffering is redefinition of the inputs/outcomes to define the victim as deserving of the suffering led to the "just world" research program (discussed below).

Research on Helping Behavior

A research area theoretically related to need-based allocation, because it has as its dependent variable behavior that relieves suffering, is the set of programs that study bystander intervention in emergencies and other helping behavior addressed to strangers (e.g., Piliavin, Dovidio, Gaertner, and Clark 1981; Batson 1987; for an extensive review see Krebs and Miller 1985; equity based accounts include Berkowitz 1972; Ickes and Kidd 1976; Walster and Piliavin 1972; research in this field continues, e.g., Dietrich and Berkowitz 1997). This research has generated several theoretical models. Most share a decision process form; that is, they propose a sequence of information processing and decision-making events that lead either to helping or not. Results (as summarized by Krebs and Miller 1985) consistently show that helping behavior is more likely to occur when: It is supported by normative processes, especially endorsement of a norm of social responsibility or need-based justice; emotional arousal caused by viewing another's suffering occurs; the potential helper expects that action is appropriate and will be effective; the potential helper recognizes the dependence of the victim (i.e., that no other persons will take appropriate action); there is perceived legitimacy of the need and the victim cannot be blamed for the condition; and costs for action are low.

Some research also has considered the consequences of helping, (e.g., Fisher, Nadler, and Witcher-Alagner 1982) and suggests that recipients of help may experience either positive or negative emotions, the latter when help is ineffective or points out a status inferiority. The helping behavior research, like the harmdoer research, shows that need-based allocation occurs when there is an instrumental justification (it is perceived as effective and low cost) and when it is normative. That is, propriety of need-based allocation occurs when it also has validity, as well as the expectation of effectiveness. Also, an intrinsic reward for need-based allocation is shown to be provided by the reduction of negative emotional arousal caused by empathy with a sufferer. Although not so explicitly mentioned by these researchers, it seems clear that there is also an intrinsic but instrumental reward from the "success" of the act of helping.

Research on the Just World

This research program originated with Lerner (1980) and presents a darker side of the norm that suffering should be alleviated. The theory derives from equity theory; Lerner asserts that people have a belief that the world is just and that they experience mental and emotional distress when this belief is contradicted by the observation of undeserved suffering. The first reaction to observation of undeserved suffering is to try to alleviate it, but if this is not possible, it is followed by readjustment of attitudes, leading to a belief that the victim must have deserved the suffering. Lerner conceives of this as a personality dimension, and paper-and-pencil scales have been developed to measure it in individuals. Of particular interest to this review is that Lerner's research shows that people do tend to accept a norm of allocation on the basis of need, and that only when this is impossible or ineffective does the denigration of the needy person occur.

Research on helping behavior and the just world phenomenon suggest that emotional reactions to suffering are doubleedged. The reduction of negative emotional arousal can provide a direct reward for need based allocation. However, when observing someone else suffering generates empathy it creates an aversive condition, one that people prefer to avoid. Reinforcement research tells us that behavior that reduces an aversive condition has powerful reinforcing properties (that is, it increases the probability of repetition of the behavior) but aversive conditions also lead to future avoidance of the situations associated with their occurrence. This is consistent with the conclusions of the equity, just world and helping behavior approaches, that is, that it is exactly when ameliorative behavior fails that people turn against the needy and/or their own complicity in that need.

The research and theory reviewed so far suggest a contradiction to the common wisdom that people who have caused their own suffering are seen as less deserving of help than those who have not. Although allocation of blame has some impact, it appears that the expectation of immediate effectiveness of the help is more important. An example is reported by Lankenau (1997), who interviewed a sample of active panhandlers in the Washington, D.C., area. Panhandlers, of course, rely on the willingness of others to respond to their need. Several of his informants reported experiencing a dilemma between appearing needy and appearing worthy; specifically (1) the degree of dishevelment; panhandlers report that they must appear shabby enough to demonstrate need, but clean enough to demonstrate that "he's trying to do something for himself"; (2) when someone has given the panhandler an item of clothing, such as a jacket or nice pair of shoes, the donor wants to see that the gift has been put to good use whereas other potential donors may question the panhandler's need if "he can afford a nice jacket like that." Apparently few potential contributors asked about the origins of the panhandler's need, or his responsibility for it. Deservingness seemed to be more a matter of the potential effectiveness of the current donation rather than the history of the need.

To summarize: In some ways need-based allocation systems are quite the opposite of the "feel good" sort of orientation often assumed for them. A need-based allocation system recognizes negative emotions and has a strong task oriented or instrumental component. For example: Bystander intervention occurs only when the bystander both recognizes an emergency and believes he/she can do something to help; denigration of victims of undeserved suffering occurs only after it is clear that no ameliorative action can be taken; persons in poverty are more deserving if they appear to be taking action to improve their situations; "caring" social settings are defined in part by their adoption of meeting needs as a legitimate group task. Psychological approaches focus on intraindividual processes, including empathy, reduction of personal distress, cognitive dissonance, and (probably) reinforcement value of success of helping. However, all of these approaches mention normative factors as essential. It is in the sociological approaches that the conditions surrounding the development and maintenance of need as a legitimate allocation norm are investigated.

SOCIOLOGICAL APPROACHES

Reward Expectation Theory

Distributive justice principles, like other social norms, are subject to agreement and negotiation among members of a collectivity, and enforced by sanctions from other persons. A distinctively sociological approach to these processes is the theoretical research program of reward expectations theory (Berger, Zelditch, Anderson, and Cohen 1972; Wagner and Berger 1993). Reward expectation theory seeks to explain the development and maintenance of shared expectations for allocation of rewards (Berger, Fisek, Norman, and Wagner 1985). The theory posits the existence of "referential structures" which provide standards for allocation. These are "socially validated beliefs that describe how the states of valued characteristics that individuals possess are associated with differences in reward levels" (Berger,

Fisek, Norman, and Wagner 1985, p. 222). Referential structures produce expectations for how rewards are/should be allocated, which "take on a moral quality...certain allocations are not simply expected; they are judged to be right or proper" (Berger, Fisek, Norman, and Wagner 1985, p. 215).

Writers in this area have not explicitly considered need as a basis of referential structures of deservingness. It would seem that a useful direction for extension of the reward expectations program would deal with relative need. Some considerations for doing this include the following. Although the morality of allocation rules based on need is clear, need cannot be defined as a "valued characteristic" in the way status characteristics are; for example, we may not wish to argue that it is better to have a high rather than a low state of need. However, status characteristics that lead to low performance expectations for a needy target may reduce legitimacy of need by reducing expectations that the target will have the ability to make good use of the aid.

Additionally, some of the theoretical questions about defining need can be addressed by using the concept of "referential structures." Referential structures may be posited to exist that help define the legitimacy of need claims as well as of need-based allocation. Examples of disputes over relative need can be found in education, medicine, social welfare, and other helping professions. (Is my patient needier than yours? On what grounds can we excuse one student from an examination but not another, when both have claimed need as an excuse? To which of several equally qualified scholarship applicants should a "need based" grant go? In other words, what constitutes the "deserving needy"?) Reward expectation theory suggests we should ask: What are the referential structures by which individuals' claims to neediness are judged legitimate? Who should make such judgments? Furthermore, not all situations will activate a referential structure legitimating need, so one of the fundamental questions such a structure must answer is: Is this a situation in which relative need should be taken into account?

When we turn to possible consequences of allocations based on relative need, reward expectations theory can help describe what happens once unequal allocations are made on the basis of need: Once need has led to unequal allocations, those inequalities may be translated into perceptions of inequalities on other dimensions. According to reward expectations theory the existence of inequalities in rewards serves as a type of standard in terms of which expectations for status ("who you are"), task ability ("what you can do"), or task outcome ("what you have done", i.e., perceived output) are formed (Wagner and Berger 1993, p. 42). Expectations for inequalities in reward "induce" expectations for inequalities in other attributes by creating paths of relevance connected to other legitimate sources of reward inequalities such as abilities or output. Thus, those who have received larger rewards come to be seen as more worthy (Lerner 1965; Cook 1975; Harrod 1980).

Evidence for this effect related to need is found in the vignette research summarized above (Elliott and Meeker 1986; Meeker and Elliot 1995). As part of those experiments, subjects were asked, after they wrote down the allocations, to rate the hypothetical group members on a number of dimensions. Results showed that targets who had both higher output *and* higher need were perceived as significantly better workers than those with lower need.

Inflation of the perception of the deservingness of needier recipients theoretically occurs when the recipients are not differentiated by previous histories of unequal reward (i.e., the need does not derive from a past history of inequality). However, when a needier recipient is also one with a past history of lower rewards, then the reward allocation processes will work in the opposite direction; less reward leading to lower expectations for performance and lower value of worthiness.

General Attitudes Toward Economic Inequality and Entitlement

Another possible source of validity for need-based allocation is general or societal norms. These have been discussed both by general theorists and by researchers on public opinion. A theoretical treatise by Heath (1976) distinguishes the society-wide justice principles of *rights* (resulting from promises, or from pre-existing status); *deserts* (resulting from previous action by the target) and *need*. Need, like desert, requires attention to the unique qualities of individuals, but these are lack or deprivation rather than desirable or admirable qualities. Needs are lacks which "must be made good before someone is able to be a fully participating member of society" (Heath 1976, p. 141). Heath hypothesizes that rights will be most endorsed in traditional aristocratic societies, desert in liberal market-oriented societies, and need in institutions like the family where each member in turn may require help meeting needs. Although consistent with the Deutsch (1975, 1985) theory, little empirical research exists on Heath's ideas.

However, a variety of researchers in different countries and over the years have inquired what ordinary citizens believe about economic need and entitlement (examples include: Alves and Rossi 1979; d'Anjou, Steijn, and Van Aarsen 1995; Hochschild 1981; Jasso and Rossi 1977; Kluegel and Smith 1986; Major 1994; Ritzman and Tomaskovic-Devey 1992; Robinson and Bell 1978; Schiltz 1970; Shepelak 1989). Two general types of questions from this sort of research are of interest; First, does the public believe that people in different life circumstances "deserve" different amounts of income because they have different levels of need; and second, does the public believe that there is a minimum amount of income that every person or household "deserves" on the basis of universal needs? The answers to both seem to be yes, for several nations and over time. For example, Will (1993), using a module from the General Social Survey, reports that respondents faced with a set of vignettes describing poor families generally seemed to believe that there is a floor below which no one should be allowed to fall (this floor being about twice what AFDC paid at the time the interviews were conducted!) but that characteristics that seem to be beyond the control of the family such as an unemployed father, and physical disability of the father produced the highest allocations, as did an indication the recipient families were actively working to help themselves. (Note the consistency with research results showing that people endorse need-based allocation oftener when they anticipate it will be effective). As Deutsch (1975) proposed, need and equality as distribution principles are closely related in many of the analyses of public opinion about distributions; the provision of a "floor" may be seen as helping people who are below average reach equality.

Research on Justice Norms within Specific Role Relationships

A fairly large literature exists on the whether or not there are norms of distributive justice that apply within families, intimate relationships, and organizations. One area of investigation of need-based allocation is analysis of the relationships between parents and their adult children when the latter have more resources than the former or the parents have health problems. Examples include Peterson (1987), Norris (1987), Wagstaff, Huggins, and Perfect (1991); Marshall, Rosenthal, and Daciuk (1987); Matthews (1987). It seems that some people see helping a needy parent as a filial obligation (a legitimate need-based allocation), while others see it more as a question of equity between parents and children or among siblings (Matthews 1987). In other words, in families there appear to be two rather different sets of legitimate allocation norms; one system in which need has priority, and another in which meeting needs is recognized as a legitimate task of the group but the primary allocation norms are equity and equality as applied to the distribution of responsibility for performing this task. Judgements by family members of what is "fair" will differ in the two types of systems.

It may also be that relieving need may be accepted as one of the legitimate tasks of a formal organization. When this occurs, the opportunity to contribute to meeting others' needs, and the amount of such contribution, can be the topic of contests for status. For example, in organizations in which the goal is the provision of help (e.g., hospitals) the opportunity to meet other persons' needs may be viewed by employees as one of the benefits of employment and is itself the subject of concerns about equitable distribution among employees (e.g., Randall and Mueller 1995).

Exchange Network Approaches: Indirect Reciprocity

One source of validity of allocation norms is the belief that behavior consistent with them will eventually be rewarded by third parties. The question of: In what kinds of social structures this is most likely to occur? is addressed by some exchange network theorists. This approach in the first place derived from anthropological theories of exchange and social structure (especially, Mauss 1925 [1966]; Malinowski 1922; Levi-Strauss 1969; Sahlins 1965; and originating with Durkheim, 1893 [1933], 1915 [1965]). Among these theorists, the dyad is not the unit of interest; the whole network of interrelated exchanges is the unit.

Exchange network theorists point out that in many social structures, an individual does not receive back a reward from the individual to whom he/she has given something but rather from someone else in the system, who has in turn received something from elsewhere in the system. For example, Levi-Strauss (1969) shows that in some kinship systems, a household does not get wives for its sons from the same kinship unit to which it sends its daughters as wives. For another well-known example, in the Kula exchange described originally by Malinowski (1922) ritual gifts travel around in a large circle, rather than being exchanged between pairs of trading partners, thus linking islands which are far distant from each other into a single network. In this kind of exchange network, what an individual wants is not direct reciprocity, but rather that his/her partner fulfill an obligation to someone else (This suggests that the first dictionary definition of "need," i.e., "necessary duty" is not so far from the sociological meaning after all). Furthermore, in such a system individuals feel confident that acts that benefit someone else will eventually be repaid although not by the direct beneficiary. Trust is thus in the system as a whole, not in individual other persons. Although many of the classic examples of nondyadic exchanges are drawn from research on non-Western societies, it was Durkheim (1893 [1933]) who proposed that it is modern industrial society that has an "organic" form of organization in which individuals do different work and are coordinated by an indirect exchange system. This contrasts with primitive societies which have "mechanical" form of organization in which individuals all do the same work and conform to all the same norms. Whether some types of exchange systems are more compatible with "modern" society than other exchange systems is an open question; all types can be found in "modern" societies.

A very useful theoretical analysis of these exchange models is Ekeh (1974). To use his theory, we must review some definitions.

First, Ekeh contrasts the "individualistic" and "collectivistic" theories of social exchange. The work on non-Western kinship and ritual gift exchange described just above is within the "collectivistic" tradition; it emphasizes exchange based on shared morality and leading to equality and social solidarity. Individualistic theories focus on individual motivations to maximize rewards (e.g., Homans' use of behaviorist models). Inequalities in reward and in power are among the predicted consequences of exchange in this approach.

Next, Ekeh distinguishes between *restricted* or dyadic exchange and *generalized* exchange. Generalized exchange uses the principle noted by Levi-Strauss of "univocal reciprocity" or indirect reciprocity. Restricted exchange further has two subtypes; *exclusive*, in which there are no other partners, and *inclusive*, in which there are possible other partners. Ekeh hypothesizes that restricted (dyadic) exchange is characterized by: high levels of accountability; a quid pro quo mentality; a short time interval in which to "balance" reciprocity; high levels of emotional involvement; and "brittleness" that is, vulnerability to tension, antagonism, and breakdown. In contrast, generalized exchange has: relatively little emotional loading; high levels of trust in other individuals and in the system; a high degree of social solidarity; a tendency to egalitarianism; and a willingness to contribute to others without an immediate or direct benefit to the actor.

The differences between restricted and generalized exchange systems are caused by the fact that in a generalized exchange an individual does not rely on the person he/she has benefitted to repay, but confidently expects sometime to be rewarded by someone else and has the sense of participating in a trustworthy social system. Although expecting that egalitarian relationships are the most frequent feature of generalized exchange systems, Ekeh does recognize that there is the possibility of exploitation and unequal power relationships in such systems.

In this theory, allocation based on the needs of others is predicted to be a specialty of generalized exchange systems, which are (consistent with Deutsch's [1975, 1985] theory) likely to have high solidarity and egalitarian relationships but (in contradiction to Deutsch's theory) low emotional intensity and relatively impersonal interactions. Individual motivations to allocate on the basis of needs come from trust in the indirect reciprocity of the system (my needs will be met at some future time) as well as validity of need-based allocation norms (i.e., the expectations that need-based allocation behavior will be rewarded by other system members).

Ekeh also distinguishes, within generalized exchange systems, between *chain generalized exchange* (a system of linked dyads), *individually focussed net generalized exchange* (individuals contribute to a group, which then benefits each individual in turn) and *group-focussed net generalized exchange* (in which individuals contribute to a group and benefit as a part of the group). He hypothesizes that individually focussed net generalized is the most receptive to a social welfare (i.e., need-based) ideology. This is, in part, because individually focused net generalized exchanges allow members of the system to assess the individual needs of members as they arise. In other words, need-based allocations require to have information about needs, and to make invidious comparisons at least in the short run.

An example of research contrasting generalized and restricted exchanges as enhancers of need-based allocation is an ethnographic study by Uehara (1990) of the informal support networks of low-income women coping with job loss. Uehara uses Ekeh's framework to identify generalized and restricted exchange systems among these women, and reports that the interactions of the people involved are consistent with Ekeh's predictions, with more emphasis on meeting others' needs in the more generalized networks. Women in more generalized networks did less detailed accounting of exchanges and had a more relaxed approach to repaying obligations.

Need-based allocation norms can also appear as norms of *mutual* help in generalized exchange systems. Several ethnographic studies of informal mutual help norms (Willer and Anderson 1981), point out both the strength and the fragility of such exchange networks in modern societies (Loukinen 1981; Southard 1981; Southard et al. 1981; Hansen, 1981). These examples, as well as the example reported by Uehara (1990), mentioned above, note the importance of information concerning need in coordinating the actions of members of a support network, and also the importance of monitoring of flows of benefit by third parties in the group.

In other words, need-based allocation systems require mechanisms for the accurate and legitimate assessment of need just as equity-based allocation systems require mechanisms for the accurate and legitimate assessment of merit. The various ethnographic studies reviewed above suggest that in generalized exchange systems patterns of visiting and gossip function to maintain the information flows. They also demonstrate that one reason members of a generalized exchange system do not feel they need to keep accounts of specific help they give one another is that they know third parties are aware of what they have done. However, there may be disputes over who is more needy relative to someone else.

Exchange Network Approaches: Power/Dependence Systems

Another exchange network approach derives from the work of Emerson (1981) on power and dependence, and of Willer and Anderson (1981) on elementary theory. In Ekeh's terminology, these deal with inclusive restricted exchange networks. Several different approaches exist within this general theoretical framework. Very briefly, these theorists suppose that the underlying individual motivation in exchanges is to maximize inclusion in rewarding exchanges, which (given the possibility of a potential partner's choosing a different exchange and leaving the actor with no reward) means that actors with fewer potential exchange partners will be at a disadvantage and in a lower power position. Thus, the structure of relationships between possible exchange partners (the organization of the network) is a crucial factor in development of inequalities.

Applying these concepts requires considering a set of concepts introduced formally by Emerson (1981). Especially, we need to recognize the distinction between *productive* and *distributive* exchange. In Emerson's terminology, *productive exchange* is an interaction in which more is produced than the total contributed by each of the participants (as when two people work on a task together, which neither could accomplish alone) while *distributive exchange* is an interaction in which a valued object or act moves from one person to another. There can also of course be destructive exchange, in which something of value is destroyed by an interaction. Stolte (1987), writing in the Emerson tradition and using these concepts, hypothesizes that distributive justice norms will form as a result of the distribution of power and type of exchange within an exchange system. Of particular interest to our discussion of need-based allocation, he hypothesizes that what he calls *consummatory need* will develop as a justice norm in distributive exchange, and where members of a previously disadvantaged group have formed a coalition to attain a power advantage. In contrast, Stolte hypothesizes that other conditions, such as productive exchange and equal or stable unequal power relations will generate justice norms based on equity or equality. This presents yet another view of the conditions for validity of need-based allocation norms; that they will be endorsed among people who have in the past been victims of unequal distribution systems but have cooperated to overcome their disadvantage. Although Stolte developed testable hypotheses, empirical evidence has yet to be presented for these hypotheses.

Among the consequences of need-based allocation hypothesized by some researchers is low status for the recipient. The idea that being seen as needy can lead to derogation or low power does seem plausible. However, much of what I have reviewed so far suggests that being seen as needy may be associated with expectations of equality or even increased merit. Considering need-based allocation rules from the perspective of power/dependence exchange networks allows us to predict the conditions under which being needy may be associated with low status or power. That is, power/dependence and elementary theory both predict that needy persons will have low power when the needy person lacks alternative sources of the good or service required to meet the need, that is, is dependent. However, need should not be confounded with dependency; the two processes theoretically work separately.

Research on Task Interdependence

Do need-based allocations have consequences for group processes? A variety of research programs on group task performance have suggested that distributive justice norms may affect task performance through processes involving communication and trust, coordination, and motivation of group members. Deutsch (1985) presents some evidence that need-based systems encourage trust and open communication, which, like egalitarian distributive justice norms, produce positive results for tasks requiring sharing of information and coordination but may interfere with tasks requiring individual concentration. Meeker (1971) points out that under some conditions of task interdependence, misplaced altruism may be just as destructive as misplaced self-interest is in situations like the Prisoner's Dilemma.

Steiner's (1972) typology of task types includes one type, the conjunctive task (in which individual contributions are combined in such a way that the group succeeds only if the poorest performer meets a minimum standard), is benefitted by attention to the needs of the weakest members. Another type, additive tasks (member's contributions are added together) also can benefit by encouraging the ability of all members to perform to capacity. Thus, we can hypothesize that need-based allocation will improve group task performance when the task is either conjunctive or additive. To the extent that group members can recognize the requirements of their tasks, they should try to meet those requirements, hence need-based allocation rules should be legitimate when a group has conjunctive or additive tasks. Another possible contribution to group task performance is that distributive justice norms, including need, may contribute to task performance by helping to resolve conflicts and coordinate group efforts (e.g., Hoffman and Maier 1959; Lerner 1987; Pruitt, 1972).

DISCUSSION AND SUMMARY

This review has produced a rich assortment of principles and propositions about the causes, concomitants and consequences of need based allocations, coming from a variety of different research programs.

Some conclusions about need-based allocation systems can be summarized as follows:

1.   Need based allocations have both expressive (emotional) and instrumental (task-related) components. The expressive features of need-based allocation systems are primarily concerned with negative emotions; suffering, failure, lack. This can be experienced both by the person in need and by empathetic observers. In operant conditioning terms, the reinforcement value of having a need met is provided by the removal of an aversive condition. This works both for the recipient and to the provider of aid through process of empathy (creating emotional ties between provider and recipient) . However, if ameliorative action is not possible or effective, avoidance or denigration may occur.

2.   The instrumental features of need-based allocations are consistent with the assumption that correcting a lack will be both necessary and sufficient to alleviate the suffering. This has two components: The ability of the allocator to perform an action that will fill a need, and the ability of the recipient to make use of the action.

3.   Thus, propriety (individual level acceptance of legitimacy) of needs and need-based allocations is promoted by individual level processes of empathy, cognitive consistency, and the reinforcement value of instrumental success in meeting another's needs. Propriety is also promoted by the existence of cultural norms supporting need-based allocations. However, the actual implementation of need-based allocations depends also on validity (collective level legitimacy).

4.   Validity of needs and need-based allocations is promoted by:

a.   Consensus on the existence and legitimacy of needs; not all personal lack or suffering qualifies for relief and bargaining or negotiation may occur over the existence and legitimacy of needs and over whether meeting needs is one of the tasks of a group. Referential structures exist that supply grounds for evaluating claims to neediness.

b.   Need claims are more likely to be legitimate if based on expectation that an ameliorative action will have an effect (be put to good use) than on attributions of blame for the need. One consequence of this is that possessing a low state of a status characteristic, leading to a lowering of performance expectations, may reduce the legitimacy of a target's need claims.

c.   Assessing need may require invidious comparisons between individuals, and place a premium on individual rather than group characteristics. Thus, need-based allocations are associated with differentiating among individuals rather than with group solidarity.

d.   Systematic exchange of information about need and allocations are necessary for assessment of legitimacy of need and implementation of need-based
allocations. Therefore, need-based allocation norms are more likely to occur in
settings in which information circulates both about individual needs and about distributions that have occurred.

5. Need-based allocations will be more likely to occur in situations in which
there is a legitimate norm to allocate on the basis of need. Need-based allocation
norms will be legitimate more often in some group structures than others. In particular, need-based norms will tend to be legitimate under generalized, especially
individually-focussed net generalized exchange, rather than restricted exchange.

6.   Individually-focused net generalized exchange, and hence need-based allocation norms, are likely to occur in:

a.   Relationships, including dyads, in which there are many different tasks and/
or a long-term time frame. In Parsons' (1951) pattern variable terms, this will be
where the relationship is *diffuse* rather than *specific* (the role partners interact in
many different situations). A long-term time frame occurs where there is interpersonal *commitment*.

b.   Groups or organizations in which allocations may be made by different persons than those whose needs are being met or who may pay the cost. Examples of
these are: Helping professionals such as medical personnel or social workers;
supervisors of work groups; redistributive taxation; participation in civic life as a
citizen.

c.   Since diffuse, committed relationships tend to be those in which high levels
of positive affect, trust, and solidarity are found, these will also be associated with
the existence of need-based distributive justice norms. This association may, however, be spurious.

d.   Since diffuse, committed, or complex relationships usually have more than
one task or basis of interaction, need-based distributive justice rules will usually
not be the only legitimate distributive justice rule. Actual allocations will tend to
represent compromises among equity, equality, need, and other possible rules.

7.   Need-based allocations are more likely to occur in groups with tasks that
are conjunctive or additive (that is, in which the contributions of the weakest performers are of value).

8.   Implementation of need-based distributive justice rules may lead to inequality through:

a.   Attention to individual differences rather than to features common to all
group members

b.   Formation of referential standards for deservingness; targets who are seen
as deserving of higher allocation based on need may be seen as more deserving in
other respects

c.   Intensifying dependency; when need-based allocation is combined with
exchange dependency (lack of alternative sources to remove the aversive condition), power effects of dependency will be especially strong. When need is asso-

ciated with a history of lower rewards, targets with greater need may be seen as less deserving.

9. The consequences of need-based allocation may include improved group task performance through:

a. Improvement of performance by weaker members
b. Coordination and exchange of information
c. Increased trust in the system.

REFERENCES

Alves, W.M., and P.H. Rossi. 1979. "Who Should Get What? Fairness Judgments of the Distribution of Earnings." *American Journal of Sociology* 84: 541-564.

Austin, W., E. Walster, and M.K. Utne. 1976. "Equity and the Law: the Effect of a Harmdoer's 'Suffering in the Act' on Liking and Assigned Punishment." Pp 163-190 in *Advances in Experimental Social Psychology*, Vol. 9, edited by L. Berkowitz and E. Walster. New York: Academic Press.

Batson, C.D. 1987. "Prosocial Motivation: Is It Ever Truly Altruistic?" Pp. 65-122 in *Advances in Experimental Social Psychology*, Vol. 20, edited by L. Berkowitz. New York: Academic Press.

Berger, J., M.H. Fisek, R.Z. Norman, and D.G. Wagner. 1985. "Formation of Reward Expectations in Status Structures." Pp. 215-261 in *Status, Rewards and Influence*, edited by J. Berger and M. Zelditch Jr. San Francisco: Jossey-Bass.

Berger, J., M. Zelditch Jr., B. Anderson, and B. Cohen. 1972. "Structural Aspects of Distributive Justice: A Status Value Formulation." Pp. 119-46 in *Sociological Theories in Progress*, Vol. 2., edited by J. Berger, M. Zelditch Jr., and B. Anderson. Boston: Houghton Mifflin.

Berkowitz, L. 1972. "Social Norms, Feelings and Other Factors Affecting Helping Behavior and Altruism." Pp.66-108 in *Advances in Experimental Social Psychology* Vol. 6, edited by L. Berkowitz. New York: Academic Press.

Berkowitz, L., and L.R. Daniels. 1963. "Responsibility and Dependency." *Journal of Abnormal and Social Psychology* 66: 429-436.

Berkowitz, L., and E. Walster. (eds.). 1976. *Advances in Experimental Social Psychology*, Vol 9. New York: Academic Press.

Blau, P.M. 1964. *Exchange and Power in Social Life*. New York: Wiley.

Cook, K.S. 1975. "Expectations, Evaluations, and Equity." *American Sociological Review*. 40: 372-388.

d'Anjou, L., A. Steijn, and D. Van Aarsen. 1995. "Social Position, Ideology, and Distributive Justice." *Social Justice Research* 8: 351-384.

Deutsch, M. 1975. "Equality, Equity and Need: What Determines which Value will Be Used as the Basis of Distributive Justice?" *Journal of Social Issues*. 31: 137-149.

Deutsch, M. 1985. *Distributive Justice: A Social-Psychological Perspective*. New Haven, CT: Yale University Press.

Dietrich, D.M., and L. Berkowitz. 1997. "Alleviation of Dissonance by Engaging in Prosocial Behavior or Receiving Ego-Enhancing Feedback." *Journal of Social Behavior and Personality* 12: 557-566.

Dornbusch, S.M., and W.R. Scott. 1975. *Evaluation and the Exercise of Authority*. San Francisco: Jossey-Bass.

Durkheim, E. 1893 [1933]. *The Division of Labor In Society*. New York: The Free Press.

Durkheim, E. 1915 [1965]. *The Elementary Forms of the Religious Life*. New York: The Free Press

Ekeh, P.P. 1974. *Social Exchange: The Two Traditions* Cambridge, MA: Harvard University Press.

Elliott, G.C., and B.F. Meeker. 1984. "Modifiers of the Equity Effect: Group Outcome and Causes for Individual Performance." *Journal of Personality and Social Psychology*, 46: 586-597.

Elliott, G.C., and B.F. Meeker. 1986. "Achieving Fairness in the Face of Competing Concerns: The Different Effects of Individual and Group Characteristics." *Journal of Personality and Social Psychology* 50: 754-60.

Emerson, R.M. 1981. "Social Exchange Theory." Pp. 30-65 in *Social Psychology: Sociological Perspectives,* edited by M. Rosenberg and R. H. Turner. New York: Basic Books.

Fisher, J.D., A. Nadler, and S. Whitcher-Alagner. 1982. "Recipient Reactions to Aid." *Psychological Bulletin.* 91: 27-54.

Galston, W.M. 1980. *Justice and the Human Good.* Chicago: University of Chicago Press.

Gouldner, A.W. 1960. "The Norm of Reciprocity: A Preliminary Statement." *American Sociological Review.* 25: 161-178.

Griffith, W.I. 1989. "The Allocation of Negative Outcomes." Pp. 107-137 in *Advances in Group Processes,* edited by E.J. Lawler and B. Markovsky, Greenwich, CT: JAI Press.

Hansen, K.L. 1981. "'Black' Exchange and Its System of Social Control." Pp. 71-92 in *Networks, Exchange, and Coercion,* edited by D. Willer and B. Anderson. New York: Elsevier.

Harrod, W.J. 1980. "Expectations from Unequal Rewards." *Social Psychology Quarterly.* 43: 126-130.

Heath, A. 1976. *Rational Choice and Social Exchange: A Critique of Exchange Theory.* Cambridge: Cambridge University Press.

Hegtvedt, K.A., and B. Markovsky. 1995. "Justice and Injustice" Pp. 257-280 in *Sociological Perspectives on Social Psychology,* edited by K.S. Cook, G.A. Fine, and J.S. House. Needham Heights, MA: Allyn and Bacon.

Hochschild, J.L. 1981. *What's Fair? American Beliefs About Distributive Justice.* Cambridge, MA: Harvard University Press.

Hoffman, L.R., and N.R.F. Maier. 1959. "The Use of Group Decision to Resolve a Problem of Fairness." *Personnel Psychology* 12: 545-559.

Homans, G.C. 1961 [1974]. *Social Behavior: Its Elementary Forms.* New York: Harcourt, Brace and World.

Ickes, W.J., and R.F. Kidd. 1976. "An Attributional Analysis of Helping Behavior." Pp. 311-335 in *New Directions in Attribution Research.* Vol. 1. edited by W. Ickes and R. Kidd. Hillsdale, NJ: Erlbaum.

Jasso, G., and P. Rossi. 1977. "Distributive Justice and Earned Income." *American Sociological Review* 42: 639-51.

Kluegel, J.R., and E.R. Smith. 1986. *Beliefs About Inequality: Americans' View of What Is and What Ought To Be.* Hawthorne, NJ: Aldine de Gruyter.

Krebs, D.L., and D.T. Miller. 1985. "Altruism and Aggression." Pp. 1-71 in *The Handbook of Social Psychology,* 3rd edition, Vol. 2. New York: Random House.

Lamm, H., and T. Schwinger. 1980. "Norms Concerning Distributive Justice: Are Needs Taken into Consideration in Allocation Decisions?" *Social Psychology Quarterly* 43: 425-429.

Lankenau, S.E. 1997. "Native Sons: A Social Exploration of Panhandling." Ph.D. Dissertation, University of Maryland, College Park.

Lerner, M. 1965. "Evaluation of Performance as a Function of Performer's Reward and Attractiveness." *Journal of Personality and Social Psychology* 1: 355-360.

Lerner, M.J. 1980. *The Belief in a Just World: A Fundamental Delusion.* New York: Plenum Press.

Lerner, M.J. 1987. "Integrating Societal and Psychological Rules of Entitlement: The Basic Task of Each Social Actor and Fundamental Problem for the Social Sciences." *Social Justice Research* 1: 102-125.

Leventhal, G.S. 1976. "The Distribution of Rewards and Resources in Groups and Organizations." Pp. 92-131 in *Advances in Experimental Social Psychology,* Vol. 9, edited by L. Berkowitz and E. Walster. New York: Academic Press.

Leventhal, G.S., J. Karuza Jr., and W.R. Fry. 1980. "Beyond Fairness: A Theory of Allocation Preferences." Pp. 167-218 in *Justice and Social Interaction,* edited by G. Mikula. New York: Springer-Verlag.

Leventhal, G.S., T. Weiss, and R. Buttrick. 1973. "Attribution of Value, Equity, and the Prevention of Waste in Reward Allocation." *Journal of Personality and Social Psychology.* 27: 276-285.

Levi-Strauss, C. 1969. *The Elementary Structures of Kinship,* rev. edition. Boston: Beacon.

Loukinen, M. 1981. "Social Exchange Networks." Pp. 85-94 in *Networks, Exchange, and Coercion,* edited by D. Willer and B. Anderson. New York: Elsevier.

Major, B. 1994. "From Social Inequality to Personal Entitlement: The Role of Social Comparisons, Legitimacy Appraisals, and Group membership." Pp. 293-355 in *Advances in Experimental Social Psychology,* Vol. 26, edited by M. P. Zanna. New York: Academic Press.

Malinowski, B. 1922. *Argonauts of the Western Pacific.* New York: E.P. Dutton.

Marshall, V.W., C.J. Rosenthal, and J. Daciuk. 1987. "Older Parents' Expectations for Filial Support." *Social Justice Research* 1: 405-424.

Matthews, S.H. 1987. "Perceptions of Fairness in the Division of Responsibility for Old Parents." *Social Justice Research* 1: 425-438.

Mauss, M. 1925 [1966]. *The Gift: Forms and Functions of Exchange in Archaic Societies* [trans by I. Cunnison] London: Cohen and West.

Meeker, B. 1971. "Decisions and Exchange." *American Sociological Review* 36: 485-95.

Meeker, B.F., and G.C. Elliott. 1987. "Counting the Costs: Equity and the Allocation of Negative Group Products." *Social Psychology Quarterly* 50: 7-15.

Meeker, B.F. and G.C. Elliott. 1995. "Equality and Differentiation: Effects of Group Structure on Allocations." *Social Justice Research* 8: 263-284.

Mikula, G. 1980. "On the Role of Justice in Allocation Decisions." Pp 127-166 in *Justice and Social Interaction,* edited by G. Mikula. New York: Springer Verlag.

Molm, L. D. and K. S. Cook. 1995. "Social Exchange and Exchange Networks" Pp. 209-235 in *Sociological Perspectives on Social Psychology,* edited by K.S. Cook, G.A. Fine, and J.S. House, Needham Heights, MA: Allyn and Bacon.

Norris, J.E. 1987. "Justice and Intergenerational Relations: An Introduction." *Social Justice Research* 1: 393-403.

Parsons, T. 1951. *The Social System.* New York: Free Press.

Peterson, C. 1987. "Need, Equity, and Equality in the Adult Family." *The Journal of Social Psychology* 127: 543-544.

Piliavin, J.A., J.F. Dovidio, S.L. Gaertner, and R.D. Clark. 1981. *Emergency Intervention.* New York: Academic Press.

Pruitt, D.G. 1972. "Methods for Resolving Differences of Interest: A Theoretical Analysis" *Journal of Social Issues* 28: 133-154.

Randall, C.S. And C.W. Meuller. 1995. "Extensions of Justice Theory: Justice Evaluations and Employees' Reactions in a Natural Setting." *Social Psychology Quarterly* 58: 178-194.

Rawls, J.A. 1971. *A Theory of Justice.* Cambridge, MA: Harvard University Press.

Ridgeway, C.L., and H.A. Walker. 1995. "Status Structures" Pp. 281-310 in *Sociological Perspectives on Social Psychology,* edited by K.S. Cook, G.A. Fine, and J.S. House, Needham Heights, MA: Allyn and Bacon.

Ritzman, R.L., and D. Tomaskovic-Devey. 1992. "Life Chances and Support for Equality and Equity as Normative and Counternormative Distribution Rules." *Social Forces.* 70: 745-763.

Robinson, R.V., and W. Bell. 1978 "Equality, Success, and Social Justice in England and the United States." *American Sociological Review* 43: 125-143.

Sahlins, M.D. 1965. "On the Sociology of Primitive Exchange." Pp. 139-52 in *The Relevance of Models for Social Anthropology,* ASA Monographs 1, edited by M. Banton. London: Tavistock.

Schiltz, M.E. 1970. *Public Attitudes Toward Social Security, 1935-1965.* Washington, DC: Government Printing Office.

Schwartz, S. 1975."The Justice of Need and the Activation of Humanitarian Norms." *Journal of Social Issues* 31: 111-136.

Schwinger, T. 1980. "Just Allocations of Goods: Decisions Among Three Principles." Pp. 95-124 in *Justice and Social Interaction*, edited by G. Mikula. New York: Springer Verlag.

Shepelak, N.J. 1989. "Ideological Stratification: American Beliefs About Economic Justice." *Social Justice Research* 3: 217-137.

Southard, F. 1981. "Normatively Controlled Social Exchange Systems." Pp. 54-69 in *Networks, Exchange, and Coercion* edited by D. Willer and B. Anderson. New York: Elsevier.

Southard, F., B. Anderson, D. Willer, N.J. Davis, J.S. Brennan, S.A. Gilham, K.L. Hansen, R. Hurst, M. Loukinen, and A. Morris. 1981. "The Theory of Mutual Benefit Systems." Pp. 95-103 in *Networks, Exchange, and Coercion*, edited by D. Willer and B. Anderson. New York: Elsevier.

Steiner, I.D. 1972. *Group Process and Productivity*. New York: Academic Press.

Stolte, J.F. 1987. "The Formation of Justice Norms." *American Sociological Review* 52: 774-784.

Thibaut, J.W., and H.H. Kelley. 1959. *The Social Psychology of Groups*. New York: Wiley.

Tornblom, K.Y., and U.G. Foa. 1983. "Choice of a Distribution Principle: Crosscultural Evidence on the Effects of Resources." *Acta Sociologica* 26: 161-173.

Uehara, E. 1990. "Dual Exchange Theory, Social Networks, and Informal Social Support." *American Journal of Sociology* 96: 521-57.

Utne, M.K., and R.F. Kidd. "Equity and Attribution." 1980. Pp. 63-93 in *Justice and Social Interaction*, edited by G. Mikula. New York: Springer Verlag.

Wagner, D., and J. Berger. 1993. "Status Characteristics Theory: The Growth of a Program." Pp. 23-63 in *Theoretical Research Programs: Studies in the Growth of Theory*, edited by J. Berger and M. Zelditch. Stanford, CA: Stanford University Press.

Wagstaff, G.F. 1994. "Equity, Equality, and Need: Three Principles of Justice or One? An analysis of 'Equity as Desert.'" *Current Psychology: Developmental, Leaning, Personality, Social* 13: 138-152.

Wagstaff, G.F., J.P. Huggins, and T.J. Perfect. 1991. "Equity, Equality, and Need in the Adult Family." *The Journal of Social Psychology* 133: 439-443.

Walker, H.A., L. Rogers, and M. Zelditch Jr., 1988. "Legitimacy and Collective Action: a Research Note." *Social Forces* 67: 216-228.

Walker, H.A., G. Thomas, and M. Zelditch Jr. 1986. "Legitimation, Endorsement, and Stability." *Social Forces* 64: 620-643.

Walker, H.A., and M. Zelditch Jr. 1993. "Power, Legitimacy, and the Stability of Authority: A Theoretical Research Program." Pp. 364-381 in *Theoretical Research Programs: Studies in the Growth of Theory*, edited by J. Berger and M. Zelditch Jr. Palo Alto, CA: Stanford Univ. Press.

Walster, E., E. Bersheid, and G.W. Walster. 1976. "New Directions in Equity Research." Pp. 1-42 in *Advances in Experimental Social Psychology*, Vol. 9, edited by E. Walster and L. Berkowitz. New York: Academic Press.

Walster, E., and J.A. Piliavin. 1972. "Equity and the Innocent Bystander." *Journal of Social Issues*. 28: 165-189.

Webster's Ninth New Collegiate Dictionary. 1985. New York: Merriam-Webster.

Will, J.A. 1993."The Dimensions of Poverty: Public Perceptions of the Deserving Poor." *Social Science Research* 22: 312-332.

Willer, D., and B. Anderson. 1981. *Networks, Exchange and Coercion: The Elementary Theory and Its Applications*. New York: Elsevier.

Zelditch, M., Jr., and H.A. Walker. 1984. "Legitimacy and the Stability of Authority." Pp. 1-25 in *Advances in Group Processes*, Vol. 1, edited by E.J. Lawler. Stamford, CT: JAI Press.

JUDGING THE CONSEQUENCES OF EVALUATION BY OTHERS IN STATUS HETEROGENEOUS GROUPS: BIASES IN THE MICROLEVEL HEURISTICS OF GROUP INFORMATION EXCHANGE

Steven D. Silver and Lisa Troyer

ABSTRACT

We present a theoretical framework describing group decision making as a function of status distributions. We propose that status distributions affect the amount and type of information that group members offer in the course of decision making. Since collective decision making depends on the information individuals offer, we conceptualize decision making as a process of information exchange among individuals. Information exchange, we emphasize, is also a form of social exchange, in which members risk the loss of social status (i.e., there is a potential social cost in the exchange). In this exchange, we conceptualize members as seeking to maintain their social statuses in the group by managing the amount and type of information they

Advances in Group Processes, Volume 15, pages 103-132.
Copyright © 1998 by JAI Press Inc.
ISBN: 0-7623-0362-X

initiate in the context of collective decision making. Status may be lost in these contexts through the receipt of negative evaluations, which are conditional on the information members initiate. In managing the exchange of information, we propose that an actor uses a heuristic in which expected status loss depends directly on the actor's status distance from a potential evaluator. We use insights from Prospect Theory on biases in an actor's judgment of gains and losses to generate explicit forms for the collective decision-making processes we describe. These forms, in turn, allow analytical inference on information exchange and quality in collective decision making. Following claims of Prospect Theory, we suggest that the status distance actors perceive in this heuristic underweights the objective distance from members who are lower in status than the focal actor, and overweights the objective distance from members who are higher in status than the focal actor. Through a formal explication of these arguments, we generate inferences on the consequences of this nonlinear weighting of status for (1) the patterns of information exchanged in the group and (2) the quality of the decision generated in groups engaged in ill-structured decision making. We also describe two empirical tests that lend support to assumptions and inference from our framework. We conclude by discussing the implications of bias in judged status distances and future directions in which our framework might be extended.

The theory and research we present here is an investigation of the process in the decision making of social groups. We focus on the social and instrumental effects of participation in collective decision making for both the individual and the group as a whole. Inasmuch as a decision-making group *thinks* and *acts*, it does so through the information that members exchange with one another in context of solving a problem or making a decision. Within the context of decision making a variety of types of information can be exchanged among members including ideas, facts, positive evaluations, negative evaluations, and interrogatives. Each of these types of information represents a contribution to the group's objectives in decision making. However, information exchange is embedded not only in a task-oriented process, but also in a social process. That is, we propose that information exchange is not only functional, but also social. As emphasized in social exchange theory (e.g., Emerson 1988; Molm and Cook 1995), exchange is a process in which reciprocation has particular importance. In fact, we argue, that it is very much reciprocation, or the *anticipation* of reciprocation, following the initiation of information by an actor that underlies the observed patterns of information exchange.

Members of social groups quickly recognize that their behavior has consequences for their social position, or status, in the group. We propose that this recognition is commonly embodied in the tacit assessment of social gains and losses that are likely to follow from information the individual considers initiating in the course of participation in decision-making groups. Social gains and losses, in turn, arise through the exchange of a particular type of information: positive and negative evaluation, respectively. That is, when actors initiate information in a group, they must confront the possibility of receiving either a positive evaluation or a negative evaluation in return for the information initiation. Positive evaluations generate social gains insofar as they enhance an actor's social status. Negative evaluations generate social losses insofar as they reduce an actor's social status. Furthermore, we assert that an important factor that moderates these assessments is the magnitude of the judged status difference between the individual who will initiate the information (i.e., the source) and the individual who is the recipient of the information (i.e., the target). In considering how these judgments affect the cognition and behavior of individuals in groups as well as group outcomes, we will conceptualize the process within a "social risk" framework of information exchange (e.g., Cohen and Silver 1989; Silver, Cohen, and Rainwater 1988). First though, we offer a brief overview of research related to social judgments. This background sets the tone for our own theoretical framework on social risk and information exchange.

THE ROLE OF JUDGMENTS OF SOCIAL DISTANCE IN SOCIAL PROCESSES

An individual's judgments of the social distance between herself and relevant others has important and well-recognized consequences for cognition and behavior. For example, Hyman (1942) found that individuals rely on self as a referent in assessing the status of others. Also, Wegener (1987) notes that regularities in evaluations of distributive justice follow from an individual's subjective scaling of social hierarchies. Wegener makes the point that one reason distributive justice is often illusory is because the perception of justice does not adequately mirror reality. In contrast to the views of previous theorists (e.g., Inkeles and Rossi 1956; Hodge, Treiman, Ross 1966), Wegener (1982) found that respondents in low-status positions tend to "shorten" their subjective judgment of the entire social order. These low-status actors give relatively depressed prestige scores to social positions at the top of the hierarchy, and relatively inflated scores to positions at the bottom. As Wegener observes, by engaging in this kind of subjective leveling of the social hierarchy, individuals in lower-status positions may see themselves more favorably (Wegener 1987). In contrast, actors in higher-status positions tend to polarize the social grading continuum. Status positions that these actors perceive as being located below their own level are lowered even more, and those of higher status actors are elevated.

Social networks researchers also find effects of referent position on status judgments and on behavioral consequences of these judgments. For example, Boster, Johnson, and Weller (1987) reported that patterns of advice seeking in an administrative office were closely related to a respondent's judgment of proximity in structural position and status of the person from whom advice was sought. At the same time, other informants do not necessarily judge the status proximities in the same manner as the respondent. In a related vein of work, prospect theorists (e.g., Kahneman and Tversky 1979) show that referent position affects preference and aversion in decision making. This line of research indicates that decisions with identical payoffs that are framed in terms of different reference points are judged very differently.

As this brief overview suggests, we find diverse indication of the biases in judgments of social distance in a range of contexts. However, biases that occur in judgments of members of small groups have not been systematically considered. Furthermore, we find little systematic inference on the *collective* consequences of biases in social judgments. This is in part because such inference requires aggregation of judgments, and the rules for such aggregation are not well known. In the sections that follow, we will directly address judgments of the status of self and others in problem-solving groups, and we will examine the behavioral consequences of these judgments. In particular, we will consider (1) how the information that individual members contributes to a group is affected by these judgments, and (2) how these behavioral consequences in the form of information exchange affect group outcomes with respect to the quality of the group's decision.

SOCIAL STATUS, INFORMATION EXCHANGE, AND ILL-STRUCTURED GROUP DECISION MAKING

Social status represents a defining feature of social interaction. In the case of formal decision-making groups, especially those that are highly visible to others, individuals face the simultaneous requirements of (1) contributing to the group objective, and (2) managing their status position in the group. Moreover, the latter requirement clearly depends to some extent on the former; contributions to the group's objective may result in either increases or decreases in status.

In considering microprocess in an individual's management of status, it is important to recognize two factors contributing to change: evaluations and the status of the source of the evaluation. First, the exchange of evaluations is an observable source of status change in collectives. Evaluations are overt and valenced judgments of individual performance by group members (Sanna and Shotland 1990). Often, though, evaluations are not objective. The same performance is more likely to be favorably judged when it originates from a higher-status group member than a lower-status group member (e.g., Foschi, Lai, Sigerson 1994; Foschi, Warriner, and Hart 1985). It is possible, though, to expect the opposite. That is, one might expect more from a higher-status actor and therefore judge her contribution lower when it is the same as the contribution of a lower-status actor. However, the former rather than the latter bias is most often observed in social groups (Driskell 1982).

Second, the expected gains and losses arising from evaluation depend on the status of the evaluator (i.e., source of the evaluations). Evaluations from higher-status sources may carry more weight than evaluations from lower-status sources. For instance, on the one hand, individuals who receive a positive evaluation from a higher-status source may feel that the evaluation is particularly status-enhancing. On the other hand, when the positive evaluation is offered by a lower-status source, the recipient may not find that it contributes much to her status at all. However, little empirical evidence exists with respect to this possibility. The dependency of the effects of the source of the evaluation on targets as well as the consequences of this dependency are not well defined. One of the goals of our work is to provide better definition to this phenomenon.

Information contributes not only to social processes, like status management, but also to the group's objective in decision making. As we previously noted, arriving at a decision in a group entails the exchange of a variety of different information types (e.g., ideas, facts, positive evaluations, and negative evaluations). While all of these information types facilitate group convergence on a decision alternative, the type of decision the group confronts may affect which types of information are most important. We are interested in a particular type of decision—ill-structured decisions. Ill-structured decisions are those which are less definable in terms that allow the application of algorithmic or heuristic rules to the decision (e.g., Mintzberg, Raisinghani, and Theoret 1976; Reitman 1964). Of the different types of information that contribute to solving ill-structured decisions, ideas are among the most important in terms of generating quality solutions in decision-making groups.

We also note that while different information types make different contributions to the quality of collective decisions, the initiation of each type has different expected consequences for status management. This is because some types of information are more likely to elicit a negative evaluation in return for the information initiation than other types. More specifically, ideas and negative evaluations are more likely to elicit a negative evaluation than positive evaluations, facts, or interrogatives. Thus, we term the former "more risky," and the latter "less risky." As a consequence of the differential risk that attaches to the type of information initiated, members may be more reticent to send more risky types of information (i.e., information types with higher likelihoods of eliciting a negative evaluation) than less risky types. The combination of insight on the differential importance of different types of information to ill-structured decision making and insight on the differential risk that different information types carry in social interaction suggests an important paradox in group decision making: One of the most important types of information (i.e., ideas) is also one of the types most likely to be negatively evaluated, and hence as a risky information type, is more likely to be withheld. Moreover, because higher-status actors are more likely to be judged more favorably than lower-status actors for the same contribution (as described previously), these risks and their behavioral consequences (i.e., reticence) are likely to be exacerbated for lower-status actors.[1] As a result of these factors, members of different status may be biased toward "specializing" in certain information types. For instance, higher status actors may tend to "oversend"[2] more risky types of information (i.e., ideas and negative evaluations), while lower status members may tend to "oversend" less risky types of information (i.e., positive evaluations, facts, and interrogatives).[3]

The role of status in risk become more paradoxical when we consider additional research on diversity in ill-structured decision making. In recent years, there have been systematic attempts to increase social heterogeneity in groups, because heterogeneity generates diversity (Pearce and Ravlin 1987). Diversity, in turn, increases the likelihood that a variety of expertise and perspective will be brought to bear on the decision that the group is considering. Such broad representation in the group is argued to increase the likelihood that a range of potential alternatives (i.e., ideas) will be proposed in the group, and thus the quality of a decision will be enhanced. The logic of heterogeneity, however, becomes more problematic when we recognize that status hierarchies arise through social differentiation (i.e., heterogeneity) among group members (e.g., Berger, Fisek, Norman, and Zelditch 1977). We again emphasize that status differences play an important role in generating social risk in groups.

A final factor worth noting in this discussion of social status, information exchange, and group decision making is the relative impact of positive and negative evaluations on these processes. The relative weighting of positive and negative evaluations reflects the relative valuing of gains and losses by group members. If negative evaluations are weighted more than positive evaluations, the "costs" of negative evaluations are seen as greater than the "gains" of positive evaluations. As a result of such differential weighting, an actor might withhold riskier information types, like an idea, until the subjective probability of it eliciting a positive evaluation (i.e., of being "correct" and/or "well-received") is greater than the subjective probability of the eliciting a negative evaluation. Because it is difficult to judge the quality of one's own ideas, if negative evaluations are weighted more heavily than positive evaluations, an increasing proportion of risky information types (like ideas) will be withheld as the decision making becomes more ill-structured. This is, of course, exactly the opposite of the exchange that would most facilitate group objectives. Moreover, this effect is likely to be greatest among lower-status members, and will significantly increase the censoring of risky information types by these members.

The foregoing observations primarily reflect individual concerns regarding information exchange in a collective. Aggregating individual effects for inference on the collective as a whole is not a straightforward operation. Biases in the information exchange of individuals of different status in a heterogeneous group are in different directions and the net effect will depend on assumptions about the magnitude of individual biases and the interaction of the effects in aggregating to a collective level. Thus, to generate inference on information exchange processes in the collective and its implications for group objectives like quality requires that such assumptions be made explicit. We now turn to a formal statement of our framework, which explicitly and systematically articulates the assumptions and arguments we have offered.

MICROLEVEL HEURISTICS IN INFORMATION EXCHANGE

On the basis of the preceding discussion, we propose that the amount and type of information that is exchanged in a collective depends on (1) differences in the weights that group members assign to positive and negative evaluations, (2) the judgments members make regarding the status distance between themselves and those who are likely to evaluate the message the members might initiate, and (3) the distribution of status among members of a collective. We expect that the theory we present in the following sections will obtain in groups whose members are collectively engaged in ill-structured group decision making. The importance of this scope condition will become clear in course of our theoretical elaboration.

Evaluations and the Expected Cost of Social Interaction

We begin our articulation of the processes involved in information exchange by modeling expected status gains and losses. We represent these losses and gains in terms of the conditional probability of receiving a positive or negative evaluation in return for initiating information in the group. Furthermore, as indicated in our previous discussion, we note that these losses and gains are conditioned by source. Evaluations from higher-status sources are weighted more heavily than evaluations from lower-status sources. We write the loss gain function for a group member in an interaction period as:

$$C_i = \sum_{i \neq j} \sum_{X=I}^{B} Pr(N_{ji}X_{ij})(f(\sigma_i, \sigma_j)) \tag{1}$$

$$G_i = \sum_{i \neq j} \sum_{X=I}^{B} Pr(P_{ji}X_{ij})(f(\sigma_i, \sigma_j)) \tag{2}$$

where Ci, Gi = the costs and gains, respectively to the ith member for initiating
  information of type, X_k;

X_{ij} = information types sent by member $\underline{i}$ to member j, such as ideas (I),
  negative evaluations (N), facts (F), positive evaluations (P), and
  blanks or "non- responses" (B);

N_{ji}, P_{ji} = negative and positive evaluations, respectively, sent by member j
  to member i,

σ_i, σ_j = the status of the ith and jth members.

In equations (1) and (2), every act or non-act (such as not responding to a message or remaining silent in an exchange) is considered to have a probability of eliciting a negative evaluation. We further argue that:

$$Pr(N_{ji}(N_{ij}) > Pr(N_{ji}I_{ij}) > Pr(N_{ji}(F_{ij}) \geq Pr(N_{ji}B_{ij}) > Pr(N_{ji}P_{ij}) \quad (3)$$

Thus, negatively evaluating another group member is seen as having the greatest probability of resulting in an negative evaluation by that member. In contrast, positively evaluating another member is seen as having the smallest probability of resulting in a negative evaluation by that member. Note that in equation (3) nonresponses are seen as having a greater conditional probability of generating a negative evaluation than initiating positive evaluations. In such a case, then, optimal behavior (i.e., behavior that best maintains an actor's status position or which minimizes status loss) for lower-status group members is unlikely to be nonparticipation. Since a member can *credibly* send only a limited number of positive evaluations, there is always some potential for negative evaluation. This potential, in turn, increases the likelihood that these lower-status members might also initiate information in the form of facts, or they may refrain from participating at some points. We formally state this as an assumption in our framework:

Assumption 1. The probability of receiving a negative evaluation as a result of initiating information in a group depends on the type of information initiated, as indicated in equation (3).

The dependencies of information exchange on the type of information exchanged and the relative status of actors we noted discussed in the previous section are evident in equations (1) and (2). We can now use these dependencies to develop formal arguments on information exchange in heterogeneous (i.e., status-differentiated) groups. We preface these arguments with additional assumptions, and use our assumptions along with mathematical operations to derive inference on the relationship between status distributions and the proportion of risky types of information exchanged in a group, as well as statements on solution quality in decision-making groups.

Relative Importance of Positive and Negative Evaluations as Regulators of Information Exchange in Collectives

We believe that a general statement on the relative weighting of positive and negative evaluations by group members is supported in several observations. First, differences in the "social etiquette" or norms of groups make positive evaluations more common than negative evaluations. This is especially the case in groups that do not have an extensive interaction history. Consequently, one can expect that the lower frequency of negative evaluations increases the weight that group members attach to this type of evaluation. Second, if members use evaluations of others to estimate expected status gains and losses of different magnitudes, then findings in other research traditions are useful to our application. In particular, the "heuristics and biases" tradition of Prospect Theory (Kahneman and Tversky 1979; Kahneman, Slovic, and Tversky 1982; Tversky and Kahneman 1992) provides insight on the valuing of positive and negative evaluations. In their early statement on the asymmetry in preferences for gains and losses of the same magnitude, these researchers proposed that losses are perceived as more "aversive" than the same sized gains are perceived as "pleasant." Additionally, they noted that shifting reference points determines whether alternatives are viewed as an opportunity to recover a loss or obtain a gain. While not uncontested (see, for example, Gigerenzer 1996), the assertion of prospect theorists on gains and losses has been supported in a range of investigations of risky choice in managerial contexts and in some cases of low risk choice (e.g., Highhouse and Johnson 1996; Sullivan and Kida 1995; Tversky and Kahneman 1991).

From these insights, we offer the following assumption:

Assumption 2. A group member judges the status loss from a negative evaluation by a member of a given status to be greater in magnitude than the status gain obtained from a positive evaluation by the same source.

Functional Form of Judged Status Distances

According to our arguments, member judgments of status distances from other members are crucial to the expected costs of initiating information, and consequently to the amount and type of information that members exchange. For example, the expected status cost of a negative evaluation or expected status gain from a positive evaluation to a medium and lower status target will differ when the target of the evaluation uses a convex or concave weighting of status distance, rather than a linear weighting of the distance. Consistent use of nonlinear weightings of objective status differences will result in "systematic" biases in the information that is initiated in the collective. While many researchers may be intuitively aware that linear representations of status effects in such cases are inadequate[4] the consequences of non-linear forms for social risks has not been addressed in a group problem-solving framework. On the basis of these insights, we offer the following assumption:

Assumption 3. A group member, A, overweights the expected status loss from a negative evaluation by a member, B, who is higher in status than A, and underweights a negative evaluation from a member, C, who is lower in status than A.

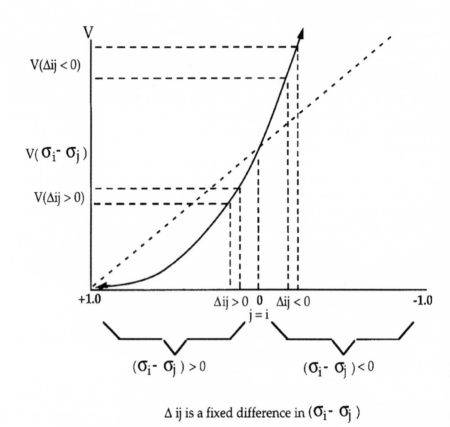

Δij is a fixed difference in $(\sigma_i - \sigma_j)$

Figure 1. Judgment of Status Loss from a Negative Evaluation as a Function of Actual Status Distance from the Evaluator

This assumption suggests that group members judge the expected status loss from a negative evaluation by a member who is z status units higher than themselves in status to be *more* than twice the expected loss from a negative evaluation by a member who is units higher than themselves. Correspondingly, this assumption indicates that group members judge the expected status loss from a negative evaluation by a member who is $\frac{z}{2}$ units lower than themselves in status as *less* than twice the expected loss from a negative evaluation by a member who is units higher than themselves. As we noted in earlier discussion, the form of this weighting has important implications for information exchange in a group. We further claim that status losses *increase* at an increasing rate for the target of a negative evaluation, as the source of the evaluation increases in the distance by which it exceeds the target in status. Correspondingly, status losses *decrease* at a decreasing rate for the target of a negative evaluation as the target of the evaluation increases in the distance by which it exceeds the source in status. A value function for the weighting distances of group members that is consistent with Assumption 3 is illustrated in Figure 1.

We now turn to the implications of the assumptions we have offered on the weighting of positive and negative evaluations. We will focus on how the weighting of status distances between the source and target of an evaluation affect patterns of information exchange in groups.

Group Status Distributions and Information Exchange

In this discussion, we will focus on the probability of initiating the information type of ideas in collectives that are composed of status-heterogeneous members. As we noted previously, this information type is perhaps the most important type exchanged in groups that are engaged in ill-structured decision making. It has been extensively argued that maximizing ideation is particularly critical in such contexts (e.g., Mintzberg, Raisinghani, and Theoret 1976; Reitman 1964). Although we focus on this key information type, our inferences can be expected to hold for other "risky" information types. In this section, we demonstrate that the likelihood of an actor initiating an idea in a decision-making group is maximized when the members of the group are equal in status.

First, we make explicit an underlying assumption in our elaboration of information exchange in decision-making groups, that group members attempt to avert the receipt of status-weighted negative evaluations.[5] This assertion is based on the arguments we have made that negative evaluations engender social costs for members (i.e., status loss), and that members seek to avoid such costs. We formalize this in our fourth assumption:

Assumption 4.   A group member is motivated to minimize the total status-weighted negative evaluations received in the exchange of information.

The convex form of the value function given in Figure 1 portrays the effects of status loss from negative evaluation as a function of the status distance of the target from the source of the evaluation. We see that this effect is consistent with a concave form for the dependence of the ith member's probability of initiating an idea on her status. As the judged distance between a source of information and one or more targets with higher status increases, the probability of idea being initiated by the source will decrease. We write a simple form of this relationship in a dyad as:

$$Pr(I_i) = k - V(\sigma_j - \sigma_i) \qquad (4)$$

where $Pr(I_i)$ = the probability of the ith member initiating an idea;

$V(\sigma_j - \sigma_i)$ = the ith member's judgment of the status distance between self and the jth member when these members are ordered $\sigma_j > \sigma_i$, and k is a constant.

Although the dependency of $Pr(Ii)$ on $V(\bullet)$ is linear in equation (4), its dependency on the status difference remains non-linear as in Figure 1. The first and second derivatives of equation (4) with respect to $(\sigma_j - \sigma_i)$ makes it clear that if V as a function of $(\sigma_j - \sigma_i)$ is convex, then $Pr(Ii)$ will be concave.[6] A natural concave form for the initiation of information in a group can be written as:

$Pr(L_i) = f(\sigma_i) = c_{-1} \sigma_i^{\beta 1}$, $\theta \in (0, 1)$ where $Pr(L_S)$ is the probability of an idea sent by the ith member.[7]

Then $Pr(L_\Sigma) = \sum\limits_{i=1}^{n} f(\sigma_i)$, where $Pr(L_\Sigma)$ is the probability of the exchange of an

idea in a group.

We also use a standard property of concave functions as it follows from Jensen's Inequality for Sums. The essential theorem is extensively used in information theory (e.g., Cover and Thomas 1991), and is stated and proven for convex functions in Karlin and Taylor (1975). The key property that follows from Jensen's Inequality can be stated as follows: Let ϕ be a concave function whose domain is some interval, M; if $x_1, ...x_n$ are n points in M, and $a_1, ... a_1$ are positive numbers such that $\sum \alpha_i = 1$, then:

$$\sum\limits_{i=j}^{n} \alpha_i \phi\left((x_i) \le \phi \sum\limits_{i=j}^{n} \alpha_i x_i \right) \tag{5}$$

For our application, we consider $Pr(L_i) = f(\sigma_i)$ a concave function representing the probability of an idea being sent. The domain of f is $\underline{M} = (0, 1)$, with $\underline{n}$ points defined as $\sigma_i, ..., \sigma_n$, the statuses of members.

If, for our case, we weight each member equally (i.e., $\alpha_1 = \dfrac{1}{n}$ for each $\underline{i}$, where $\underline{n}$ is the number of group members), we can show that the number of messages sent is maximized when all status are equal; namely when $\alpha_i = \dfrac{1}{n}$ for all i, that is $c_1 \Sigma$

$f(\sigma_1) \le c_1 \sum\limits_{i=1}^{n} f\left(\dfrac{1}{n}\right)$. This can be shown as follows:

$$Pr(I_i = \sum\limits_{i=1}^{n} f(\sigma_i) = n \sum\limits_{i=1}^{n} \dfrac{1}{n} f(\sigma_i) \tag{6}$$

$$Pr(I_i) = \sum_{i=1}^{n} f(\sigma_i) = n \sum_{i=1}^{n} \frac{1}{n} f(\sigma_i)$$

$$\leq nf\left(\sum_{i=1}^{n} \frac{\sigma_i}{n} \right) \text{ by Jensen's Inequality}$$

$$= nf\left(\frac{1}{n} \sum_{i=1}^{n} \sigma_i \right)$$

$$= \sum_{i=1}^{n} f\left(\frac{1}{n} \right) \text{ since } \sum_{i=1}^{n} \sigma_i = 1$$

Therefore, there is no distribution of σ_i such that the function for the probability of an idea initiation, $\sum f(\sigma_i)$, is greater than $\sum f\left(\frac{1}{n} \right)$. On the basis of our assumptions and these operations, we derive the following inference when information initiation by a group member is a concave function of her status:

Inference 1.   The probability of an idea being initiated in a group will be maximized when the members of the group are equal in status.

Member Status Distributions and the Quality of Solutions Generated by Problem-Solving Groups

We now address how the status distribution in a group affects the quality of group solutions to "ill-structured" problems. As we have previously noted, groups are commonly faced with such problems. Quality as it relates to such decisions has been difficult to define in both conceptual and empirical terms. However, as we have suggested, quality often depends on the number of ideas as well as the adequate filtering of ideas. Negative evaluations can be an important filter, and as such we conceptualize negative evaluations as making an important contribution to decision quality. However, we note that while ideas contribute to quality when they are maximized in number, negative evaluations are likely to contribute most when they are kept in a bounded interval. Too high a number of negative evaluations can rapidly increase the expected costs of initiating ideas, thereby inhibiting their exchange. Also, though, too low a number of negative evaluations can result in inadequate filtering of ideas. In fact, such inadequate filtering may lead to the phenomenon of "groupthink" described by Janis (1982).

Consequently, we conceptualize quality-maximized decisions as those in which group members (1) maximize the total number of ideas initiated, and (2) initiate negative evaluations in proportion to the number of ideas that other members offer. The former condition on the number of ideas follows from the finding that idea originality increases monotonically with the number of ideas initiated in a group (e.g., Christensen, Guilford, and Wilson 1957). The latter condition on negative evaluations provides for adequate filtering of ideas, while not excessively increasing the expected costs of initiating ideas or reducing the cohesiveness of the group. We may write the quality contribution (Q) of an individual member of an n-member group as:

$$Q_i = I_i - \alpha \sum_{j=1}^{n} (I_j - RN_{ij})^m, m > 1. \tag{7}$$

where I_i = the number of ideas initiated by the ith group member;
$\quad N_{ij}$ = the number of negative evaluations sent by the ith group member to the jth group member;
$\quad R$ = the "ideal" ratio of ideas to negative evaluations.

Such a form for quality contribution makes explicit the interdependence between members in group decision making. In previous work, we have demonstrated that a quadratic form for the second term of equation (7) is suitable for predicting idea uncommonness. This form predicts idea uncommonness as a measure of quality from $\frac{1}{R}$, the ratio of negative evaluations to ideas (Silver and Troyer 1994).

Consistent with these conditions, we write the quality-maximizing solution, Q^*, in terms of the total number of ideas and the ideal ratio of ideas to negative evaluations in a dyadic case as:

$$Q^* = \max(Q) = I_i + I_j - \alpha(I_j - RN_i)^2 - (I_i - RN_j)^2 \tag{8}$$

where I_k = the number of ideas initiated by the kth group member;
$\quad N_k$ = the number of negative evaluations initiated by the kth group member;
$\quad R$ = the "ideal" ratio of negative evaluations to ideas, and $k = i, j$.

We state our arguments on quality-maximizing decisions formally as our fifth assumption:

Assumption 5. The quality of ill-structured decisions is maximized when the number of ideas initiated by group members is maximized and negative evaluations are initiated by group members in proportion to the number of ideas that other members offer [as given in equation (8)].

In previous discussion, we noted that the probability of idea initiations and initiations of negative evaluations would be increasing with a group member's status. Since we also consider the total number of messages that a member initiates to be increasing with the member's status, we write the dependence of the number of ideas and negative evaluations a member offers as a monotonically increasing function of the member's status. That is, $I_i = \sigma_i^\beta$, and $Ni = \sigma_i^\gamma$, respectively, where β, γ, and $\in = (0,1)$. On this basis, we write the quality function in relation to status as:

$$Q(\sigma_k) = c_j\left(\sigma_i + \sigma_j^\beta - c_1\sigma_i^\beta - c_2R\sigma_j^\gamma\right)^2 - \alpha\left(c_1\sigma_j^\beta - c_2R\sigma_i^\gamma\right)^2 \qquad (9)$$

Our interest is in examining how status homogeneity affects solution quality, in accord with equation (9). Thus, we assess whether $\sigma_i = \sigma_j = 0.5$ is a global maximum for Q (i.e., that and $Q'(0.5) = 0$ and $Q''(0.5) < 0$). By the symmetry at $\sigma_i = \sigma_j = 0.5$, this point is a critical point of Q, when the function is considered in its dependency on σ_i as in (9). Hence, $Q'(0.5) = 0$. However, the sign of $Q''(0.5)$ is not readily evaluated by analytical methods, given the form of equation (9) and its dependency on β, γ, and R. Therefore, numerical methods are used to indicate the functional form of $Q(\sigma)$ implied by equation (9) and to test whether $\sigma = 0.5$ is a global maximum for Q. To accomplish this, we set the constants c_1 and α to 1, and examine equation (9) for a range of values that β, γ, and R can assume. Given the assumption on the concavity of the I and N functions, β and γ are bounded by 0 and 1. We investigate a range of parameter values in all but the extremes of parameter ranges (i.e., a case of β, γ, $\in$ (.20 to .85). We also use results of a previous study to bound the interval of $\frac{1}{R}$ to $0.10 \leq \frac{1}{R} \leq 0.25$.[8] We used a direct search procedure to examine the levels of σ_i at the maximum Q for gradations of 0.05 in the defined interval of β, γ, and R. For all points inside this interval, Q was found to be obtained at $\sigma_i = \sigma_j = 0.5$.

These results demonstrate the important consequences of the weighting heuristics that members use when judging the amount and type of information to initiate. On the basis of these operations and the simulation, we derive the second inference of our theory, which relates the quality of collectively-generated solutions for ill-structured decisions to the status distribution in the group:

Inference 2.   The quality of an ill-structured decision by a group will be maximized when the members of the group are equal in status.

Our theoretical framework is premised on key assumptions for which we have
noted indirect support. However, the form of these assumptions is eventually an
empirical question. The second and third assumptions are of particular interest
because these claims represent the adaptation of insights from Prospect Theory to
our arguments on social judgments that determine patterns and outcomes of information exchange in problem-solving groups. To date, we are unaware of any
research that directly tests such claims. Consequently, these assumptions represent
important candidates for empirical testing. We turn now to a brief summary of two
studies directed at assessing two of the assumptions used to derive our inferences,
as well as an examination of the first inference.

EMPIRICAL INVESTIGATION OF THE FRAMEWORK

To initially assess assumptions and one of the inferences comprising our theory,
we conducted two studies. The first, Study 1, employs a vignette strategy to investigate (1) the comparative valuing of negative and positive evaluations asserted in
Assumption 2, and (2) the differential weighting of negative evaluations from
higher and lower status sources represented in Assumption 3. In the second study,
Study 2, we test Inference 1, the claim that the probability of idea initiations in a
group will be greatest when members of the group are equal in status.

Study 1:   The Valuing of Social Gains and Losses

In this study, participants read a vignette that asked them to consider themselves
members of group involved in a decision-making task. The vignette instructed the
subjects to judge the status gains and losses from positive and negative evaluations
that might hypothetically be initiated by six other putative members of the group
portrayed in the vignette. Other group members represented in the vignette were
described in terms of their variation on the status attributes of year-in-school and
grade point average (GPA).

Respondents

Nineteen junior and senior undergraduates at Stanford University volunteered to
participate in the study. Participants were each paid $10, and completed the
vignette-based questionnaire independently in sessions with three to five other
participants that were administered by one of the authors.

Table 1. Mean Judgments of Status Losses and Gains from
Evaluations by Grouping Factors
(Standard Deviations in Parentheses)

Factor	Loss from Negative Evaluation	Gain from Positive Evaluation
Between Subjects Factors		
Gender:		
Female (n = 10)	55.38	44.15
	(12.33)	(14.73)
Male (n = 9)	57.59	46.46
	(11.42)	(14.08)
Class:		
Junior (n = 10)	58.42	46.60
	(11.00)	(14.88)
Senior (n = 9)	54.22	43.74
	(12.57)	(13.86)
Within Subjects Factor		
Source:		
1st Year Grad, 3.8 GPA	72.74	58.79
	(5.04)	(11.61)
Junior, 3.8 GPA	61.26	49.32
	(7.39)	(12.78)
1st Year Grad., 2.4 GPA	55.53	48.21
	(8.30)	(11.51)
Freshman, 3.8 GPA	50.32	38.05
	(10.78)	(13.71)
Junior 2.4 GPA	53.74	45.42
	(8.82)	(11.94)
Freshman, 2.4 GPA	45.00	31.68
	(8.45)	(9.84)
Grand Mean	56.43	45.25
	(11.96)	(14.48)

Procedures and Instrument

Respondents were told that the study they were participating in was one in which they would be asked to make judgments about working with hypothetical others described in terms of their year-in-school and GPA. They were advised that they would begin by reading a brief summary of the other members of this hypothetical group as well as a short description of the hypothetical group's task. The respondents were then given the instrument, which consisted of a vignette and a set of social judgment scales. In the vignette, six members of a group were described in terms of their year-in-school and GPA. Three levels of year-in-school (freshman, junior, first-year graduate student) were crossed with two levels of

GPA (2.4 or 3.8 on a 4.0 scale) to define the six members of the group. This manipulation was intended to produce a status hierarchy in the hypothetical group. The
respondents were instructed to consider themselves to be members of this group.

The vignette next described the problem with which the group was responsible
for developing a solution. The problem indicated that the group was responsible
for developing a recommendation for the use of a grant that the university had
received to design a new computing facility. The vignette also noted that in the
course of the task, participants should expect that the ideas of group members
would be evaluated. More specifically, it was noted that a positive evaluation
would increase a person's status in the group, while a negative evaluation would
lower a person's status in the group.

Following the vignette were two sets of social judgment scales. When all
respondents in a session had finished reading the vignette, they were instructed
to read and complete the first set of scales. This set elicited respondents' rat-
ings of the status costs and gains of receiving a negative or positive evaluation,
respectively from each member of the group. For each scale, the respondents
were instructed to make a vertical stroke on a horizontal line to indicate the
cost or benefit of receiving a negative evaluation or positive evaluation from a
particular group member (identified in terms of year-in-school and GPA). The
scales were anchored at the minimum with the label "Not at All Costly" or
"Not at all Beneficial," and at the maximum with the label "Highly Costly" or
"Highly Beneficial." The horizontal line was 80 millimeters in length. Consequently, the costs and benefits were operationalized in terms of the measured
distance from the low end of the line to the point at which the respondent made
the vertical mark.

When all respondents had completed the first set of scales, they were
instructed to read and complete the second set. The second set of social judgments included instructions directing the respondent to rate of each of the six
group members on the dimension of prestige. In addition, respondents rated
themselves with respect to prestige. Prestige was defined within the instrument
as, "One's judgment of the relative social standing of another; i.e., how an individual is ranked in relation to the other people that she or he is compared
with." The scale was anchored at the minimum with the label "Very Low Prestige," and at the maximum with the label "Very High Prestige." As in the first
set of scales, respondents were asked to indicate their judgment of each group
member's (and their own) prestige by placing a vertical mark on a horizontal
line. The line for these scales was 130 millimeters in length. Thus prestige was
operationalized in terms of the measured distance from the low end of the line
to the point at which the respondent made the vertical mark. After all respondents had completed the second set of scales, the study administrator debriefed
the study participants.

Study 1 Results

Judgments of the Magnitude of Gains and Losses from Positive and Negative Evaluations

We analyzed the respondents' judgments of the magnitude of costs and benefits from negative and positive evaluations, respectively, in 2 (gender of the judge) by 2 (year-in-school of the judge: junior vs. senior) by 2 (type of evaluation: positive vs. negative) by six (position of the evaluating group member in the vignette) MANOVAs with repeated measures on type of evaluation and positions of group members. We also included GPA of the respondent as a covariate in the analysis. Interactions higher than first-order were pooled in the error term, since we did not predict such effects. Means for these analyses are provided in Table 1.

Main effects of gender and year-in-school of respondent were not significant (gender: $F(1, 16) < 1.0$; year-in-school: $F(1, 16) < 1.0$). The GPA covariate was also not significant. However, main effects of both type of evaluation the position of the hypothetical source of evaluation (as determined by year-in-school and GPA) were highly significant (type of evaluation: $F(1, 169) = 48.4, p < .001$; position of evaluator: $F(5, 169) = 16.5, p < .001$). Respondents rated the magnitude of the cost of a negative evaluation as significantly greater than the magnitude of the gain from a positive evaluation. None of the first-order interactions were significant ($p > .10$). These results are consistent with Assumption 2.

Judgments of the Cost of a Negative Evaluation as a Function of the Status of the Evaluator

We again note that the respondents provided judgments of prestige of each hypothetical group member, as well as for themselves. For each respondent and each assessment of prestige, we calculated the difference between the respondent's rating of herself/himself and the rating of the particular group member. This provides an operationalization of the respondent's perceived status distance from each hypothetical group member. We then analyzed each subject's judgment of the expected cost of a negative evaluation from each hypothetical group member as a function of the judged prestige of the member. The value function in Figure 1 predicts that this function should be convex. This requires that the best fit of the function have a positive and significant quadratic component. A nonlinear least squares procedure yielded a coefficient for the quadratic component of $\beta = .106$, s.e. $= .041$ ($t(114) = 2.58$, one-tailed $p < .01$). The relation between perceived status distance and expected cost of a negative evaluation is illustrated in Figure 2. These results provide support for Assumption 3 of our framework, which asserts that group members overweight the expected status loss from a negative evaluation by members higher in status than themselves, and underweight the losses from members lower in status than themselves.

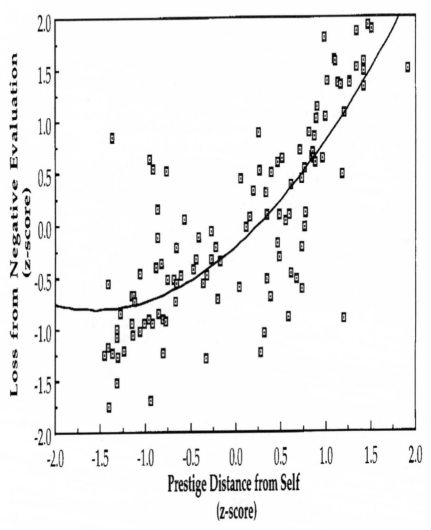

Figure 2. Loss from Negative Evaluation by Prestige and
Status Distance from Self

Study 2:   Status Distribution and Idea Generation in Interactive Groups

Our objective in the second study was to test Inference 1, which proposes that
the probability of idea initiations is greatest when group members are equal in
status.

Subjects

Ninety-six freshmen and sophomore undergraduates at the University of California, Berkeley received course credit for participating in this study. Twelve male and twelve female groups of four persons were formed from these participants. We constructed same-sex groups since an actor's sex has been found to have significant effects on participation in mixed-sex groups (e.g., Lockheed 1985; Strodtbeck and Mann 1956) Aside from this constraint, subjects were randomly assigned to groups, and groups were randomly assigned to one of two experimental conditions.

Task

An adaptation of the "Winter Survival Exercise" (e.g., Johnson and Johnson 1987 was used as the idea generation task. This exercise requires that the group evaluates the usefulness of salvaged items for survival in a hostile environment. In our adaptation of the task, the group is asked to generate as many survival-related uses as possible for each of six salvaged survival items (six feet of rope, a newspaper, a pistol, a can of shortening, a chocolate bar, and a bottle of whiskey).

Dependent Variables: Number and Proportion of Messages

The number of ideas exchanged and the probability of an idea initiation in the group represent the dependent variables in this study. Idea number was the sum of survival ideas group members generated for the six salvaged items. The unconditional probability of an idea initiation was operationalized as the ratio of the number of idea initiations to the total of all types of initiations generated in the group.

Independent Variable: Group Status Distribution

To manipulate the group status distribution, each group member independently completed a "Desert Survival Test" (e.g., Johnson and Johnson, 1987) prior to the group's work on the "Winter Survival Exercise." After completing the test, members were given fictitious feedback on their own scores as well as the distribution of other scores in the group (though not the scores of specific individuals). Each member of the group was randomly assigned a score. In the status-differentiated condition (SD), the distribution of test scores members received was 2, 4, 5, and 8, where 10 was the maximum possible score. In the status undifferentiated condition (SU), the score distribution members received was 4, 4, 5, 5. Based on Inference 1, we hypothesized that groups in the SU condition would generate more and higher proportions of ideas than groups in the SD condition.

Study 2 Results

As predicted, groups in the SU condition generated significantly more ideas than groups in the SD condition (Means: SU = 1.204, SD = 87.7; $F(1,22) = 5.10$, $p < .05$). Proportions of ideas initiated in SU groups were also higher than in SD groups, however, these differences were only marginally significant (Means: SU = .514, SD = .466; $F(1,22) = 4.02$, $p < .07$). Neither the effect of sex-type of the group (i.e., whether it was composed of male or female members) nor the interaction of sex-type and condition generated significant differences with respect to number or proportion of ideas initiated in the groups. These results indicate support for Inference 1.0.

DISCUSSION

Our theoretical account uses a well-recognized and general insight with respect to a range of social phenomena: that subjective judgments predominate over objective realities in determining social behavior. Moreover, subjective judgments often depart significantly from objective realities. Although the direction and magnitude of such bias may vary with the context, the existence of departures from objective information has been consistently demonstrated and related to cognition and behavior. The theory and research we present is unique in its application of the general phenomena of subjective bias to judgments of social gains and losses. Furthermore, we demonstrate how those judgments affect member participation in the exchange of information that characterizes decision-making groups.

Information exchange is fundamental to group decision making. Consequently, understanding how groups reach decisions requires understanding the factors that condition information exchange. We have begun to address this issue by formally developing arguments on subjective bias in judgments of social gains and losses that occur in the course of information exchange. These arguments are then linked to the social meaning and implications of information initiation and reciprocation in groups. Most importantly, we note that (1) different types of information carry different risks of generating a social loss (through likelihood of eliciting a negative evaluation in return), (2) negative evaluations are viewed as more costly to one's social status than positive evaluations are beneficial to social status, (3) evaluations from higher-status actors are viewed as having greater effects on one's own status than evaluations from lower-status actors, (4) actors seek to minimize the receipt of status-weighted negative evaluations, and (5) solution quality in ill-structured problem solving is maximized when the number of ideas initiated in the group is maximized and when negative evaluations are initiated in proportion to the number of ideas initiated in the group. Through formal representation of these assertions, we also derive inferences on the effects of status heterogeneity on (1) the information exchange behavior of actors in a group, and (2) the quality of decisions that are likely to be generated through information exchange in groups. We expect these arguments to hold in groups whose members are collectively engaged in solving ill-structured decisions.

The preliminary empirical studies we presented support our theoretical framework. The first study indicated that actors do view negative evaluations as more costly than positive evaluations are beneficial. Also, this study supported our assumption that group members tend to view the evaluations from a higher-status source has having greater impact on their own status than those from a lower-status source. Of particular interest, though is how these processes affect the content of information exchanged in groups engaged in ill-structured decision making. As we have elaborated, in these contexts, ideas represent a particularly important type of information. A paradox arises, though, within the context of our framework because this type of information that has a high likelihood of eliciting a negative evaluation. From our formal model, we show that the risk is minimized in status-homogeneous groups, and consequently we would expect higher rates of idea initiation in such groups. The second empirical study we presented supported this inference.

The fact that status processes bias group interaction is not a new insight. Researchers studying status and social influence within the tradition of Status Characteristics Theory have directed attention to biases arising from status processes (e.g., Berger et al. 1977). In particular, these researchers have focused on the opportunities that higher status group members take and are given in social interaction. Furthermore, this line of theory and research has demonstrated that actors tend to view the contributions of higher status group members more favorably than those of lower status members. In addition, the domination of "action opportunities" by higher status group members is commonly seen as both expected and legitimate by other group members (Ridgeway and Berger 1988). Findings from this program of research have advanced our understanding of status and social influence in groups. We note that our assumption on the differential *importance* of evaluations from higher vs. lower status actors is consistent with the notions of favoritism and legitimacy accorded to higher status actors within Status Characteristics Theory.

Of paramount importance in our framework is how status *distributions* affect the formal objectives of group through the impact of these distributions on the information exchange occurring in the group. We emphasize the internal judgment processes of group members in the context of a status-heterogeneous group. We propose that decisions regarding information exchange are motivated in part by judgments on the expected status gains and losses. One way to consider our assertions is to examine how they inform the regulatory processes through which action opportunities are taken by a group member according to the member's structural position in the group. Our conceptualization suggests that, all else equal, the difference between the expected costs of "risky" information types (such as ideas, opinions, and negative evaluations) and the expected costs of less risky information types (such as positive evaluations, facts, and silence) is likely to increase with the distance of the group member from the high status group member. As a consequence of this, domination by higher status group members is likely to be concentrated in the types of information initiations, ideas, that contribute most to quality in group decisions. At the same time, lower-status group members are likely to oversend information types that may undermine decision quality. In particular, lower-status group members are likely to oversend positive evaluations and facts, as well as engage in nonresponses (i.e., silence). As evidenced in Janis' (1982) groupthink studies, this type of interaction pattern can lead to premature acquiescence to a dominant decision alternative that is actually detrimental to the group's objective. We can appreciate the threats to quality in decision-making groups that these processes engender even more when we recognize that status differences are often generated on the basis of social characteristics that are at best minimally related to actual competence (e.g., Cohen and Roper 1972; Pugh and Wahrman 1983).

As this discussion suggests, we believe that our framework on social risk also highlights policy considerations for decision-making groups. Current approaches to decision making recognize the benefits of diversity in dealing with uncertain and turbulent environments (Gruenfeld, Mannix, Williams, and Neale 1996; Jackson, Brett, Sessa, Cooper, Julin, and Peyronnin 1991; Pearce and Ravlin 1987; Watson, Kumar, and Michaelsen 1993). This recognition most often comes with little or no appreciation of the internal consequences of unmanaged diversity. Diversity commonly increases distance in status hierarchies, with attendant effects on internal status risk for medium and lower status members. Driskell and Salas (1991) note that environments that produce high uncertainty and "threat" to the collective can also rigidify internal status hierarchies and increase the effects of status on group performance. Our theoretical framework emphasizes the detrimental impact that diversity can have on group outcomes through the microlevel processes it affects. However, we emphasize that we are not suggesting that external risk is overemphasized or that it should be managed less diligently. Rather, we are suggesting that a group's internal processes in high-risk environments and the consequences of these processes may require more management than is commonly recognized.

We note that there are a number of procedures that may facilitate management the effects of bias in information exchange that arise from status distributions. For instance, Connolly, Jessup, and Valacich (1990) have extensively studied and implemented procedures that introduce anonymity in decision-making groups. Our arguments on information exchange may contribute to refinement of such procedures. In particular, it may be optimal to invoke anonymity in particular phases of decision making when risky information types (like ideas) are likely to make important contributions. These points in decision making might be derived, in turn, from rules differentiating the phases of a decision-making process (e.g., Stodolsky 1981). Another procedure that has been proposed to manage decision-making groups include proscribing or limiting evaluation, as in nominal group methods (e.g., Bartunek and Murnighan 1984). We note, however, that procedures that directly proscribe negative evaluations may lead to inadequate filtering of information that is exchanged in the group. Also, group members may develop alternatives to verbal communication in order to convey evaluations. These alternatives are often tacit and have the counter-productive effect of introducing greater uncertainty into the group interaction.

We believe that altering the social meaning of evaluation by increasing trust in a group represents a potentially fruitful alternative to proscribing evaluation. When trust is in place, individuals are likely to maintain higher commitments to a group in the presence of risk or uncertainty (e.g., Kollock 1994; Lawler and Yoon 1996). Conditions that develop and maintain trust are often generally described in guidelines for managing interactive groups. Fine and Holyfield (1996) note that the importance of these conditions merits their increased integration into our understanding of group processes. Toward these ends, we believe that a systematic explication of the conceptual role of trust-enhancing would benefit our theoretical framework on information exchange in interactive groups.

Another manner in which risks in information exchange may be managed is related to research on framing within "heuristics and biases" arguments (e.g., Sullivan and Kida 1995; Tversky and Kahneman 1992). This line of research suggests that if group members change the reference points that they use in the exchange of negative evaluations, then the expected costs of this information type may be reduced. For example, compared to a direct negative evaluation, an evaluation that is framed by its source as a distinction between amounts of positive evaluation (or positive and no evaluation) rather than positive and negative evaluation may have less of an effect on member perceptions of social costs of initiating risky information. The framing of evaluation in terms of degrees of positive evaluations and nonresponses (i.e., no evaluations) may lead actors to assess the evaluation (and hence information initiations it may elicit) in terms of gains alone rather than gains and losses. In other words, the framing of an evaluation may change the salience of gains as opposed to costs. This explication also points to the importance of nonresponses in information exchange. Silence may replace an initiation of information because of the information's expected risk (and hence, potentially high cost). Alternatively, silence may itself reflect critical evaluation by group members. As such, these arguments suggest that conceptual and empirical examinations of silence may contribute to our understanding of group information exchange processes.

Clearly, there are a number of directions to extend the framework. Currently, our theoretical framework is oriented toward cross-sectional examinations of information exchange in groups. Time-varying elaborations of information exchange may be of particular importance, though, since analyses of interactive groups have traditionally emphasized change processes (McGrath 1984). Interactive process and status effects are more difficult to represent in dynamic forms. Nonetheless, a more complete account of social processes in decision-making groups requires such elaboration.

We also envision our framework moving toward greater incorporation of how social environments affect group decision-making processes. Environments may introduce indirect and often unanticipated risks to an actors social standing. This is because environments interact with group structure to impose enduring effects on group behavior (Orasanu and Salas 1993). In particular, environments may introduce additional dependencies, and as such may disturb the status and information exchange processes that would otherwise prevail in a "closed" social system (e.g., Ancona 1993; Knottnerus 1997; Troyer 1995). While environments are, of course, complex and difficult to represent in the closed form of our current framework, their representation appears essential to a comprehensive explanation of social processes.

Finally, we propose that more definitive assessments of status judgments are needed. Since the metric of such judgments is often at issue (e.g., Baker 1977; Wegener 1982), it may be that status distributions that follow continuous and interval scaled objective criteria (such as GPA or years of tenure in a position) can be examined with psychophysical methods in laboratory studies. We again emphasize that judgments of social gains and losses in interpersonal exchange are important to a wide range of social processes. As such, systematic attempts to definitively state the rules of these judgments and demonstrate their effects represents a research agenda with far-reaching effects for social science.

In conclusion, we have conceptualized how social risk can bias member participation in group decision making, and how this, in turn, can influence the quality of the group's decision. In developing this conceptualization, we have come to appreciate the complexity of collective decision making. There are stakes at both the group and individual levels involving both instrumental and social considerations. A central goal of our research involves disentangling the sources of risk at these different levels, ascertaining their relations, and examining the processes through which they affect group outcomes. In this endeavor, we have integrated research and theory from social, behavioral, and cognitive conceptualizations of decision making. Our theory and research suggest that social judgments by actors in decision-making groups are subject to the same types of cognitive biases that characterize monetary and social dilemmas. Moreover, these cognitively biased judgments are the basis for decisions on participation in such groups. These results are encouraging to us, suggesting that the explicit and systematic incorporation of insights from a variety of research traditions represents a promising strategy for the study of group processes.

NOTES

1. Silver, Cohen, and Crutchfield (1994) provide direct evidence on this effect by coding both the ideas that members exchange and those that they actually record. Even when groups are explicitly

instructed to record *all* ideas, status-differentiated groups evidenced significantly greater "censoring" of ideas than status-equal groups, and the more uncommon (i.e., unusual) ideas were the ones most likely to be censored.

2.   "Oversend" here means to send more than their expertise would ordinarily be expected to merit.

3.   Differences in the total number of messages individuals send as a function of their statuses are not as easily defined as sometimes commonly assumed. As we will note, nonresponses or "blanks" often have a nonzero probability of being negatively evaluated (silences can be costly). If this is true, filling time with positive evaluations, facts, and questions, can be an optimal strategy for minimizing status loss. In such a case, lower-status members could actually send more messages in certain information categories than higher-status members, although the proportion of information types that comprise the total messages would be very different. Here, as elsewhere, this suggestion is likely to be context dependent and needs to be examined empirically. Most data we have examined show that more total messages are sent by higher-status actors, but differences are less often statistically significant than the differences in the number of "riskier" message types sent by higher- and lower-status actors.

4.   For example, a linear weighting would lead to a claim that if a group moves from a status distribution which is indexed as 4, 4, 5, 6, 6 to one which is indexed as 2, 2, 5, 8, 8, then the perceived cost of initiating an idea or negative evaluation to the member with the status score of 5 would stay the same, since the distribution remains symmetric about this mean. Such a claim is counterintuitive and not supported in our own empirical results.

5.   This is clearly not the only motive actors have for participation in social groups. See Silver (1995) for a treatment that supports the inferences we offer when a motive to contribute to the group's objective is also recognized.

6.   Another possibility with respect to equation (4) is that the relationship of $Pr(I_i)$ to the V function itself is nonlinear, as in:

$$Pr(I_i) = k - V^m, \text{ where } m \text{ is a parameter.}$$

$$\text{Then, } \partial \frac{Pr(I_i)}{\partial \sigma_i} = -m V^{m-1} \frac{\partial V}{\partial \sigma_i} \text{ and}$$

$$\frac{\partial^2 Pr(I_i)}{\partial \sigma_i^2} = -m \ (m-1) \left(V^{m-2} \left(\frac{\partial V}{\partial \sigma_i} \right)^2 - m V^{m-1} \left(\frac{\partial^2 V}{\partial \sigma_i^2} \right) < 0 \right)$$

$$\text{if } m \ \geq 1, \text{ since Figure 1 implies } \frac{\partial^2 V}{\partial \sigma_1^2} > 0.$$

So $Pr(I_i)$ will be a concave function of $(\sigma_j - (\sigma_i))$, as in equation (4), if $m > 1$.

The case $\underline{m} < 1$ is indeterminate. This case implies that the change in the probability of an idea imitiation for a unit change in the status distance between the source of the idea and source of a potential evaluation is greater when the status differences are small than than when they are large. This is, at the least, counter-intuitive.

7.   Concavity in production functions for a diversity of social and physical outputs is also a common assumption (see, for example, Intriligator 1984). The importance of assumptions on concavity in rates of infomration exchange has also been demonstrated in information theory (e.g., Cover and Thomas 1991) where emphasis is on "noise" is signals and the amount of factual information that can be extracted from a message.

8.   In this study (Silver and Troyer 1994), the relationship between (1) idea uncommonness as a measure of idea quality and (2) the ratio of negative evaluations to ideas was empirically examined in 19 problem-solving groups. Nine of the ten groups with the highest mean uncommonness scores were in the interval $0.10 \leq \frac{1}{R} \leq 0.25$. Mean uncommonness for this group was .18, while the mean for the groups outside this interval was .04. The mean uncommonness for the entire sample was .11.

REFERENCES

Ancona, D.G. 1993. "The Classics and the Contemporary: A New Blend of Small Group Theory." Pp. 225-293 in *Social Psychology in Organizations: Advances in Theory and Research*, edited by J. Keith Murnighan. Englewood Cliffs, NJ: Prentice-Hall.

Baker, P.M. 1977. "On the Use of Psychophysical Methods in the Study of Social Status: Replication and Some Theoretical Problems." *Social Forces*. 55: 898-920.

Bartunek, J.M., and J.K. Murnighan. 1984. "The Nominal Group Technique: Expanding the Basic Procedure and Underlying Assumptions." *Group and Organization Studies*. 9: 417-32.

Berger, J., M.H. Fisek, R.Z. Norman, and M. Zelditch Jr. 1977. *Status Characteristics and Social Interaction*. New York: Elsevier.

Boster, J.S., J.C. Johnson, and S.C. Weller. 1987. "Social Position and Shared Knowledge: Actors' Perceptions of Status, Role, and Social Structure." *Social Networks*. 9: 375-387.

Christensen, P.R., J.P. Guilford, and R.C. Wilson. 1957. "Relations of Creative Response to Working Time and Instructions." *Journal of Experimental Psychology*. 53: 82-88.

Cohen, B.P., and S.D. Silver. 1989. "Group Structure and Information Exchange: Introduction to a Theory." Pp. 160-181 in *Sociological Theories in Progress: New Formulations*, edited by J. Berger, M. Zelditch Jr., and B. Anderson. Newbury Park, CA: Sage.

Cohen, E.G., and S.S. Roper. 1972. "Modification of Interracial Interaction Disability: An Application of Status Characteristics Theory," *American Sociological Review*. 37: 643-757.

Connolly, T.L., L. Jessup, and J.S. Valacich. 1990. "Effects of Anonymity and Evaluative Tone on Idea Generation in Computer-Mediated Groups." *Management Science*. 36: 689-703.

Cover, T.M., and J.A. Thomas. 1991. *Elements of Information Theory*. New York: Wiley.

Driskell, J.E. 1982. "Personal Characteristics and Performance Expectations." *Social Psychology Quarterly*. 45: 229-237.

Driskell, J.E., and E. Salas. 1991. "Group Decision Making Under Stress." *Journal of Applied Psychology*. 76: 473-478.

Emerson, R.M. 1988. "Social Exchange Theory." In *Social Psychology: Sociological Perspectives*, edited by M. Rosenberg and R.H. Turner. New York: Basic Books.

Fine, Gary A., and L. Holyfield. 1996. "Secrecy, Trust, and Dangerous Leisure: Generating Group Cohesion in Voluntary Organizations." *Social Psychology Quarterly*. 59: 22-38.

Foschi, M., G.K. Warriner, and S.D. Hart. 1985. "Standards, Expectations, and Interpersonal Influence." *Social Psychology Quarterly* 57: 326-339.

Foschi, M., L. Lai, and K. Sigerson. 1994. "Gender and Double Standards in the Assessment of Job Applicants." *Social Psychology Quarterly* 57: 326-339.

Gigerenzer, G. 1996. "On Narrow Norms and Vague Heuristics: A Reply to Kahneman and Tversky." *Psychological Review*. 103: 592-596.

Gruenfeld, D.H., E.A. Mannix, K.Y. Williams, and M.A. Neale. 1996. "Group Composition and Decision Making: How Member Familiarity and Information Distribution Affect Process and Performance." *Organizational Behavior and Human Decision Processes*. 67: 1-15.

Highhouse, S., and M.A. Johnson. 1996. "Gain/Loss Asymmetry and Riskless Choice: Loss Aversion in Choices Among Job Finalists." *Organizational Behavior and Human Decision Processes* 68: 225-233.

Hodge, R.W., D.J. Treiman, and P.H. Rossi. 1966. "A Comparative Study of Occupational Prestige." Pp. 309-334 in *Class, Status, and Power*, edited by R. Bendix and S.M. Lipset. New York: Free Press.

Hyman, H.H. 1942. "The Psychology of Status." *Archives of Psychology*: 269.

Inkeles, A., and P.H. Rossi. 1956. "National Comparisons of Occupational Prestige." *American Journal of Sociology*. 61: 329-339.

Intriligator, M.D. 1978. *Econometric Models, Techniques, and Applications*. Englewood Cliffs, NJ: Prentice-Hall.

Jackson, S.E., J.F. Brett, V.I. Sessa, D.M. Cooper, J.A. Julin, and K. Peyronnin. 1991. "Some Differences Make a Difference: Individual Dissimilarity and Group Heterogeneity as Correlates of Recruitment, Promotions and Turnover." *Journal of Applied Psychology* 76: 675-689.

Janis, I. 1982. *Groupthink*, 2nd edition. Boston: Houghton-Mifflin.

Johnson, D.W., and F.P. Johnson. 1987. *Joining Together: Group Theory and Group Skills*, 2nd edition. Englewood Cliffs, NJ: Prentice-Hall.

Kahneman, D., and A. Tversky. 1979. "Prospect Theory: An Analysis of Decision under Risk." *Econometrica*. 47: 263-291.

Kahneman, D., P. Slovic, and A. Tversky. 1982. *Judgment under Uncertainty: Heuristics and Biases*. Cambridge, UK: Cambridge University Press.

Karlin, S., and H. Taylor. 1975. *A First Course in Stochastic Process*, 2nd edition. New York: Academic Press.

Knottnerus, J.D. 1997. "The Theory of Structural Ritualization." In *Advances in Group Processes*, edited by B. Markovsky, M. Lovaglia, and L. Troyer . Vol. 14. Stamford, CT: JAI Press.

Kollock, P. 1994. "The Emergence of Exchange Structures: An Experimental Study of Uncertainty, Commitment, and Trust." *American Journal of Sociology*. 100: 315-45.

Lawler, E.J., and J. Yoon. 1996. "Commitment in Exchange Relations," *American Sociological Review*. 61: 89-108.

Lockheed, M.E. 1985. "Sex and Social Influence: A Meta-Analysis Guided by Theory." Pp. 406-429 in *Status, Rewards, and Influence: How Expectations Organize Behavior*, edited by J. Berger and M. Zelditch Jr. San Francisco: Jossey-Bass.

McGrath, J.E. 1984. *Groups: Interaction and Performance*. Englewood Cliffs, NJ: Prentice-Hall.

Mintzberg, H., D. Raisinghani, and A. Theoret. 1976. "The Structure of Unstructured Decisions," *Administrative Science Quarterly*. 21: 246-275.

Molm, L.D., and K.S. Cook. 1995. "Social Exchange and Exchange Networks." Pp. 209-235 in *Sociological Perspectives on Social Psychology*, edited by K.S. Cook, G.A. Fine, and J.S. House. Boston: Allyn and Bacon.

Orasanu, J., and E. Salas. 1993. "Team Decision Making in Complex Environments." Pp. 327-345 in *Decision Making in Action: Models and Methods*, edited by G.A. Klein, J. Orasanu, R. Calderwood, and C.E. Zsambok. Norwood, NJ: Ablex Publishing.

Pearce, J.A., and E.C. Ravlin. 1987. "The Design and Activation of Self-Regulating Work Groups," *Human Relations*. 40: 751-782.

Pugh, M.P., and R. Wahrman. 1983. "Neutralizing Sexism in Mixed-Sex Groups: Do Women Have to Be Better than Men?" *American Journal of Sociology*. 88: 746-762.

Reitman, W.R. 1964. "Heuristic Decision Procedures, Open Constraints, and the Structure of Ill-Defined Problems." In *Human Judgments and Optimality*, edited by M.W. Shelly and G.L. Bryan. New York: Wiley.

Ridgeway, C.L., and J. Berger. 1988. "The Legitimation of Power and Prestige Orders in Task Groups." Pp. 207-231 in *Status Generalization: New Theory and Research*, edited by M. Webster Jr., and M. Foschi. Stanford, CA: Stanford University Press.

Sanna, L.J., and R. L. Shotland. 1990. "Valence of Anticipated Evaluation and Social Facilitation," *Journal of Experimental Social Psychology*. 26: 82-92.

Silver, S.D. 1995. "A Dual Motive Heuristic for Information Exchange in Interactive Groups: Managing Risk and Commitment." *Decision Support Systems.* 15: 83-97.

Silver, S.D., and L. Troyer. 1994. "Managing Information Exchange to Increase the Quality of Group Decisions: Conceptual Foundations for an Event-Sensitive GDSS." In *Proceedings of the Twenty-Third Annual Meeting of the Western Decision Sciences Institute,* edited by A.S. Khade and R.B. Brown .

Silver, S.D., B.P. Cohen, and J.H. Crutchfield. 1994. "Status Differentiation and Information Exchange in Face-to-Face and Computer-Mediated Idea Generation." *Social Psychology Quarterly.* 57: 108-123.

Silver, S.D., B.P. Cohen, and J. Rainwater. 1988. "Group Structure and Information Exchange in Innovative Problem Solving." Pp. 169-194 in *Advances in Group Processes,* edited by E.J. Lawler and B. Markovsky, Vol. 5. Stamford, CT: JAI Press.

Stodolsky, D. 1981. "Automatic Mediation in Group Problem Solving." *Behavior Research Methods and Instrumentation.* 13: 235-242.

Strodtbeck, F.L., and R.D. Mann. 1956. "Sex Role Differentiation in Jury Deliberations." *Sociometry.* 19: 3-11.

Sullivan, K., and T. Kida. 1995. "The Effect of Multiple Reference Points and Prior Gains and Losses on Mangers' Risky Decision Making." *Organizational Behavior and Human Decision Processes.* 64: 76-83.

Troyer, L. 1995. "Team Embeddedness: The Relations between Team Social Structures, Organization Social Structures, and Team Performance." Unpublished Ph.D. dissertation, Stanford University, Stanford, California.

Tversky, A., and D. Kahneman. 1991. "Loss Aversion in Riskless Choice: A Reference-Dependent Model." *Quarterly Journal of Economics.* 106: 1039-1061.

Tversky, A., and D. Kahneman. 1992. "Advances in Prospect Theory: Cumulative Representation of Uncertainty." *Journal of Risk and Uncertainty.* 5: 297-323.

Watson, W.E., K. Kumar, and L.K. Michaelsen. 1993. "Cultural Diversity's Impact on Interaction Process and Performance: Comparing Homogeneous and Diverse Task Groups." *Academy of Management Journal.* 36: 590-602.

Wegener, B. 1987. "The Illusion of Distributive Justice." *European Sociological Review.* 3: 1-13.

———. (Ed.). 1982. *Social Attitudes and Psychophysical Measurement.* Hillsdale, NJ: Erlbaum.

AN EXPERIMENTAL INVESTIGATION OF MOTIVES AND INFORMATION IN THE PRISONER'S DILEMMA GAME

Michael J.G. Cain

ABSTRACT

A large and growing body of experimental evidence indicates people not only cooperate in repeated prisoner's dilemma games but also in single-play prisoner's dilemma games. Game theory can explain some of these experimental findings by assuming players have strong social motives or strong moral preferences that transform the nature of a strategic interaction and make cooperative choices rational. However, rational cooperation requires that players know the motivations of their opponents under conditions of complete information. This paper explains and tests for rational cooperation in the prisoner's dilemma game without this assumption. Instead rational cooperation is interpreted as a game of incomplete information where players choose strategies based on their motivations and expectations about the cooperative intentions of their opponents. The experimental results reported in this paper provide evidence consistent with this model and suggest that most cooperative behaviors are the result of weak social or weak moral influences on preferences, conditioned by beliefs about an opponent's cooperative attitudes.

Advances in Group Processes, Volume 15, pages 133-160.

The problem of cooperation in the prisoner's dilemma game has become one of the most studied problems in social sciences during the latter half of the twentieth century. Scholarly attention to this problem is well deserved because the game presents us with a genuine dilemma of individual versus social rationality and forces us to consider the logical and empirical basis of cooperation in both small-and large-group interactions. This paper focuses exclusively on the possibility of rational cooperation in small groups. The first part of this paper shows how rational cooperation can emerge among players in single-play prisoner's dilemma games when the standard assumption of self-interested rationality is modified to include other nonselfish incentives. The second part of this paper shows how information combines with nonselfish decision making to induce rational cooperation. An experimental test of this model shows that most people choose defection as game theory predicts. However, the results also show that some people rationally cooperate because of social or moral influences. These influences on preferences normally manifest themselves in behavior only when others can be expected to reciprocate. Therefore, social or moral influences should not be understood as categorical influences on behavior, but conditional influences which are state dependent.

THE PRISONER'S DILEMMA GAME AND THE PROBLEM OF COOPERATION

The attraction of the prisoner's dilemma game derives from the simplicity of the dilemma. In this game two players are assumed to have similar orderings of payoffs defined over four possible outcomes (See Figure 1). (The ordering $T > R > P > S$ refers to standard labels for payoffs which mean temptation T, reward R, punishment P, and sucker S respectively.) Each player can choose to cooperate or defect, but if both players cooperate, both are better off than if they defected. However, the cooperative choice of each player is dominated by each player's defect choice, meaning that defect choices yield higher individual payoffs, regardless of the strategy used by an opponent. Since defection is a dominant strategy for each player, the Nash equilibrium prediction in a single-play prisoner's dilemma game is for both players to defect. This prediction presents the following problem or dilemma: if both players choose their individually best strategy of defection, both players are worse off than if they had chosen their dominated strategy of cooperation. Rationality leaves everyone worse off, whereas the irrational strategy of mutual cooperation results in a situation where everyone is better off. Cooperation in the prisoners' dilemma game therefore appears difficult to explain using traditional game theoretic analysis.

Player   Column

		Cooperate	Defect
Player Row	Cooperate	R, R	S, T
	Defect	T, S	P, P

Player Preference Orders: $T > R > P > S$ and $2R > T + S$

Figure 1.   The Prisoner's Dilemma Game

The Rationality of Cooperation

The prisoner's dilemma is an interesting model for investigating voluntary cooperation among members of a group because it forces us to consider how cooperative behaviors can be explained without resorting to the claim that cooperators are irrational. We know cooperation often occurs in society and most of us believe it is reasonable. How then does *rational cooperation* occur? Two general types of answers have been proposed to explain the rationality of cooperation in the prisoner's dilemma game. One approach relies on the existence of exogenous incentives that are known to influence rational behavior in different contexts of choice. For example, the threat from a central authority to punish a player if a defect choice is discovered can be used to induced cooperation in may economic, political, or social contexts of decision making (Ostrom 1990). Either positive incentives associated with cooperative behaviors or penalties associated with defect choices can be used to induce cooperation. This approach to the problem of cooperation has been used frequently when external incentives are available to a central authority with monitoring capabilities. However, whenever these incentives are not available or whenever monitoring is not possible or too costly, rational cooperation cannot be explained using exogenous influences on behavior.

Another approach used to explain the rationality of cooperation in a prisoner's dilemma game does not rely on the existence of external incentives or external monitoring capabilities; instead, endogenous features associated with the nature of the strategic interaction and individual rationality are used to explain cooperative choices. The most celebrated example of this approach was proposed by Axelrod and Hamilton (1981). According to their argument, rational players may choose to cooperate in the first play of a prisoner's dilemma game in order to induce long-term cooperation using the strategy known as tit for tat. A tit-for-tat strategy is a conditional strategy used in a repeated prisoner's dilemma game that permits cooperation to emerge among selfish players without a central authority (Axelrod 1984; Bendor and Swistak 1997). Under suitable conditions, tit for tat can explain the emergence of cooperation by assuming players interact continuously and by assuming players possess a sufficiently high present valuation of future payoffs. However, if the probability of additional interactions is unlikely or if the present valuation of future payoffs too small, mutual defection again becomes the best strategy.

Each of these solutions to the prisoner's dilemma game potentially resolves the problem of cooperation in different social contexts. A central authority can make cooperative choices attractive to rational egoists because of the special incentives they provide to cooperators and defectors, while tit for tat can explain how cooperation can emerge among egoistic players without any central authority. Yet neither approach fully explains the rationality of cooperation in a single-play prisoner's dilemma game. When there is a small likelihood of continued interactions or when there is no central authority to induce cooperative behavior, the problem of rational cooperation in the prisoner's dilemma remains unexplained.

An alternative approach used to explain the rationality of cooperation in the single-play prisoner's dilemma game builds on naturally occurring endogenous differences in individual rationality. For example, when players possess a sufficient degree of altruism (Taylor 1987), or when players are motivated by considerations of fairness (Harsanyi 1955; Frohlich 1992) or when preferences are influenced by certain kinds of moral judgments (Sen 1974; Raub 1990) the nature of the strategic interaction changes. Whenever this occurs, prisoner's dilemma preferences can be modified in ways that transform the interaction from a prisoner's dilemma game to some other game where mutual cooperation is preferred. These possibilities are explored in the next section.

TRANSFORMING INFLUENCES IN THE PRISONER'S DILEMMA GAME

According to traditional interpretations of the prisoner's dilemma game, defection is always the best strategy for each player because it dominates their cooperative strategy. If both players choose their dominant strategies, the Nash equilibrium prediction for a one-shot game is the (P, P) outcome. However this Nash prediction is based on the assumption that *rationality responds only to selfish payoff information in outcomes*. Other information in the outcome space, according to this assumption, does not influence a player's preference or strategy choice. Although this assumption is certainly reasonable for many strategic interactions, in mixed motive games like the prisoner's dilemma it tends to restrict the behavioral possibilities that can occur in cognition when players make rational choices.

While it is true that most people respond to selfish or egoistic incentive information, it has also been argued that rationality frequently responds to moral considerations associated with actions or nonegoistic incentives in outcomes. The ethical system of Kant (1970) or the impartial reasoning arguments of Rawls (1971) or Harsanyi (1955) are examples of normative systems of reasoning that recommend individually rational choices at odds with rational, self-interested decision making. When applied to individual decision making in the prisoner's dilemma game, these systems—in contrast to standard game theoretic interpretations of rationality—suggest that rational players should choose cooperative strategy choices (Sen 1974).

Yet the influence of selfishness and morality on individual behaviors need not be understood only in categorical terms. Utilitarian authors, such as Hume and Smith, have argued that welfare influences similar to benevolence or sympathy often combines with self-interest to produce rational choices. If utilitarian analysis is applied to the prisoner's dilemma game, several distinct predictions about behavior would be expected for a population of rational actors. Some individuals may defect because they have selfish motivations, whereas others may cooperate because of differing degrees of concern for others. Utilitarianism implies that rational behavior in a prisoner's dilemma game will depend on diversities in motivations that exist in a population of rational actors and that the preferences individual players possess are conditioned by different kinds of welfare motivations.

These competing views of individual rationality—egoistic views associated with game theory and strong moral views associated with different ethical systems—raise important issued about the true nature of individual rationality. Descriptive issues associated with these viewpoints can be evaluated using the prisoner's dilemma game, because equilibrium predictions about behaviors in this game partially depend on one's theoretical views on rationality.[1] Since each viewpoint makes specific but often divergent predictions about behavior in the prisoner's dilemma, we can evaluate the descriptive capabilities of each viewpoint as applied to small-group behaviors. However, before evaluating these viewpoints, we first need to develop predictions about behavior and show how these predictions follow from each viewpoint. To accomplish this, it will be necessary to relax the standard assumption of self-interested, rational behavior used in game theory.

Preferences, Motives and Transformations

When the standard assumption of rational self-interest is relaxed, different questions arise about changes in preferences, in behavior, and in strategic interactions. For example, given different moral or social influences on rationality, we can ask how strong these influences must be to produce changes in preferences or changes in behavior. To fully answer this, define a utility function U_i which uses a player's own payoff information (π_i) and their opponents's payoff information (π_j) to evaluate any outcome (X_ϕ). Assume players use all payoff information available in an outcome space to rank outcomes and that each player assigns a weight to their own (θ_i) and their opponent's payoff (θ_{-i}).[2] Players then make a decision in a prisoners' dilemma game by maximizing the function,

$$U_i (X_\phi) = \theta_i \pi_i + \theta_{-i} \pi_j$$

subject to a preferred distribution of payoffs to oneself and others (θ_i, θ_{-i}).[3] If players have utility functions consistent with this model, a player's true preferences in the prisoner's dilemma game need not be the same as the stipulated payoffs, but rather depends on the relative weight a player assigns to their own payoff and their opponent's payoff. This suggests that the preference orders of players in a prisoners' dilemma game may be subjectively modified to produce changes in the "apparent" prisoner's dilemma game players face.

The subjective modification of payoffs in a game is normally understood to be the result of different kinds of utility maximization attitudes.[4] Behaviorally speaking, however, such modifications are probably the result of different social or moral influences on motivation or preferences.[5] These influences can also result in transformations of games. Although many possible transformations can occur as a result of different behavioral influences, I investigate only two classes of transformations. An *essential transformation* of a game is defined as a transformation which results in a change of strategy for a one or more players. Transformations that do not result in changes of strategy are called *inessential transformations*. In this section I investigate two types of essential transformations and the changes in strategy choice that occur.

The first type of essential transformation occurs whenever an influence on individual preferences results, in what is called *Assurance Preferences*.[6]

Assurance Preferences: $[(\theta_i R + \theta_{-i} R) > (\theta_i T + \theta_{-i} S)] \supset [R > T > P > S]$

Assurance preference are derived by allowing player i to get value from both their payoff and their opponent's payoff. This statement assumes player i is concerned about j's payoff only if j cooperates, but not otherwise. Assurance preferences presuppose that player i does not value j's payoff in all states of the game. But if player i places a sufficiently large value on j's payoff when j cooperates, then apparent prisoner's dilemma preferences are transformed. The conditional statement above describes the degree of value player i must place on player j's payoff to transform their prisoner's dilemma preferences to assurance preferences. This statement is true for any player whenever the following inequality is satisfied:

Assurance Condition: $\theta_{-i} > T - R/R - S$.[7]

Whenever player i values another player's payoff in this degree, prisoner's dilemma preferences are transformed to assurance preferences. This condition can be understood as *the minimum degree* of value i must place on j's payoff to result in a change of preference in a prisoner's dilemma game.

Associated with the assurance condition is another condition which describes the upper limit on θ_{-i} in the prisoner's dilemma game necessary to achieve assurance preferences:

$$Assurance\ Boundary: \quad 1 > \theta_{-i} > T - R/R - S.$$

The assurance boundary implies that prisoners' dilemma preferences can be transformed even when θ_{-i} is less than one. In behavioral terms this means players need not value another's welfare more than their own to transform their preferences in a prisoner's dilemma game. Therefore, the strength of a social motivation needed to transform preferences to assurance preferences in *any* prisoner's dilemma game need not be stronger than a selfish motivation.

These two conditions are important not only because of their implications for understanding the kind of motives associated with them, but also because of their implications for behavior. Whenever the assurance condition is satisfied for any player i, cooperation in the prisoners' dilemma game is a best reply strategy choice (Raub 1990). Whenever a player has a best reply strategy, their choice is conditional on the choice of another player. A cooperative best reply is a rational strategy choice for a player with assurance preferences if, and only if, (1) player j has assurance or moral preferences, (2) both players are fully informed about the preferences of their opponent, and (3) both players know the other is informed and knows the other knows this, and so forth. If these conditions are satisfied, cooperation is the best choice for player i. If one of these conditions is not satisfied, however, defection is the best choice.

The second type of essential transformation of a prisoner's dilemma game occurs whenever an influence on individual preferences results in what I call *Moral Preferences*.[8]

$$Moral\ Preferences: \quad \{[(\theta_i R + \theta_{-i} R) > (\theta_i T + \theta_{-i} S)] \& [(\theta_i S + \theta_{-i} T) > (\theta_i P + \theta_{-i} P)]\} \supset [R > T > S > P].$$

According to this statement, if a player has a particular kind of welfare motivation or a particular moral attitude such that their opponent's payoff *always matters regardless of how the other player behaves*, then the original prisoner's dilemma preferences order is transformed. (Note that the ordering of outcomes for moral preferences is different from the ordering determined by assurance preferences.) This statement is true provided that θ_{-i} satisfies the assurance condition and the following dominance condition:

$$Dominance\ Condition: \quad \theta_{-i} > P - S/T - P.$$

If the assurance and dominance conditions are satisfied for any player i, cooperation can be a *dominant strategy* for player i. It has been argued that moral preferences may result from altruistic welfare influences (Taylor 1987), moral concerns (Sen 1974; Raub 1990), or desires for egalitarian welfare distributions (Harsanyi 1955; Frohlich 1992). But moral preferences are important because players who have these preferences will always cooperate in a single-play prisoner's dilemma game regardless of the preferences of another player.

Both kinds of essential transformation can lead to rational cooperation in the prisoner's dilemma game. Moral preferences can lead to a dominant strategy of cooperation and assurance preferences can lead to a cooperative best reply strategy. But a few inessential transformations of this game need to be mentioned to round out this discussion about the influence of motives on strategy choice. Besides social motives which are too weak to transform a player's preferences in the prisoner's dilemma game, there are motives which are more malevolent than the standard assumption of self-interest. Malevolent motivations are of little strategic interest in the two-person prisoner's dilemma game, because they merely make defect choices more attractive to players by increasing the utility value of defection to that player. Unlike positive social motives or moral influences, malevolent attitudes neither transform, nor change rational strategy choices in single-play, prisoner's dilemma games. If the assurance condition is not satisfied for some player, then there is no transformation of preference. Players therefore have the same ordering of preference:

Dilemma Preferences: $[(\theta_i R + \theta_{-i} R) \leq (\theta_i T + \theta_{-i} S)] \supset [T > R > P > S]$

Whenever the influence on payoffs satisfies this condition, players have dilemma preferences where defection is a dominant strategy choice.

The Influence of Motives on Preference and Behaviors

Given this analysis of changes that can occur in the prisoner's dilemma game, it is possible to fully summarize the effects of different influences on the transformation of preference and strategy. First, negative influences such as malevolence yield inessential transformations of dilemma games; they only make them "more severe" in the sense that the distance between the temptation payoff (T) and the cooperative payoff (R) increases. This means defection is always the best strategy choice for either malevolent of selfish players. Second, weak social motivations, such as sympathy or altruistic attitudes, also result in inessential transformation of the prisoner's dilemma if the valuation of another player's payoff (θ_{-i}) is greater than zero, but less than the assurance condition. In this case a prisoner's dilemma game becomes "less severe" in the sense that the distance between the temptation payoff (T) and the cooperative payoff (R) decreases. Defection again remains the

Table 1. Transformation in the Prisoner's Dilemma Game

Influence	Condition	Preference	Strategy
Egoism and Negative Social Influences	$[\theta_i > \theta_{-i}]$ and $\theta_{-i} \leq T - R/R - S$	$T > R > P > S$ Dilemma Preferences	Defect is a *dominant* strategy
Weak Social or Moral Influences	$\theta_i > T - R/R - S$	$R > T > P > S$ Assurance Preferences	Defect or cooperate is a *best reply* strategy
Strong Social or Moral Influences	$\theta_i > T - R/R - S$ and $\theta_i > P - S/T - P$	$R > T > S > P$ "Moral" Preferences	Cooperate is a *dominant* strategy

best strategy choice. Third, essential transformation of the prisoners' dilemma game occur if social motivations are strong enough to satisfy the assurance condition. In this case defection is no longer a dominant strategy; instead, cooperation is a best reply strategy when your opponent cooperates. Fourth, another essential transformation of the prisoners' dilemma game occurs if social or moral motivations are strong enough to satisfy both the assurance and dominance condition. In this case cooperation is a dominant strategy choice and players will cooperate regardless of the behavior of other players. These influences and their results are summarized in Table 1.

Diverse behavioral influences on rationality can be associated with any of these transformation conditions. For example, some normative views of rationality suggest that players should always cooperate regardless of the expected choice made by the other player. Players with this type of motivation will likely have moral preferences. Traditional game theoretic views of rationality suggest that players should always defect, regardless of what other players might do (Luce and Raiffa 1989). Players with this type of motivation will likely have dilemma preferences. Utilitarian views of rationality make no unique predictions about strategy choices in the prisoner's dilemma game. Instead this view implies that welfare attitudes can modify interactions in prisoner's dilemma games in these general ways: welfare attitudes can result in a more or less severe dilemma games where cooperation is dominated, or welfare attitudes can result in either cooperative best reply or cooperative dominance strategies where defection is no longer necessarily the best choice.

Although philosophers and moralists may insist otherwise, many social scientists would expect players to have moral preferences less frequently than assurance preferences. There are several reasons for this. First, for some prisoners' dilemma games, players may need to value another person's payoff more than their own to have moral preferences.[9] Since we would expect most players to have selfish motives which are stronger than social or moral motives, most players, *ceteris paribus* cannot be expected to have moral preferences.

Second, there is experimental evidence which shows that altruistic and egalitarian players react rationally to increase in the cost of altruistic or fair choices

(Frohlich and Oppenheimer 1984). This means the relative frequency of such players in a population decreases with increases in "egoistic" costs. Similar reasoning can be applied to the analysis of assurance and moral preferences. Players with moral preferences can be "egoistically" harmed when others fail to cooperate. However, players with assurance preferences cannot be egoistically harmed since they will cooperate only on the condition that the other player cooperates. We would therefore expect players with dilemma preferences and players with assurance preferences to occur with greater frequency than players with moral preferences.

TESTING FOR RATIONAL COOPERATION UNDER INCOMPLETE INFORMATION

The argument outlined above explains how rational cooperation can emerge in a single-play prisoner's dilemma game when there is no central authority and when the probability of future interactions is small under conditions of full, complete, and perfect information. According to this argument, different types of rationalities can change preferences and strategy choices so cooperation becomes a rational choice for decision makers. Whatever the merits of this approach, there are several limitations associated with this explanation of rational cooperation. It was argued that cooperation always occurs if players are motivated by strong social considerations that result in moral preferences. This assumption about rationality may strike many as much too optimistic; in the very least it demands empirical support beyond the claims made by philosophers and moralists. The other reason to expect rational cooperation to occur is because players have assurance preferences. Optimism about the frequency of assurance players aside, the information conditions necessary for cooperation appear rather demanding. Players with assurance preferences can be expected to cooperate on the condition that they know their partner will cooperate and their partner knows they will cooperate. While this may be necessary for rational cooperation, it assumes a degree of information about others that is simply not available to most players in actual prisoner's dilemma interactions.

The transformative approach to cooperation describes how rational cooperation can emerge in a single-play prisoner's dilemma game, but the assumptions required by this approach appear too strong. Perhaps a careful review of previous experimental studies will indicate that motives are important in cooperative behaviors; yet even if this is true, we shall need to ask if rates of cooperation in the prisoner's dilemma can be explained on the basis of positive social motives and moral judgments alone, or if there are other factors associated with rational cooperation.

The review of recent empirical studies outlined below suggests that social and moral motivations are related to cooperative behaviors. However these studies also show another important factor related to increases in cooperative behaviors:

communication among players. To incorporate the role of communication into the transformative approach, a modified version of rational cooperation is proposed. This modified approach assumes players do not know the preferences of their partner nor exactly how they will behave. Instead, players estimate the choice behavior of opponents under conditions of incomplete and imperfect information and then make decisions on this limited informational basis. This modified model of rational cooperation is then tested to determine if players cooperate in single-play prisoner's dilemma games using information about other player types.

Previous Experimental Evidence

No empirical studies deal with the transformation of games specifically, but many studies provide indirect or suggestive support for each transformation condition mentioned earlier. One set of studies relevant to these claims are empirical investigations into the motivations of players in two-person and n-person prisoner's dilemma games. Researchers have found that several motives are strongly correlated with different choices in the prisoner's dilemma game. Defect choices, for example, have been found to be correlated with the desire not to be cheated and the desire to do better than others (Rapoport and Chammah 1965; Rapoport 1988; Saijo and Nakamura 1995), while cooperation has been found to be strongly correlated with "motivational orientations" (Kuhlman and Marshello 1975; Sawyer 1966) "social motives" (Liebrand and van Run 1985, Messick and McClintock 1968) and "social values" (Kramer, McClintock, and Messick 1986; McClintock and Allison 1989). These experiments on cooperative motivations in the prisoner's dilemma game are consistent with the hypothesis that social motives or moral considerations may be transforming preferences in ways that make cooperation rational.

Although positive social motives may foster cooperation, the precise influence of these motives on strategy cannot be fully determined from these experiments. When subjects made choices in prisoner's dilemma games, they did not have information about their opponents. As a result, we cannot know the type of preference subjects possessed and the strategy they would play against varied player types. Subjects may have had moral preferences prompting them to cooperate unconditionally with other players, or subjects may have had assurance preferences prompting them to cooperate conditionally. Though supportive of the transformative approach to rational cooperation, these experiments cannot tell us about the relative importance of motives and information in fostering cooperation.

Related experimental findings support the importance of communication for cooperation in the prisoner' dilemma game. In two-person and n-person prisoner's dilemma experiments a replicable and strong finding is that communication increases the probability of cooperation, especially in environments with no provision points (Ledyard 1995; Sally 1995). Sharing information somehow prompts players to cooperate. Perhaps communication fosters trust among players that tends to encourages cooperative behaviors. Trust among players, independent of communication, has also been found correlated with cooperative strategy choices in prisoner's dilemma games (Rapoport 1973).

Of course these experimental finding cannot be explained within standard game theoretic analyses. Social or moral motives may be correlated with cooperation, but so what? Since a player can do better by having egoistic preferences, these influences on preference are strictly speaking, irrational. Communication with other players also should have no influence on cooperative choices. Defection is the best strategy choice regardless of whether or not we talk about it. In the language of game theory preplay communication is simply "cheap talk" which should not influence a player's dominant strategy choice. A related argument holds for motives of trust. Trust or favorable expectations about another player's choices can never lead to rational cooperation in a single-play prisoner's dilemma game regardless of the level of strength of this motivation or the intensity of the cooperative expectation. You may trust the other player to cooperate but defection still yields a higher payoff.

Transformation and Information

Standard game theoretic analysis cannot explain these findings, but what about the transformative approach? The transformative approach appears superior to game theory because it shows how different motives may be important for rational cooperation. But how can the role of communication be explained and integrated into this framework? To answer this question, the informational conditions on rational cooperation need to be more carefully scrutinized. For example, if a strategy choice depends on knowledge about another player's rationality, then communicating or signaling your rationality to another player should influence the behavior of players disposed to cooperate. In other words, if both players have reliable information about their opponent's choice behavior and if this information suggests an opponent will cooperate, this could induce players with assurance preferences to cooperate. Under this interpretation we would expect that positive estimates about an opponent's cooperative strategy choice may lead to rational cooperation.

But this explanation is not fully consistent with findings in game theory. Even if both players have assurance preferences and even if both players believe the other player has similar preferences, common knowledge between players is necessary for rational cooperation. I may know you have assurance preferences but if I cannot be sure you believe that I have the same preferences as you, you may decide I am likely to defect. Therefore, I should defect since I believe you think I will. Both player have assurance preferences and both may believe the other player has assurance preferences, but if there is no common knowledge of these facts between players, defection remains the best strategy choice.

This argument suggests that common knowledge among players may be important for rational cooperation in the prisoner's dilemma game for players with assurance preferences. In addition to this, players with assurance preferences require a positive expectation that their opponent will cooperate. But if player with assurance preferenecs are paired with other players who have moral preferences, then common knowledge is not required for cooperation. Common knowledge between players is not always necessary for rational cooperation, but rather depends on the player type of an opponent.

These additional informational factors provide us with a basis to determine how motives and information combine to produce rational cooperation in the prisoner's dilemma game. Information about other players should not influence the behavior or rational players with *Egoistic or Strong Moral Preferences*, since both players have dominant strategies. Players should choose their dominant strategies regardless of the choice made by the other player. Information about other players should influence the behavior or rational players with *Assurance Preferences*. Corresponding to these claims are the following hypotheses:

Hypothesis 1.   The choice behavior of players with assurance preferences will be influenced by information about other player types.

Hypothesis 2.   The choice behavior of players with dilemma preferences will not be influenced by information about other player types.

Hypothesis 3.   The choice behavior of players with moral preferences will not be influenced by information about other player types.

Experimental Design

This experiment attempts to measure the influence of diverse motives on choice behaviors in a strategic environment of decision making and attempts to determine if information about another player influences strategy choice. This model of decision making assumes players make choices in the prisoner's dilemma game under conditions of incomplete and imperfect information. To test this model, three types of information about subjects need to be revealed: (1) the type of utility function a player possesses and its influence on orderings in a prisoner's dilemma game, (2) a player's expectation about the behavior of the other players, and (3) their preferred strategy in the prisoner's dilemma game. If cooperative behaviors in the prisoner's dilemma game are a function of transformed preferences and information about other players, then attributions about the principle cause of cooperative behavior must independently measure both.

How can the influence of diverse welfare information on preference be measured in a prisoner's dilemma game to approximate a player's utility function? Because different factors influence choices in strategic contexts, individual motivations cannot be inferred from the observation of strategy choices alone. Instead, individual motives must be approximated through other techniques. Recent literature investigating the influence of motives or social values on strategic decision making have used different survey techniques or weak monetary incentives to reveal differences in motivation. This experiment attempts to reveal diverse preferences from a choice perspective using a dictator game.

In a dictator game, a player's positive social attitudes or egalitarian preferences toward others can be revealed by asking player i to split a pie between themselves and another person. This split results in payoff of size α_i to player i and a payoff of size $(1-\alpha_i)$ to another player. The proportion of a pie a decision maker awards to themselves and another person can then be used to approximate the kinds of preferences *they would have* in a strategic context of decision making. To determine this, assume $\theta_i = \alpha_i$ and $\theta_{-i} = (1 - \alpha_i)$. If the ratio of the split preferred by player i is defined as $(1 - \alpha_i)/\alpha_i$, then whenever this ratio satisfies the assurance condition, player i is predicted to have either assurance or moral preferences. If the ratio of the split preferred by player i does not satisfy this ratio, player i is predicted to have dilemma preferences.[10] A dictator game therefore provides the basis to develop predictions about preferences in the prisoner's dilemma game based on choice behavior alone.

A player's expectations about the cooperative behavior of their opponents can be revealed by asking them to predict the choices their opponent will make in a prisoner's dilemma game. As an incentive to predict correctly, players are rewarded for correct predictions about their opponent's choice. The experimental design requires that all players are provided information about their opponents' preferred split in the previous dictator game before making a decision in the prisoner's dilemma game. Dictator splits are the only information players shared and therefore the only basis for developing expectations about the behavior of other players.

According to the modified transformative approach to rational cooperation, we can expect information to influence only a subset of players. Define a player's expectation about j's behavior in the prisoners' dilemma game as:

Cooperative Expectations: p_i = player i's expectations
that player j will cooperate.

Defect Expectations: $(1 - p_i)$ = player i's expectation that player j will defect.

The expectations of players with assurance or moral preferences should be conditioned by the information they receive about their opponent's play in the dictator game. Player with assurance or moral preferences can be expected to predict cooperation by their opponents or $p_i > 1 - p_i$, provided their opponent's preferred split in the dictator game satisfied the assurance condition. If the other player kept most of the pie, then we would expect players with assurance or moral preferences to predict defection or $p_i > 1 - p_i$. However, for players with dilemma preferences, we would expect little differentiation. If these players assume the other player is rational, then they should expect others to defect or $p_i > 1 - p_i$ for all opponents.

Observing the choices players reveal through their decision on the proportion of the split of a pie, their predictions on how they expect others to choose, and their preferred strategy choice in a prisoner's dilemma game will allow us to distinguish among different player types and the role information may have on expectations and strategy choices. Both game provide incentive compatible information on the kind of utility functions players possess. This information can then be used to compare the predicted effects of social attitudes on choice behaviors in strategic contexts and to compare these effects with the influence of positive expectations for cooperative choice behaviors.

Experimental Procedures

The experiments were conducted during the spring of 1996 using 64 inexperienced subjects from the Jagiellonian University in Crakow, Poland. The subjects were recruited using an announcement asking them to participate in a paid experiment on group decision making. A preselection survey was used to minimize the number of participants who previously knew each other before they were assigned to a group. Subjects were then assigned to eight groups consisting of eight players. Subjects in each experimental group were randomly assigned to desks separated by partitions. Throughout the experiment, subjects were unable to see or communicate with other participants in the group. Subjects were informed that any choices they made would be anonymous and that they would be paid at the conclusion of the experiment based on the choices they and others in the group made.

For the first decision, referred to here as the Dictator Game, subjects were given a total of 10 points (1 point = 1.5 zloty) and they were asked to decide an allocattion of these points between themselves and another randomly selected person in the group.11 For points they decided to keep, they were told to place them in an envelop marked Your points and any points allocated to another went into an envelop marked only with numbers. Subjects were also informed that it was possible someone would later view the contents of the numbered envelop, although their identity would not be revealed at any time either during or after the experiment (See Appendix B for a description of the instructions).

After subjects made dictator choices allocating points to themselves and another person, subjects were introduced to the prisoners' dilemma game. Subjects were first asked to complete a set of questions on this game and then answers were checked by the experimental assistant. When subjects answered incorrectly, the correct answers were carefully explained to the subject. After all explanations were complete, subjects were asked to play two different prisoner's dilemma games with the assistant. The experimental subjects were told that they would not be paid for these choices, but that they could earn money for correct answers on questions which followed each play of the game.

Table 2.   Distribution of Choices in the Dictator Game

	Amount of Points Dinated to Others in Dictator Game						
Amount	0	1	2	3	4	5	6 or more
Subjects	4	5	9	8	4	8	2
(%)	(0.1)	(0.125)	(0.225)	(0.2)	(0.1)	(0.2)	(0.05)
Mean = 2.93							
Subjects	2	8	*	*	8	6	*
(%)	(0.083)	(0.33)			(0.33)	(0.25)	
Mean = 2.92							

In the next part of the experiment, referred to here as the *Prisoner's Dilemma Game,* subjects were asked to make a decision in a group. Subjects were informed that they would be randomly paired with another person in the group and that the payoff they received would be based on their joint set of choices (See Appendix C for a description of the instructions). Subjects were randomly paired three times with three different players. Before making any choice however, subjects were given an envelop of the person they were paired with for that round. This envelop contained the amount of points their partner donated to another person in the Dictator Game. In another words, each subject knew how they and their partner played in the dictator game, and since both players knew the other was similarly informed, common information about player types was approximated.

After subjects recorded the number of points their partner kept and the number of points that person gave away in the Dictator Game, subjects were asked to make a choice in the prisoner's dilemma game. After making this choice, subjects were asked to record their predictions about how the other player would choose in the game and the level of confidence they had in their prediction. At the conclusion of the experiment, before they left the laboratory, subjects were asked to complete several exit surveys.

Experimental Results

The dictator game was played under two separate conditions: unrestricted and restricted choice. In the unrestricted condition subjects were asked to choose any division of 10 points (whole numbers only). In the restricted condition subjects were also asked to choose a division of ten points, but they could only choose splits of (10, 0), (9, 0), (6, 4) and (5, 5). There were 40 subjects in the unrestricted choice condition and 24 subjects in the restricted choice condition. How much did subjects keep for themselves and how much did they give away to others? The average amount donated to another anonymous subject in the group for both groups was less than 3 points ($\bar{X}$ = 2.9). Less than 10 percent of all subjects kept the entire endowment of 10 points for themselves and over 20 percent of the

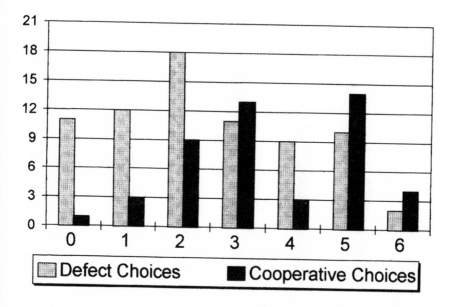

Figure 2. Prisoner's Dilemma Choice

subjects split the pie evenly between themselves and another. The distribution of choices made by all subjects is described in Table 2.

The choice behaviors of the experimental subjects appears consistent with previous experimental studies of the single-play prisoner's dilemma game. This suggests that the dictator game is not influencing the behavior of subjects in the prisoner's dilemma game. Subjects defected more often than they cooperated. Fifty-eight percent (109) of all choices were defect choices, while 42 percent (80) were cooperative choices.[12] The 95 percent confidence interval for the mean proportion of defect choices is greater than half (0.51, 0.65). Figures 2 and 3 show the distribution of different choices in the prisoners' dilemma game according to the amount subjects donated to others in the dictator game (for both restricted and urestricted conditions).

For the purpose of analysis, subjects are divided into two different player types, depending on the choice a player made in the dictator game. A *stingy player* is defined as a subject who gave away less than three points to another person, and a *nice player* is defined as a subject who gave away three or more points to another person. This distinction between players approximates the predicted difference between players with dilemma preferences and players with assurance or moral preferences. Stingy players ($n = 28$) made up 44 percent of the sample, while nice players ($n = 36$) made up 56 percent of the sample.

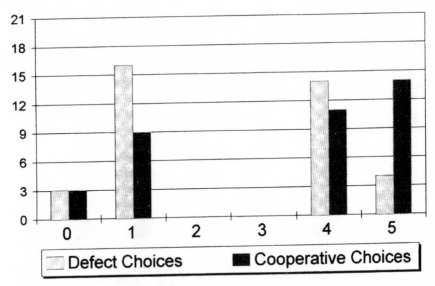

Figure 3.   Prisoner's Dilemma Choice
(Restricted Dictator Game)

The behavioral differences among stingy and nice players are significant. Stingy players tended to defect much more frequently than nice players. Stingy players defected 71 percent of the time while nice players defected only 47 percent. The differences in the choice behaviors of stingy and nice player types in the prisoner's dilemma game is significant at $\alpha = 0.001$ ($t = -3.63$, $df = 185$; $p < 0.001$). But differences in behavior among these player types can also be found in the expectational judgments made by subjects. Stingy players predicted that other players would defect 66 percent of the time, while nice players predicted defection only 47 percent of the time. The differences in the expectational judgments of stingy and nice player types in the prisoner's dilemma game is also significant at $\alpha = 0.05$ ($t = -2.40$; $df = 181$; p 0.017).

Because subjects were always randomly paired with other subjects in the prisoner's dilemma game, a possible explanation for these differences in behavior could be pattern of random pairings which occurred in the experiment. It is possible, for example, that stingy players were more often paired with other stingy players while nice players were more often paired with nice players. This would indeed explain the observed differences in behaviors. However, this was not the case. On average, stingy players were more often paired with nice players ($\bar{X} = 6.62$ kept for self) and nice players were more often paired with stingy players ($\bar{X} = 7.47$ kept for self). Therefore, these differences in behavior cannot be explained by random pairings with similar player types.

Table 3. Choices and Predictions in The Prisoners' Dilemma Game

	Stingy Player Choices			Nice Player Choices		
Choices	Stingy	Nice	Totals	Stingy	Nice	Totals
Cooperation	6	18	24	21	35	56
Defection	23	37	60	33	16	49
Totals	29	55	84	54	51	105

	Stingy Player Predictions			Nice Player Predictions		
Expectations	Stingy	Nice	Totals	Stingy	Nice	Totals
Cooperation	8	20	28	19	34	53
Defection	21	35	56	35	17	52
Totals	29	55	84	54	51	105

When the choices of different player types is analyzed in terms of the types of opponents they faced in the prisoner's dilemma, we again see important aggregate differences in the behaviors of stingy and nice players. Stingy players in general tended to expect both kinds of players to defect (See Table 3). The odds of a predicted defection by a stingy player ranged from 2.62 when meeting stingy players to 1.75 when meeting nice players (See Table 4). Stingy players were therefore less optimistic about the possibility of stingy player cooperation. However this pattern of predictions is different for nice players. Nice players on averaged expected stingy players to defect, but then switched their predictions when facing nice players, expecting nice players to cooperate. When comparing stingy players to nice players, stingy players were almost two and a half times more likely to defect when facing other stingy players (2.43) but five times more likely to defect when facing nice players (5.43).

The only information players had to form beliefs about their opponent was information concerning how many points their opponent gave to another player in the dictator game. This information appears to be playing a role in the behavior of subjects in the prisoner's dilemma game. But how significant is this influence in contributing to the behavior of each type of player? For stingy players, information about other players was not a significant factor in their behavior ($\chi^2 = 1.35$; $df = 1$; $p > 0.10$). For these players we cannot reject the null hypothesis that information was influencing strategy choices. But for nice players, the results are different. Information about other players was a significant factor in their behaviors and appears to have caused them to switch choices ($\chi^2 = 9.32$; $df = 1$; $p < 0.001$).

An investigation of odds ratios for choices gives us greater indication of how player preferences and information about others influenced behaviors for subjects in each group. As Table 4 indicates, stingy players tended to chose defection more than they predicted defection. This shows that some stingy players were expecting

Table 4.   Odds Ratios for Choices and Predictions

	Odds Ratios	
	Stingy Players	Nice Players
Stingy	2.62 Predict Defection	1.75 Predict Defection
	3.83 Chose Defection	2.5 Chose Defection
Nice	1.84 Predict Defection	2.0 Predict Cooperation
	1.57 Chose Defection	2.18 Chose Cooperation

to receive the temptation payoff. By contrast, nice players tended to chose defection less than they predicted and tended to chose cooperation more than they predicted cooperation. This suggests that some nice players expected to be cheated by others, yet still played cooperative strategies.

DISCUSSION

The experimental results confirm earlier studies on the importance of positive social motives and moral attitudes for fostering cooperatives behavior.[13] Despite differences in design between this experiment and other experiments on motivations reviewed above, nice players tended to cooperate in the prisoner's dilemma game much more frequently than stingy players in ways consistent with earlier studies. However given the above analysis, information about other players also appears to be an important factor in cooperate behaviors. Nasty or selfish players tended to recognize potential cooperators, but this did not significantly affect their behaviors. Nice players, in contrast to nasty players, tended to respond favorably to potential cooperators and unfavorably to potential defectors. Information therefore appears to influence the choice behavior of only a subset of players, just as the transformative approach predicts.

But what about the differences between players with assurance preferences and players with moral preferences? Although this experimental design does not allow us to directly infer who has moral preferences on the basis of dictator splits alone, we can use choice and expectational data in the prisoners' dilemma game to infer this. Among nice players, two players who preferred even splits appear to have exhibited moral preferences in the prisoner's dilemma game: they cooperated even though they believed the other person would defect. This was inferred not only on the basis of their choice behaviors in the prisoner's dilemma game, but also using exit surveys administered to subjects on preferred distributions.

These experimental results illustrate the complex role social values and morality play in behavior. Very few subjects revealed purely selfish behavior and very few subjects revealed purely moral behaviors. Instead social values and the influence of morality are conditioned by the potential costs associated with having such values. Cooperation appears to gain a weak foothold when social values influence behavior along with standard selfish motives. Nice players tended to cooperate when they thought the other player would also cooperate, otherwise they defected like everyone else.

These results also have important implications for theories of rationality. Traditional views of rational choice theory can explain most of the observed choice behaviors: 58 percent of all choices were defect choices. This suggests that 42 percent of the choices were irrational. Normative theories of rationality explains the least amount of the behaviors exhibited by subjects. But neither viewpoint on rationality can explain why information has an influence on nice players but not nasty players. Utilitarian theory fits nicely with the transformative approach to behavior because it allows for a range of human motivations. Although people tend to be self-interested, this motive is conditioned by social or moral motives. Because the degree of conditioning varies throughout the population, there is a wide distribution of different motives among rational actors.

CONCLUSION

Traditional analyses of the prisoner's dilemma game imply that rational players will choose their dominant strategy of defection. However, the analysis presented in this paper suggests that some players may *rationally cooperate* in prisoners' dilemma games if their behavior is influenced by particular kinds of social motivations, such as altruism, or by particular types of moral considerations, such as fairness. Three related predictions about rational behaviors were derived when strategy choices are influenced by different kinds of motivations. First, because egoistic or selfish influences will not change preference orders, defection remains a dominant strategy choice for egoistic or selfish players. Second, social or moral influences can also change preference orders and if these influences are strong enough, cooperation may become a dominant strategy choice. Third, weaker social or moral influences can also change preference orders to induce cooperative choices. However, cooperation is not always guaranteed and depends directly on the rationality of the other player. This latter prediction suggests that information about the rationality of other players may be a factor in rational cooperation for certain kinds of players.

These predictions about choice behavior in the prisoner's dilemma game were evaluated using an experimental design that attempted to reveal not only diverse social and moral motivation among players, but also the expectations players had about their partner in the game. The experimental investigation of behavior revealed choices in two environments of choice. Subjects were first asked to decide the best allocation of points between themselves and another anonymous person in the group, and subjects were then asked to make a decision and a prediction about their partner's choice in a prisoner's dilemma game. There was no communication permitted in this experiment, however, subjects in the prisoner's dilemma game were required to share information about how they and their partner behaved in the dictator game. In this very restricted informational environment, subjects formed expectations about how other players might choose.

The results of this experiment show that many people rationality defect as traditional analyses of game theory predicts. But the results also show that many people cooperate, especially people who played nicely in the dictator game. Among nice players, a small percentage of rational cooperation appears to be the result of strong social considerations. However most rational cooperation appears to be the result of weaker social or moral motivations. These weaker motivations combine with expectations players have about their partner's cooperative intentions and influence strategy choices. When nice players have positive social or moral motives and positive expectations that their partner will cooperate, nice players tended to cooperate.

These experimental results provide support for an incomplete information model of rational cooperation in a single-play prisoner's dilemma game. This model suggests that social and moral motivations together with information about player type influences cooperative decision making for most players. Rational strategy choices for all players appear conditioned by welfare information to oneself, welfare information about another player, and information about the kind of player type one faces. If players have no concern for another's welfare, then dominant defect choices can be expected.

This experiment also provides evidence that explains an observed tendency in other social dilemma experiments: cooperation among subjects increases when communication among subjects is permitted. Under traditional interpretations of the prisoner's dilemma game, communication should have no influence on strategy choice. However, according to the incomplete information interpretation of transformation in games, communication can be useful for players with assurance preferences when making strategy choices. If tests of prisoner's dilemma games are interpreted as games of incomplete information, communication can contribute to rational cooperation if subjects have assurance preferences.

This experiment also suggests an important amendment to earlier studies on cooperation in the prisoner's dilemma game. Social values such as altruism and equality are likely to be important factors in contributing to cooperation in small groups. However, the importance of these values needs to be understood in the context of other information. If cooperative players suspect another player does not share their values, they are very likely to chose defection, rather than be penalized for their beliefs. Therefore social values or moral considerations are playing an important role in fostering cooperation, but this role is conditioned by their beliefs about others.

ACKNOWLEDGMENTS

I wish to thank Jacek Szmatka for his permission to use the Group Processes Laboratory in the Institute of Sociology at the Jagiellonian University. I am also grateful to Joanna Mazur and Tadeusz Sozański for their help in performing the experiments described in this chapter. Tadeusz Sozański, Paweł Poławski, and Aleksander Surdej provided Polish translations of the experimental materials. I wish to thank J. Joseph Hewitt and David Lalman for their comments on an earlier version of this paper and Virginia Foran for her editorial suggestions. I also received helpful comments on the experimental design from Beth Blake, Keith Dougherty, John Guyton, Joe Oppenheimer, Piotr Swistak, Tadeusz Tyszka, and Mark Van Boening. I gratefully acknowledge the American Council of Learned Societies, the International Research and Exchange Board, and the Graduate School of the University of Mississippi for their financial support.

APPENDIX A

Minimum Boundary Condition

Set $\theta_i = 1$

$$[R + \theta_{-i} R] > [T + \theta_{-i} S]$$

$$[\theta_{-i} R - \theta_{-i} S] > [T - R]$$

$$\theta_{-i}[R - S] > [T - R]$$

$$\theta_{-i} > T - R / R - S$$

Assurance Boundary

$$2R > [T + S]$$

$$R > [T + S]/2$$

Since R is closer to T than S in the interval

$$T - R < R - S$$

$$T - R / R - S < 1$$

$$1 > \theta_{-i} > T - R / R - S$$

Dominance Condition

Set $\theta_i = 1$

$$[S + \theta_{-i}T] > [P + \theta_{-i}P]$$

$$[\theta_{-i}T - \theta_{-i}P] > [P - S]$$

$$\theta_{-i}[T - P] > [P - S]$$

$$\theta_{-i} > P - S/T - P$$

APPENDIX B

PLEASE DO NOT SPEAK TO ANYONE OTHER THAN THE EXPERI-
MENTER THROUGHOUT THE EXPERIMENT. IF YOU DO NOT UNDER-
STAND SOMETHING, PLEASE RAISE YOUR HAND.

Before you are two envelops: one marked with the words "Your Points" and the
other marked only with numbers. The envelop labelled "Your Points" contains 10
blank pieces of paper and the envelop marked only with numbers contains 10
pieces of green paper. Each green piece of paper is worth 1 point each. Blank
pieces of paper have no value.

Count the number of points you have in your possession. You should have 10
points (10 pieces of green paper and 10 blank pieces of paper. If there are more or
less than this, raise your hand immediately. Remember that each green piece of
point is worth 1.5 złoty.

For this round, you are requested to make a decision about who receives these
points: yourself or another person who has been randomly selected by the experimenter. You will not know which person has been selected at any time either during or after the experiment.

If you decide to give this person points, they will not know which person gave
these points to them. *No participant in the experiment will be able to determine
who made this choice, other than yourself.* It is possible, however, that some participants in the experiment will later view the contents of the *other envelop* now in
your possession. If someone views the contents of this envelop later in the experiment, they will not be able to determine who made this decision, although they
will be able to determine what decision was made in this round. No one will see
the envelop marked "Your Points."

How do you go about making a decision for this round?

To keep points for yourself, place the green pieces of paper in the envelop labeled "Your Points." Whenever you place a point in this envelop, remove a white piece of paper. The reason for replacing these points with blank sheets is so all envelops look the same when they are returned to the experimenter. When you are finished there should be 10 pieces of paper in each envelop.

For example, if you decide to keep 9 points for yourself and give 1 point to this other person, then remove 9 pieces of green paper from the envelop marked with numbers and replace the points with 9 blank pieces of paper. Place the 9 points in the envelop labeled "Your Points." You will receive money for these points at the conclusion of the experiment.

To give points away to another person, do not remove points from the envelop labeled with numbers. In other words, any points you leave in the envelop will go to another person and any points you place in the envelop labeled "Your Points" will go to you.

For example, if you decide to give 9 points to another person and keep 1 point for yourself, then remove 1 point from the envelop labeled with numbers. Place the point in the envelop labeled "Your Points." Remember, your decision are anonymous and you may keep or give away any amount of money you choose. No participant in the experiment will be able to determine who made this choice, other than yourself. Please make your decision now. You have several minutes to make your choice. When everyone is finished, the envelops will be collected.

APPENDIX C

For this round you have been paired with a another person in the experiment. This pairing is not the same as any from the previous rounds. Like the previous rounds, you will not know who you have been paired with either during or after the experiment and no one has been given information about the choices you made from previous rounds.

Before you is an envelop used by the other person you are now paired with. Please look at the contents of that envelop to determine how much that person took for him or herself and how much they gave to some other person during round 1. This person was **not** paired with you in the previous round.

To determine how much that person kept for him or herself, count the number of blank pieces of paper. To determine how much that person gave to another person in the experiment, count the number of green pieces of paper. Please record the amounts below:

The other person kept _____ point(s) for him or herself.
The other person gave _____ point(s) to someone else in the group.

Please replace the entire contents of this envelop after you record the amounts above and raise your hand for the envelop to be collected.

After your envelop is collected turn to the next page.

In this round, you and the person you are paired with are being asked to make a group choice, similar to the choices you made in *the Practice Round*. For this choice, the money you earn depends on your choice and the choice the other person you are paired with makes. Each of you will make a decision in this round, although any money you earn will be paid to you at the end of the experiment. There is a one third chance of receiving payments from this round at the conclusion of the experiment.

The following table presents two sets of payoff similar to the previous round and the practice round. Like before, the first set represents what you can receive and the second set represents what the other person may receive. The payoffs you can receive in this round are printed in **bold.**

Both you and the person you are paired with have the following information about payoffs:

The person you are paired with can choose either #1 or #2		
	Choice #1	Choice #2
Your **A** Choice	**7.00**, 7.00	**0.00**, 10.00
Your **B** Choice	**10.00**, 0.00	**3.00**, 3.00

What you earn for this choice depends on what you and the other person choose in this round. You will be paid for your choices at the end of the experiment.

Make your choice by placing a check mark next to the choice you most prefer:

_____ *My A Choice* for this round.
_____ *My B Choice* for this round.

Now that you have recorded your choice, record your best guess about what you think the other person you are paired with will choose.

You will be paid 2.00 points for a correct guess. Check your best guess here:

_____ The other person I am paired with will pick *Choice #1* for this round.
_____ The other person I am paired with will pick *Choice #2* for this round.

How confident or certain are you about this answer?
_____ Very confident
_____ Somewhat confident

_____ Neither confident nor unsure
_____ Somewhat Unsure
_____ Very unsure

Given your choices, how many points will you and the other player receive?

NOTES

1. Later in this section I show that predictions also depend on informational conditions among actors in the game.

2. Assume θ_i can only be positive and θ_{-i} can be either negative or positive and allow (θ_i, θ_{-i}) to vary between states, but not actions.

3. We can think of these preferred weights as either unreflectively part of a person's utility function or intentionally chosen by a rational actor.

4. Compare Messick and McClintock (1968).

5. Compare (Liebrand and van Run (1985), Kramer et al. (1986), and Liebrand, Wilke, Vogel, and Volters (1986).

6. This term was introduced by Sen (1974). He called it assurance preferences because if both players had these preferences a prisoner's dilemma game is transformed to an assurance game.

7. See Appendix A for a proof of this condition and other conditions.

8. The term *moral preference* does not imply that individuals must be moral. However, as I argue below, the moral or social motivation necessary to have such preferences is stronger than the motivation for *assurance preferences*.

9. Unlike assurance preferences, moral preferences do not have a similar boundary condition. The maximum upper bound for the ratio $P - S/T - P$ is greater than 1 for some values of $[T, S] \varepsilon$ (-∞, + ∞). As a result, for some prisoner's dilemma games and some values of the interval $[T, S]$, players may need to value another's welfare more than their own to have moral preferences.

10. The conditions on preferences stated in the first part of this paper assume $\theta_{-i} = \theta_{-i}/\theta_i$ where $\theta_i = 1$. Therefore to approximate these conditions using a dictator game $\theta_{-i} = (1 - \alpha_i) / \alpha_i$

11. The exchange rate at this time was $1.00 = 2.4 zl$. However the equivalent purchasing power of $1.00 in the United States was approximately 1.5 zl. Therefore 1 point had the purchasing power in Poland of approximately $1.00 in the United States.

12. There were 189 valid observations for 63 experimental subjects. The choices of one subject was removed because the subject recorded too many incorrect answers in both the practice and experimental sessions.

13. See the studies reviewed above.

REFERENCES

Axelrod, R., and W. Hamilton. 1981. *Science* 211, 1390-1398.

Axelrod, R. 1984. *The Evolution of Cooperation*. Basic Books.

Bendor, J., and P. Swistak. 1997. "The Evolutionary Stability of Cooperation." *American Political Science Review* 91(2): 290-307.

Cain, M.J.G. 1993. Social Values and Individual Rationality: An Investigation of the Effects of Diverse Welfare Values on Decision-making. Ph.D. dissertation. University of Maryland.

Frohlich, N. 1992. "An Impartial Reasoning Solution to the Prisoner's Dilemma." *Public Choice* 74: 447-460.

Frohlich, N., and J. Oppenheimer. 1984. "Beyond Economic Man." *Journal of Conflict Resolution* 28: 54-73.

Harrison, G., and K. McCabe. 1992. "Expectations and Fairness in Simple Bargaining Experiments." Economic Working Paper. University of South Carolina.

Harsanyi, J.C. 1955. "Cardinal Welfare, Individualistic Ethics, and Interpersonal Comparisons of Utility." *Journal of Political Economy* 63: 309-321.

Kant, I. 1907. *Fundamental Principles of the Metaphysics of Ethics*, 3rd edition. [Translated by T.K. Abbott]. London: Longman Press.

Kramer, R.M., C.G. McClintock, and D.M. Messick. 1986. "Social Values and Cooperative Response to a Simulated Resource Conservation Crisis." *Journal of Personality* 54: 576-592.

Ledyard, J.O. 1995. "Public Goods: A Survey of Experimental Research." In *The Handbook of Experimental Economics*, edited by J. Kagel and A. Roth. Princeton, NJ: Princeton University Press.

Liebrand, W.B.G., and G.J. van Run. 1985. "The Effects of Social Motives on Behavior in Social Dilemmas in Two Cultures." *Journal of Experimental Social Psychology* 21: 86-102.

Liebrand, W.B.G., H.A.M. Wilke, R. Vogel and F.J.M. Volters. 1986. "Value orientation and Conformity." *Journal of Conflict Resolution* 30: 77-97.

McClintock, C.G., and S. Allison. 1989. "Social Value Orientation and Helping Behavior." *Journal of Applied Social Psychology* 19: 353-362.

Messick, D.M., and C.G. McClintock. 1968. "Motivation Bases of Choice in Experimental Games." *Journal of Experimental Social Psychology* 3: 85-101.

Ostrom, E. 1990. *Governing the Commons.* Cambridge: Cambrige University Press.

Rapoport, A., and A.M. Chammah. 1965. *Prisoners' Dilemma.* Ann Arbor, MI: University of Michigan Press.

Rapoport, A. 1973. *Experimental Games and Their Uses in Psychology.* Morristown, NJ: General Learning Press.

Rapoport. A. 1988. "Experiments with N-Person Social Traps I and II." *Journal of Conflict Resolution* 32: 457-488.

Raub, W. (1990). "A General Game-Theoretic Model of Preference Adaptations in Problematic Social Situations." *Rationality and Society* 2: 67-93.

Rawls, J. 1971. *A Theory of Justice.* Oxford: Clarendon Press.

Saijo, T., and H. Nakamura. 1995. "The 'Spite' Dilemma in Voluntary Contribution Mechanism Experiments." *Journal of Conflict Resolution* 39: 535-560.

Sally, D. 1995. "Conversation and Cooperation in Social Dilemmas." *Rationality and Society* 7(1): 58-92.

Sen. A. 1974 [1982]. "Choice, Orderings and Morality." *Choice, Welfare, and Measurement.* Cambridge: MIT Press.

Taylor, M. 1987. *The Possibility of Cooperation.* Cambridge: Cambridge University Press.

Van De Kragt, A.J.C., R.M. Dawes, and J. Orbell. 1988. "Are People Who Cooperate 'Rational Altruists'?" *Public Choice* 56: 233-247.

DEPENDENCE AND COOPERATION IN THE GAME OF TRUMP

R. Thomas Boone and Michael W. Macy

ABSTRACT

Although the effects of dependence on power in social exchange have been widely studied, there is relatively little work on the effect of dependence on cooperation. Game-theoretic analysis of the iterated Prisoner's Dilemma suggests that cooperation increases with dependence on an ongoing partner. An alternative hypothesis is that cooperation increases with a decrease in self-reliance, even in one-shot games, where cooperation is not rational. We tested both hypotheses in laboratory experiments with human subjects. Using a new cardgame representation of a Prisoner's Dilemma ("Trump"), we manipulated self-reliance by changing the value of the cards dealt to subjects. We crossed this factor with the subject's attachment to an ongoing partner, which we manipulated by allowing an option to change or keep a partner. We found that cooperation increased with both factors, low card value and attachment. However, increased cooperation appeared to mainly reflect reduced self-reliance, not the inability to change partners. Cooperation was greater with a permanent partner, but only when self-reliance was high.

Advances in Group Processes, Volume 15, pages 161-185.
Copyright © 1998 by JAI Press Inc.
All rights of reproduction in any form reserved.
ISBN: 0-7623-0362-X

THE DEPENDENCE-COOPERATION HYPOTHESIS

A mutual interest in helping one another is often insufficient to guarantee that cooperative efforts will be forthcoming. Game theorists have formalized the problem as the Prisoner's Dilemma (or PD), a mixed-motive game between two players, each with two choices, to *cooperate* (e.g., help the other) or *defect* (e.g., refuse to help). These two choices intersect at four possible outcomes, each with a designated payoff. *R* (for reward) and *P* (for punishment) are the payoffs for mutual cooperation and defection, respectively, while *S* (for sucker) and *T* (for temptation) are the payoffs for cooperation by one player and defection by the other (free riding). By definition, $T>R>P>S$. These payoffs create tension between individual and collective interests. From a self-interested standpoint, no matter what the partner chooses, the best strategy is to defect (either out of *greed* if the partner is naïve, or out of *fear* if the partner is not). The dilemma is that the optimal choice for each player can lead to the worst possible collective outcome.

The standard game-theoretic solution is to assume that the game is ongoing (or iterated) between the same two players. Each side can then use reciprocity and retaliation to reward and punish the partner's behavior. The "shadow of the future" (Axelrod 1984) thus creates an opportunity for tacit collusion, which is not possible in the one-shot game.

Pruitt and Kimmel (1977) surveyed twenty years of experimental research on iterated PD and noted a widespread tendency for tacit collusion to emerge from a series of mutual defections. At the outset, the players distrust and/or try to cheat one another, leading to a series of mutual defections. Eventually, however, the players learn that defection is not a viable option, and that mutual cooperation is a better strategy. With that as the primary goal, the players come to regard their partner not as predator or prey, but as a potentially—someone whose help is needed. Although the players are also interdependent in the one-shot game, it is only in the iterated game, Pruitt and Kimmel argue, that "long-range thinking" can reveal each side's dependence on the relationship itself. "Perceived dependence on the other, i.e., a recognition of the importance of the other's cooperation" is the key to the development of mutual cooperation (1977, p. 375).

This dependence-cooperation hypothesis has broad theoretical implications, ranging from Durkheim's functionalism to Hechter's utilitarianism. Durkheim (1933) argued that the division of labor increases interdependence, which in turn gives rise to organic solidarity. Hechter's (1987) theory of group solidarity contends that members' dependence on the group creates more extensive obligations to contribute to the collective good.

The dependence-cooperation hypothesis is also relevant to "power-dependence theory" (Cook, Emerson, Gillmore, and Yamagishi 1983). There is a large and growing body of experimental evidence that dependence on an exchange partner causes an actor to accept inferior terms in cooperative bargaining games (where binding agreements preclude cheating).[1] If so, then perhaps dependence might also cause a player in Prisoner's Dilemma (a *noncooperative* game) to settle for less than what might be obtained by cheating the partner. However, while the effect of dependence on power has been widely studied, the effect on cooperation has been largely neglected.[2]

The principal exceptions are laboratory experiments on "helping behavior" (Carnevale, Pruitt, and Carrington 1982) and "reward contingencies" (Burgess and Buschell 1968; Michaels and Wiggins 1976; Molm 1980). Carnevale et al. focused on the subject's need for a partner's future help and found that this produced "helping behavior" only between people who liked one another and who therefore expected their help to be reciprocated. However, the choice problem was not a Prisoner's Dilemma; there was no "sucker's payoff" nor did subjects have an opportunity to exploit the partner.

In "reward contingency" research, a subject's rewards depend partly or wholly on another's choices. These studies have also suggested that dependence promotes social behavior, but the reward structure was not a Prisoner's Dilemma; thus, the results may not be generalizable to cooperation. Moreover, reward contingency is not equivalent to "future dependence" in the study by Carnevale and colleagues. These studies did not distinguish between these two dimensions of dependence, even though it is likely that both were present in the designs.

We believe the dependence-cooperation theory has sufficient theoretical importance to warrant a systematic test. In this paper, we report results of two experiments that measured the effect of dependence on cooperation under controlled conditions. We also elaborate the theory by distinguishing two dimensions of dependence that are confounded in previous research. We call these "relational" and "resource" dependence. Relational dependence refers to the inability to choose a different exchange partner. Following Pruitt and Kimmel, Carnevale et al. hypothesized that the need for future help from a reliable partner increases the willingness to cooperate. If so, then the lower the probability that both partners will remain, the weaker the incentive.

Resource dependence refers to the inability to obtain a desired outcome by one's own efforts, without the partner's cooperation. It is the opposite of self-reliance, and corresponds to reward contingency in an earlier generation of studies. Players with greater resources are less in need of a partner's help, although some resource dependence is implied by the tension between individual and collective interests that defines all Prisoner's Dilemma games. Put differently, resource dependence refers to the need for *any* partner's help, while relational dependence refers to the need for a *particular* partner's help. We hypothesize that resource dependence reduces the risk of exploitation: If you have few resources, you have little to lose by cooperating. Conversely, relational dependence reduces the temptation to exploit your partner: If you have no one else to turn to in the future, you have a lot to lose by defecting.

To independently manipulate each dimension, we designed a new research tool that embeds the Prisoner's Dilemma in a card game called Trump. The

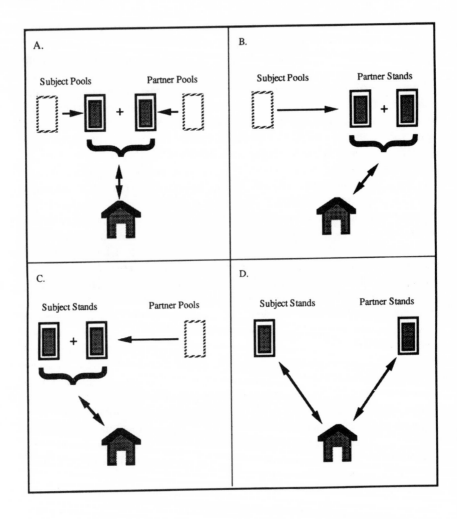

Figure 1. Outcomes when Subject and Partner Cooperate
(Pool) or Defect (Stand)

design highlights awareness of dependence on a partner's help and allows us to control resource dependence using the value of the card dealt to the subject. The lower the card, the more difficult it is to win without the partner's help. We manipulated relational dependence using the rule for partner selection to control the subject's ability to leave or keep the current partner. We then measured the independent effects on cooperation of each dimension as well as their interaction.

TRUMP

Trump is an online, computer-run card game based on a three-way interaction between the subject, a "partner," and the "House." The object of the game is to win as many chips as possible by beating the House. The basic unit of play is a hand, and each round of Trump consists of 21 hands. At the beginning of a hand, each player receives a card that only the owner can see. Hence, the House's and partner's cards are always face down on the subject's screen, while the subject's card is face up.[3] The subject's card ranges in value from two to ten, as does the partner's card, while the House's card ranges from six to ten. The subject has to make two choices, whether to stand (defect) or pool (cooperate) and how much to bet on the hand. All bets range from 5 to 25 in increments of 5. The House matches the pot (the total bet by both players), so that for any given hand, the total amount awarded is twice the combined bets of the subject and partner.

The payoff is based on the decisions made by both the subject and the partner and the relative values of the three cards. Figure 1 shows how the decisions to cooperate or defect change the relative payoffs. If both the subject and the partner cooperate ("pool"), the values of the two player's cards are added together and compared to the value of the House's card (Figure 1a). If the combined cards of the subject and partner exceed (or trump) the value of the House's card, both the subject and the partner win. The pot (the subject's and partner's bet, and the House's matching bet) are then divided equally between the subject and the partner. If the combined cards of the subject and the partner fail to exceed (are less than or equal to) the value of the House's card, then both the subject and the partner lose their bets.

If the subject cooperates but the partner defects ("stands"), the partner takes the subject's card and plays alone with both cards against the House (Figure 1b). If the combined cards, now solely in the possession of the partner, exceed the value of the House's card, then the partner wins the pot. If the combined cards fail to beat the House's card, then the House wins the pot. Either way, the subject receives nothing.

Alternatively, if the subject chooses to stand, but the partner pools, the outcomes are reversed (Figure 1c). In this case, the subject takes the partner's card and plays alone with both cards against the House. If the combined cards, now solely in the possession of the subject, trump the House, the subject wins the pot. Otherwise, the subject loses his or her bet. Either way, the partner receives nothing.

Finally, if both the subject and the partner choose to defect ("stand"), each takes on the House independently (Figure 1d). The subject either wins or loses a side bet against the House, and the outcome has no effect on the partner (and vice versa).

Given the use of cards that vary from hand to hand, Trump deviates from the traditional formulation of the PD design by having a stochastic payoff matrix. The expected payoff is the probability of beating the House, multiplied by the size of the pot, minus the amount bet. If the House wins, the subject loses the bet and gets back nothing, regardless of either player's decision to stand or pool. If the House loses, the subject either gets the whole pot, half the shared pot, the subject's side bet with the House, or nothing. The probability of each of these outcomes depends on the cards dealt to each player and the decisions to stand or pool. The size of the pot depends on the amount bet by each player. The change in cards and bets from hand to hand means that the game moves around a Prisoner's Dilemma "game space" that includes areas that border the PD. The core of the game space is defined by the expected payoff for each of the four combinations of player choices, given the probability distribution for card values and bets.

To simplify, let us regard the amount bet as a "sunk cost" and focus only on the relative "payback." Suppose Alter defects (stands). If Ego cooperates (pools), the probability of winning is zero, even if Alter beats the House with the combined cards. Hence, the "sucker's payoff" is zero ($S = 0$). If Ego defects, the probability of winning increases with the value of Ego's card, with a total of 10 possible winning card combinations out of 45 total combinations, or $P = 0.22$.

Suppose Alter cooperates (pools), and the combined cards trump the House. All else being equal (including the amount bet by each player), the size of Ego's winnings will be the same if both players cooperate (R) or if both defect (P). However, the probability of beating the House with two cards is much greater, giving $R = 0.83$.

For any given pot, the size of the winner's share doubles when Ego stands (T) rather than pools (R). Hence $T = 2R$, or $T = 1.66$. The K statistic for this payoff matrix is 0.37, about equal to the index of cooperation for the most commonly used PD game in experimental research ($K = 0.4$).[4]

We do not assume that subjects have the cognitive ability or inclination to calculate expected payoffs. However, validity checks confirm that subjects knew they were better off if their partner cooperated, no matter what the subject chose to do. They also were aware that cooperation carried the risk of exploitation by their partner, while defection posed the opportunity to keep the whole pot without having to share. This tension between individual and collective interests is the critical requirement for a test of the effect of dependence on cooperation in a mixed-motive game.

We are also confident that subjects knew they could not win alone against the House with a card less than seven. The value of the subject's card was revealed to the subject before they decided to stand or pool, and this information alters the game's incentive structure. We used this to test whether resource dependence induced cooperation by negating the use of defection as an aggressive or defensive strategy. If defection is *aggressive*, motivated by greed (the opportunity to free ride), then higher cards should increase defection as they increase the probability of winning with the partner's help. If defection is *defensive*, motivated by fear (the opportunity to go it alone and avoid being suckered), then higher cards should increase defection as they increase the probability of winning without the partner's help. The need for a seven or higher to beat the House allowed us to distinguish between these two possible motivations for dependent cooperation. For card values of six or below, the subject cannot win without the partner's help. Hence, below seven, higher cards increase the ability to win by exploiting the partner, but do not increase the ability to defect and win alone. For values above six, higher cards increase self-reliance as well as the ability to win by taking the partner's card. If resource dependence induces cooperation by restraining greed (Don't cheat when you can't win), we should expect defection to increase monotonically across the full range of card values (2-10). If resource dependence induces cooperation by negating fear (Cooperate if you have nothing to lose), defection should remain flat as card values increase in the region 2-6, and increase sharply with card value in the region 7-10.

Trump also differs from the conventional PD game in allowing players to "exit," that is, to leave their partner in favor of another.[5] We manipulated relational dependence using three exit conditions:

- No-exit (permanent pairings).
- Elective-exit (an option to leave the partner and request reassignment from the "single's pool" of unattached and rejected players).[6]
- Forced-exit (partners were always reassigned after each hand).

In the first experiment, we compared the exit option to a no-exit game in which the partner never changed. Subjects in the elective-exit condition had the option to *leave* an unwanted partner. In the second experiment, we compared the exit option to a game in which the partner always changed after each hand. In this design, subjects in the elective-exit condition had the option to *remain* with a desired partner.

Trump requires 12 players, the subject and 11 potential partners. This number makes random pairings highly unlikely to generate ongoing interaction with the same partner. Although subjects were told they were interacting with one of the other 11 subjects seated around the room, in actuality, the partner was always a computer simulant. In order to reinforce this illusion, all computers appeared to link into a local area network. Realistic delays were also built into the game at moments when a real partner might be expected to take time to respond.

All 11 of the simulated partners were programmed to follow the same rules of interaction when playing each other as they used when interacting with the subject. In other words, each subject played with 11 simulated partners, 10 of whom played one another when they were not paired with the subject. Each computer was entirely independent, so that each subject's choices had no effect on the stimuli received by other subjects. This allowed individual-level analysis of the data. All subjects received the same series of cards in the same pseudo-random order. The cards dealt to the partner and the House were also identical across subjects.

After each hand, the computer displayed the following information: the other two cards (belonging to the partner and the House), the partner's decision to stand or pool, how much the partner bet, and the respective winnings of each player and the House. When the subject was ready to continue, the subject initiated the next hand. New cards were dealt and the partnerships were updated. The computer designated each player by a letter that was consistent throughout each round of play. The screen displayed the pairings, including the number of hands each pairing lasted. This provided the subject with information about the relative stability of all relationships. The display made it very easy for subjects in the elective pairing condition to know which members chose to stay together.

We did not convert subject's winnings into cash, another difference with most PD experiments. Instead, subjects were eligible for one of several cash prizes. The top 10 percent of the subjects who had the highest earnings across six randomly selected hands (out of 42) received $40. This payment system motivated subjects to win as many hands as possible. Previous PD researchers have used a pay-as-you-go design in which each decision to cooperate or defect changed the subject's earnings by only a few cents. This incentive may be too small to motivate defection, especially as cumulative earnings increase over time (Snijders and Raub 1996). In contrast, our lottery design confronted subjects with an all-or-nothing earnings opportunity. Any given hand could be the one that determined who won a prize. Hence, the choice was not simply a matter of a few cents more or less; it was a choice in which $40 could be at stake.

We did not want competition for prizes to make the game zero-sum or undermine an interest in mutual cooperation. Therefore, we had subjects compete against everyone who signed up to participate in the experiment, not just the 11 others in the room at a particular time. In addition, with multiple prizes, a subject could win by being part of one of the more successful dyads. That the partner might also win would not prevent the subject from enjoying the full value of the prize. Unless one was blessed with naïve partners, mutual cooperation was the next best hope of winning a prize, even though one of the partners might win as well.

Advantages of Trump over Conventional PD Designs

In addition to the motivating effect of an all-or-nothing prize, our card-game format has two additional advantages over conventional "give-some, take-some" experimental designs in PD research. First, the Trump game allows the independent manipulation of multiple dimensions of dependence. The pairing rules manipulate relational dependence, the ability to keep or leave the current partner. By controlling the subject's card, we could also vary resource dependence, or self-reliance. The latter could also be achieved by changing the values in a formal payoff matrix, but we were concerned that subjects might not perceive a change in the payoffs as increased or decreased need for the partner's help. Cards provided a tangible representation of a valued asset whose quantity could vary from hand to hand.

Second, the game reinforces the perception of collective interests by pitting the two partners against a "common enemy," a construct that is missing in conventional experimental PD designs. A Prisoner's Dilemma is actually a three-actor coalition game, not a dyadic conflict. In the didactic presentation of the problem, the coalition target is readily apparent. It is the policeman trying to extract confessions from two prisoners by playing them against one another. However, the third player is often missing in conventional give-some, take-some experimental designs. In these designs, the target of the coalition is hidden: It is the experimentalist who must pay out more money if the subjects can successfully collude. Yet the experimentalist typically remains invisible to the players. This is accomplished by embedding subjects' mutual interests in a highly abstract payoff structure. Without a tangible target, "goal interdependence is rather difficult to understand for most naïve subjects" (Rabbie 1991, p. 246). Trump addresses this problem by introducing a third player, the House. The need to pool resources against a common opponent makes subjects palpably dependent on help from their partners.

EXPERIMENT 1: DESIGN

Experiment 1 tested the effects of resource and relational dependence on cooperation, as well as their interaction. We manipulated relational dependence by giving subjects an option to leave the partner in favor of a new partner randomly selected from the "single's pool" of unattached players. The option to exit allows aggressive players to use a strategy of "hit and run" and creates uncertainty about the prospects for tacit collusion with an on-going partner. Hypothesis 1 predicts the main effect of relational dependence:

Hypothesis 1. Holding card values constant, cooperation is greater with permanent pairings (the no-exit condition) than with elective pairings.

The ability to exploit is affected not only by the prospect of future interaction but also by the value of the subject's card. Hypothesis 2a predicts the main effect of resource dependence:

Hypothesis 2a. For a given pairing condition, cooperation decreases with the value of the card.

The effect of card value on cooperation may not be linear. For card values below seven (the minimum required to beat the House), higher cards have no effect on the ability to win alone, but they increase the ability to beat the House by taking the partner's card. Hence, if perceived weakness restrains greed (the willingness to take the partner's card without sharing the pot), then we should expect cooperation to decrease monotonically as card values increase over the entire range, from two to 10. However, if resource dependence allays the fear of being suckered, we should expect cooperation to remain flat for cards between two and six, and to increase with the value of the card thereafter:

Hypothesis 2b.   Cooperation decreases with the value of the card only for cards above six.

Finally, dependence on the partner for help in the future may moderate the effect of resource dependence on cooperation. Specifically, the willingness to defect with a low card indicates greed but not fear (given the inability to win without the partner's help). If relational dependence constrains greed, then we can expect:

Hypothesis 3a.   Cooperation with low cards is more likely with a permanent partner than with elective pairings.

Alternatively, subjects with a high card (who do not need the partner's immediate help) may nevertheless anticipate the need for future help from an ongoing partner. However, they will then cooperate only if they are willing to risk the loss of a valuable asset. If defection is motivated by fear, not greed, and if relational dependence allays the fear of being suckered, then we can expect:

Hypothesis 3b.   Cooperation with high cards is more likely with a permanent partner than with elective pairings.

Subjects

A total of 43 undergraduates, counterbalanced for gender, participated in the first experiment. All subjects were recruited from introductory psychology and sociology courses and received course credit for participation. In addition, subjects competed for one of four cash prizes. The four subjects with the highest point-totals across six randomly selected trials (out of 42) received $40. Subjects participated in groups of twelve (including confederates used to fill out the group as necessary). Subjects were aware that they were competing for prizes not only with the other eleven subjects in their group but with subjects recruited to other groups as well.

Stimulus

Experiment 1 involved each subject in two rounds of Trump, each consisting of 21 hands. One round offered an exit option and the other did not, with the sequence balanced across subjects as a control on exposure effects.[7] In the no-exit condition, subjects had the impression they were paired with the same partner for the duration of the round. The six player-pairings listed on the computer display never changed. In contrast, in the elective-exit condition, subjects had the opportunity to keep or change their partner at the beginning of each hand (before cards were dealt). Any subjects who elected to change their partners were placed in a singles pool consisting of other players who either elected not to remain with their partner or were rejected by their partner.

Simulated Partner Strategies

Simulated partners chose to stand or pool with fixed probabilities that were not dependent on the subject's previous move. This made it easier for subjects in the elective-exit condition to identify the most desirable partners. (Post-experiment validity checks were used to confirm subjects' ability to discriminate among their potential partners.) Simulated partners differed in the probability of cooperation, ranging from 0.1 to 0.9, with an expected cooperation rate of 0.5 and a standard deviation of 0.3. The probabilities were based on pseudo-random numbers to standardize stimuli for all subjects. In addition, simulants played a strategy of "exit for tat." Whenever the subject defected, they were randomly assigned a new partner.

The simulant strategy was identical across all treatment groups. We only manipulated the *representation* of the partner to the subjects, not the actual simulant programming. In contrast to the elective-exit condition, subjects in the no-exit condition did not know they could be assigned a new partner, nor did they have the opportunity to request reassignment. In this condition, the simulant's "exit for tat" strategy was behaviorally equivalent to a change in the simulant's propensity to cooperate, following defection by the subject. In effect, the simulant played a variant of the "Pavlov" strategy (Nowak and Sigmund 1993; Macy 1995) in which the probability of cooperation changes when the outcome is unsatisfactory (the partner defects).

Procedure

Upon arrival at an on-campus computer lab, subjects were seated at twelve computers arranged around the perimeter of the room, facing outward and placed so that subjects could not inadvertently see a neighbor's screen. Subjects were told that the partner could be any one of the eleven other players. The experimenter then gave each subject a card with an ID code and ID number. The ID code was used as an identifier for each subject's data. The ID number was used to randomly assign each subject to one of two treatment sequences (exit followed by no-exit or no-exit followed by exit).

After entering their identifying information, subjects participated in an interactive demonstration of the rules of the game. The demonstration ended with a three-question quiz that tested the subject's comprehension of the game. The quiz included a question that specifically checked whether subjects understood that they could still beat the House with a low card (such as a "3") if the partner chose to pool and they chose to stand. Subjects who did not answer all three questions correctly were shown a summary of the rules of the game and asked to retake the quiz. The demonstration included a display similar to Figure 1, showing the four outcomes corresponding to the four combinations of stand and pool by each of the two players. This visual aid remained in view during the entire game in order that subjects could refer to it if they needed a reminder.

To insure that all subjects started playing at the same time, subjects were required to enter a password that the experimenter announced only after all subjects had completed the demonstration. Once this password was entered, the computers appeared to link into the local area network, and once this was completed, the subjects began to play. The total time of play was 20 minutes. The first round ended after 21 hands; the second round ended at the end of the 20-minute period, but only the first 21 hands were included in the data analysis. The time limit was necessary to maintain the deception that subjects were interacting with one another. (They could not tell when other subjects started the second round, but obviously knew when the experiment had ended.) Two subjects failed to complete the second round and were subsequently dropped from the study, leaving a total of 41 subjects.

The computer recorded the treatment sequence, the decision to stand or pool, and the amount bet in each hand (by the subject and the 11 simulants), the six pairings, the decision to exit (where applicable), the outcome of each hand for each player, and their accumulated winnings.

Upon completion of play, subjects were administered a nine-item survey designed to measure the motivations underlying their behavior. Within two weeks, a longer survey was mailed to each subject. This instrument was designed to measure social value orientations, using the Van Lange (Van Lange and Kuhlman 1994) and Mach tests (Christie and Geis 1970). In addition, the instrument included several personality measures, as well as three items designed to test the credibility of the deception (without disclosing it).[9] The affective measures are not used in this study but will be considered (along with gender) in a future paper on cooperation, dependence, and social value orientation.

EXPERIMENT 1:   RESULTS

Effect of Dependence on Cooperation

We tested the effect of dependence using repeated-measures analysis of variance in cooperation. Cooperation was measured in each round as the proportion of hands in which the subject chose to pool. The analysis was based on a 2 (card: high, low) by 2 (exit: yes, no) by 2 (sequence: exit first, exit last) factorial design, with repeated measures for card value and exit, the two dimensions of dependence manipulated in this study. Sequence was a between-subject factor used to control for exposure effects. Half the subjects experienced the exit condition first; the others experienced the no-exit condition first. Cards were classified as low (2-6) or high (7-10) based on the inability to trump the House without the partner's help. (The House's minimum card was a six, which could only be trumped by a seven or higher.) The results are summarized in Table 1 and illustrated in Figure 2.

Contrary to Hypothesis 1, we found no significant main effect of relational dependence. The rate of cooperation was not significantly greater in the no-exit condition, compared to the exit. However, we found a highly significant main effect of card, $F(1, 39) = 92.26$, $p < 0.001$. Cooperation levels were on average twice as high in the low-card condition compared to the high-card condition, as predicted by Hypothesis 2a.

We also found a significant interaction between card value and exit condition, $F(1,39) = 22.51$, $p < 0.001$. A post hoc analysis using the Tukey procedure (Stevens 1992) revealed that when subjects were dealt a high-card, cooperation was significantly higher in the no-exit condition (0.45) compared to the exit group (0.31), as predicted by Hypothesis 3b. In other words, when subjects had a high card (and thus did not necessarily need their partner's cooperation), they were more likely to pool than when they believed they were permanently paired with their partner. (Nevertheless, cooperation remained well below the rate observed when subjects were dealt a low card).

In contrast, with low cards, we found no difference in the level of cooperation between the exit and no-exit groups, contrary to Hypothesis 3a. Relational dependence appears to have reduced the fear of losing a high card, but it had no effect on the temptation to try to win alone with a low card by taking the partner's card. This aggressive behavior was relatively uncommon in both the no-exit and exit treatments (with 0.72 and 0.76 rates of cooperation, respectively).

To give a more precise measure of the effect of card value, we calculated the within-subject correlation between cooperation and card value and then tested whether the correlation depended on the ability to win alone against the House. We also tested for interaction between resource and relational dependence, using repeated-measures analysis of variance in the association between card value and cooperation. The results are summarized in Table 2 and illustrated in Figure 3. In the low-card region (2-6), higher card values had no effect on cooperation, even though they increased the ability to successfully exploit the partner's help by choosing to stand. In the high-card region (7-10), higher card values had a strong linear effect on cooperation, with $r = -0.254$ in the no-exit condition and $r = -0.371$ in the exit condition. The difference in card-effect above and below the critical value was highly significant ($p < 0.001$), regardless of exit condition ($p = -0.419$). This strongly supports Hypothesis 2b. Cooperation tended to decrease with the ability to win alone against the House. Otherwise, the ability to win with the partner's card had no effect on cooperation.

Table 1. Repeated Measures Analysis of Variance in
Cooperation by Card Value (Low, High), Exit (Yes, No), and
Sequence (Exit Æ No-Exit, No-Exit Æ Exit)

Source	DF	MS	F	p
Between Subjects Effects				
Sequence	1	165.44	.09	.765
Error	39	1827.69		
Within Subjects Effects				
Card Value	1	49967.74	92.96	<.001
Sequence * Card Value	1	128.56	.24	.628
Error	39	537.51		
Exit	1	910.10	1.28	.264
Sequence * Exit	1	1578.33	2.23	.144
Error	39	708.41		
Exit * Card Value	1	3353.17	22.51	<.001
Sequence * Card * Exit	1	8.12	.05	.817
Error	39	148.99		

EXPERIMENT 1:   DISCUSSION

This experiment confirmed previous research showing that dependence increases
the willingness to cooperate. However, the effect of resource dependence is much
stronger than relational dependence. The weak main effect of relational dependence suggests that the opportunity to "hit and run" is not as important as conventional game-theoretic analysis would suggest. On the contrary, cooperation in
permanent relationships was higher than in elective pairings only when resource
dependence was low (that is, when the subject had a high card). This suggests that
relational dependence reduced subjects' fear of exploitation, not their temptation
to exploit. This pattern parallels what we observed with resource dependence.
Cooperation decreased with higher cards only when card values exceeded the
minimum required to beat the House. Subjects appear to have used a strategy of
helping when help was needed.

EXPERIMENT 2:   DESIGN

Experiment 1 compared a game with an option to exit and a game where exit was
precluded. Subjects were required to remain with a permanent partner or were
given the option to leave. In Experiment 2, an identical exit decision had the opposite framing. We compared a game with an elective exit to a game where exit was

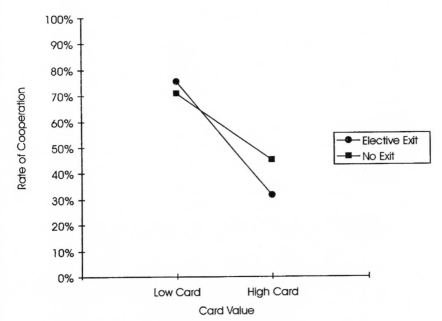

Figure 2. Rate of Cooperation by Card Value (Low, High) and
Exit Condition (No-Exit, Exit)

Table 2. Repeated Measures Analysis of Variance in Card-Effect by
Card Value (Low, High) and Exit (Yes, No)

Source	DF	MS	F	p
Card Value	1	2.86	25.43	<.001
Error	40	.11		
Exit Condition	1	.27	3.05	.089
Error	40	.09		
Exit Condition * Card Value	1	.05	.67	.419
Error	40	.08		

compulsory. In this design, subjects were required to change partners after each
hand, or were given the option to stay. Relational dependence varied with the ability to *remain* with a partner, instead of the ability to *leave*.

This experiment tested whether the effect of resource dependence on cooperation was a rational response to changing incentives or a heuristic response to perceived weakness. In a game with a very low probability of re-encounter, the
optimal strategy is hit and run, regardless of the value of the card. Even if the

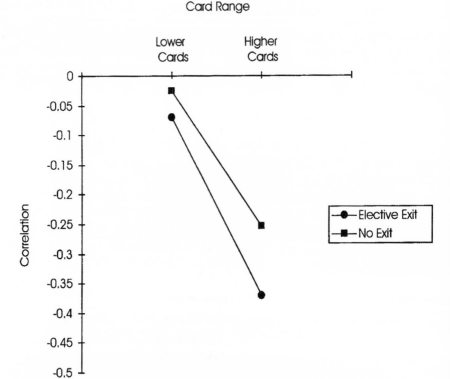

Figure 3. Correlation between Card Value and Cooperation by
Exit Condition (No-Exit, Exit) and Card Range (2-6,7-10)

subject's card is too low to win alone against the House, there is a nontrivial
chance that the partner will cooperate. If so, the subject's payoff for defection will
be double the payoff for cooperation. With no opportunity for tacit collusion,
rationality dictates defection, regardless of the value of the card. Hence, Hypothesis 4 predicts less cooperation with zero relational dependence:

Hypothesis 4. Holding card values constant, cooperation is lower with compulsory exit than when exit is optional.

An alternative hypothesis is that the response to dependence is *heuristic* rather
than *rational*. The need for the partner's help may activate a rule to "cooperate
when you need help from others." Subjects can then be expected to pool when they
feel they need their partner's help, even though they are better off choosing to
stand. Hence, the effect of resource dependence on cooperation should be as

strong in the random-pairing condition as it is when subjects have the opportunity to remain with a partner. Hypothesis 5a predicts the main effect of resource dependence:

Hypothesis 5a. For a given pairing condition, cooperation decreases with the value of the card.

We saw in Experiment 1 that the effect of card value on cooperation was highly nonlinear. For cards below seven, higher cards had no effect on the ability to win alone, but they increased the ability to beat the House by taking the partner's card. Hypothesis 5b predicts a nonlinear effect of resource dependence:

Hypothesis 5b. Cooperation decreases with the value of the card only for cards above six.

Although we found little evidence that subjects in Experiment 1 were using an aggressive strategy, a game with ever-changing partners may encourage predatory behavior. If relational dependence constrains greed, then we can expect:

Hypothesis 6a. Cooperation with low cards is more likely with elective than with compulsory exit.

Alternatively, subjects with high cards (who have less need for the partner's immediate help) may nevertheless anticipate the need for future help from an ongoing partner. However, they will cooperate only if they are willing to risk the loss of a valuable asset. If relational dependence allays this fear, then we can expect:

Hypothesis 6b. Cooperation with high cards is more likely with elective than with compulsory exit.

Subjects

A total of 40 undergraduates, counterbalanced for gender, participated in the second experiment. Recruitment, experimental procedure, payment, and follow up were identical to that in Experiment 1, except that the partnership rules were changed. In one condition, subjects had the option to keep or change partners, identical to the elective-pairing condition used in Experiment 1. In the other condition (forced-exit), instead of playing with a permanent partner, subjects were randomly assigned a new partner for each new hand. Although the partner appeared to change after every hand, in reality, the simulants continued to play the same "exit for tat" strategy as in the elective exit condition. As in Experiment 1, the two treatment conditions differed in the appearance of an option to exit but not in the actual behavioral responses of the simulated partner. In the course of playing the two rounds, all subjects experienced both the forced-exit and the elective-exit conditions. The sequence of rounds was reversed in a balanced design.

EXPERIMENT 2: RESULTS

Effect of Dependence on Cooperation

As before, we measured cooperation as the number of times a subject choose to pool within a given round of 21 hands. We tested the effect of elective exit on cooperation using an eight-factor, 2 (card: high, low) by 2 (exit: elective, forced) by 2 (sequence: elective first, elective last) analysis of variance, with repeated measures for exit and card. Effects are reported in Table 3 and depicted in Figure 4. As predicted in Hypothesis 5a, we found only a main effect of card, $F(1, 38) = 163.20$, $p < 0.001$, and no other significant main effects. As before, cooperation was twice as frequent in the low-card condition compared to the high-card. However, contrary to Hypothesis 6a and Hypothesis 6b, the effect did not depend on the opportunity to form a committed relationship (the elective-exit condition). In the forced-exit condition, there was no rational reason to pool a low card, given the low probability of remaining with the current partner. Yet subjects continued to follow the rule to cooperate when in need. Contrary to Hypothesis 4, the rate of cooperation was no greater when exits were optional.

Table 3. Repeated Measures Analysis of Variance in Cooperation by Card Value (Low, High), Exit (Forced, Elective), and Sequence (Forced → Elective, Elective → Forced)

Source	DF	MS	F	p
Between Subjects Effects				
Sequence	1	1133.78	3.21	.081
Error	38	3635.96		
Within Subjects Effects				
Card Value	1	77480.01	177.37	<.001
Sequence * Card Value	1	402.07	.92	.343
Error	38	436.83		
Exit Condition	1	33.89	.08	.778
Sequence * Exit Condition	1	5511.82	13.14	<.001
Error	38	419.37		
Card Value * Exit Condition	1	208.68	.72	.402
Sequence * Card * Exit Condition	1	12.40	.04	.837
Error	38	290.00		

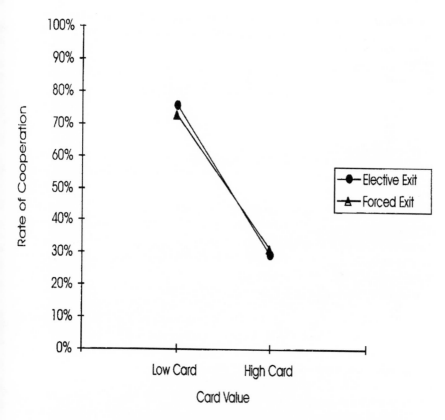

Figure 4.   Rate of Cooperation by Card Value (Low, High) and
Exit Condition (Elective, Forced)

To give a more precise measure of the effect of card value, we calculated the within-subject correlation between cooperation and card value and then tested whether the correlation depended on the ability to win alone against the House. We also tested for interaction between resource and relational dependence, using repeated-measures analysis of variance in the association between card value and cooperation. The results are summarized in Table 4 and illustrated in Figure 5. The difference in card-effect above and below the critical value was highly significant ($p < 0.001$), regardless of exit condition ($p < 0.973$). The effects for the elective-exit condition were identical to those observed in this same condition in Experiment 1. In the low-card region, higher card values had no effect on cooperation, even though they increased the ability to successfully exploit the partner's help by choosing to stand. In the high-card region, higher card values had a

Table 4. Repeated Measures Analysis of Variance in Card-Effect by
Card Value (Low, High) and Exit (Forced, Elective)

Source	DF	MS	F	p
Card Value	1	4.05	23.68	<.001
Error	39	.17		
Exit Condition	1	.31	4.50	.040
Error	39	.07		
Exit Condition * Card Value	1	.00	.00	.973
Error	39	.11		

strong linear effect on cooperation ($r = -0.348$), as predicted by hypothesis
Hypothesis 5b. However, in the forced-exit condition, higher cards reduced cooperation more so than in the elective-exit condition ($p < 0.040$). This was the case
even as cards increased in the region that was too low to win alone against the
House ($r = -.118$). Not surprisingly, with high cards, the effect of resource
dependence was even more pronounced ($r = -0.438$).

EXPERIMENT 2:   DISCUSSION

The second experiment replicates and extends the findings of Experiment 1. Once
again, the impact of resource dependence was strikingly demonstrated. Subjects
were more likely to stand when they did not need their partner's help and more
likely to pool when they did. The new finding is that dependence induced cooperation even when there was no chance of building a committed relationship, and
hence, nothing to be gained by pooling. It is possible that subjects simply failed to
understand that they could win with a low card if the partner pooled. However, this
possibility was emphasized in the instructions and subjects were specifically
tested on this point before the experiment began. Therefore, it is unlikely that
subjects chose to pool out of ignorance. It is also possible that subjects in the
forced-exit condition nevertheless glimpsed the "shadow of the future," since it
was likely that a partner would be revisited at least once over 42 hands. However,
subjects had no way to record a partner's behavior for later recall. Thus, while the
forced-exit condition was not equivalent to a one-shot PD, the level of relational
dependence was effectively zero, and certainly much lower than in a game with the
option to remain permanently paired with a single partner. Yet we found no difference in the levels of cooperation between elective and forced exit. Subjects pooled
their low cards in the forced-exit condition, even though, with constantly changing
partners, they had little or nothing to gain by doing so. A reasonable interpretation
is that the effect of dependence on cooperation is heuristic rather than rational,
based on a rule to "offer help when help is needed."

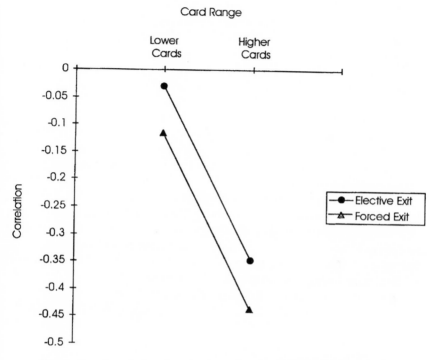

Figure 5. Correlation between Card Value and Cooperation by Exit Condition (Elective, Forced) and Card Range (2-6,7-10)

The increase in defection with high cards appears to be largely a defensive response to the fear of being suckered, not an aggressive response to "strength," a pattern also observed in Experiment 1. The effect of greater resources was relatively weak until the resource-level reached the critical point required to win without the partner's help. Nevertheless, we did observe indications of greater aggressiveness with very low relational dependence. In the forced-exit condition, defection increased slightly with the ability to win by taking the partner's card, a strategy that was rarely indicated in either the elective-exit or no-exit conditions.

GENERAL DISCUSSION

When dealt a low card, subjects tended to pool, regardless of their relational dependence on the partner. Their need for their partner's help caused them to act cooperatively, despite the opportunity to receive that help without reciprocating. Instead, subjects appear to have used a heuristic that says, "If you need your partner's help, offer yours." This was even the case in the forced-exit condition, where cooperation could not be used to engineer a tacit collusion. With zero relational dependence, there was no rational reason to pool, regardless of the card the subject had been dealt. Thus, the strong effect of resource dependence on cooperative behavior does not appear to be instrumentally motivated. However, further study is required to determine if this heuristic is a learned behavioral response to perceived weakness or an internalized social norm that proscribes receiving help without offering one's own.

When dealt a high card, subjects tended to stand. However, in the no-exit condition, subjects were less prone to stand with a high card. In this treatment, subjects did not have the option to exit and believed they remained paired with the same partner for the entire round. The higher level of relational dependence in this condition appears to have induced "helping behavior" by reducing the risk of exploitation. This helping behavior was much less frequent when the partner was not permanently attached, due to either an optional or compulsory exit.

Finally, the effect of resource dependence appears to be mainly a *defensive* response to increased self-reliance. Higher cards prompted subjects to defect only after the card value exceeded the critical point required to win without the partner's help. Subjects were clearly reluctant to win by taking the partner's card without offering their own. Moreover, this reluctance appears to be related to the level of relational dependence. The need for the partner's help in the future, in the no-exit and elective-exit conditions, may have nullified the temptation to aggressively exploit the partner.

Scope Conditions and Directions for Future Research

This study is the first step in a program of incremental research on exit effects, dependence, and cooperation in social dilemmas. In this first round of experiments, resource dependence clearly overshadowed relational dependence. Subjects apparently used their card value as a simple heuristic for when to pool. With a low card, they tended to cooperate, regardless of the embeddedness of their relationships. Relational dependence only induced cooperation in the absence of resource dependence, that is, when subjects were dealt a high card and were less in need of the partner's help.

We found no evidence that the opportunity to exit encouraged a strategy of hit and run. However, it is possible that the opportunity to exploit was offset by a tendency to "flee rather than fight," that is, to abandon an unsatisfactory relationship rather than retaliate. In addition, mutual defection with a permanent partner may have led to resignation, which was attenuated in the elective-exit condition by the opportunity to walk away and create a "fresh start." We leave these possibilities for future research.

As a further test of the effect of relational dependence, we are currently replicating Experiments 1 and 2 but with all cards face down, such that the subjects' cards are not revealed until after the decision to stand or pool. If they do not know the card they are dealt, subjects may attend more carefully to the partner that they have been dealt, and to the opportunity to look for someone better. We hypothesize that uncertainty about the need for the partner's help may increase the effects of relational dependence.

The exit option allowed subjects to abandon a partner but did not give them any control over the partner they would be paired with next. The effect of elective pairing on cooperation might be increased if subjects could influence the selection of the partner. We plan to test this by adding the option to request specific partners.

Finally, we plan to eventually replace simulated partners with human subjects. This will compromise our ability to control the individual-level stimulus, which is why we began with simulated partners. However, by using groups as the unit of analysis, we can test whether the exit option leads to the segregation of cooperative and predatory players, thereby protecting the former from exploitation and facilitating the rehabilitation of predators by foreclosing opportunities to exploit. If so, then dependence on a permanent partner may have negative effects on cooperation that have been overlooked in previous research, including this study.

ACKNOWLEDGMENT

This research was supported by a grant from the National Science Foundation, #SBR 95-11461.

NOTES

1.   Along with Cook et al. (1983), see Skvoretz and Willer (1993); Bienenstock and Bonacich (1993); Markovsky, Willer, and Patton (1988).

2.   See Molm (1994) and Tallman, Gray, and Leik (1991) for discussions of "mutual dependence" and "interdependence" in social exchange. See also Bonacich (1995) and Willer and Skvoretz (1997).

3.   Trump can be played with any of the eight possible combinations of visible and nonvisible cards by House, subject, and partner. We used "own-card-up" in these experiments. In another study, we manipulate knowledge of card values, using three additional treatments: "both cards down," "both cards up," and "partner's card up." "Both cards up/down" tests the effect of uncertainty on cooperation, and "partner's card up" tests the effect of the partner's dependence on cooperation by the subject.

4.   According to Rapoport and Chammah (1965), $K = (R-P)/(T-S)$ and increases with the incentive to cooperate. A typical PD payoff matrix in experimental research has $T = 5$, $R = 3$, $P = 1$, and $S = 0$, giving $K = 0.4$

5.   For a rare laboratory study of Prisoner's Dilemma with an option to exit, see Orbell and Dawes (1993). They showed that subjects who intended to cooperate were less prone to exit than were those who intended to defect. However, they did not test whether the exit option made subjects more prone to cooperate.

6.   Note that when the single's pool is empty, the "exit" option can be exercised but to no avail.

7.   Cooperation was somewhat lower in the second round of play, and this may indicate a decline in initial naiveté as subjects gained experience. We controlled for this effect with a counterbalanced design, and we found no significant interactions between treatment order and other independent variables in the experiment.

8. Thirteen out of 83 subjects in the two experiments had to repeat the quiz three times. They were allowed to complete the experiment, but their quiz scores were recorded as a check against data anomalies and none were found.

9. Less than eight percent of subjects who completed the survey indicated suspicion that they might be playing a simulated partner. Rabbie (1991, p. 251) cites an unpublished meta-analysis that found less cooperation when subjects believed the partner was a computer rather than another person. We therefore checked these subjects carefully for behavioral anomalies but found none. By posing the possibility, the survey may have planted the suspicion post hoc.

10. We found a significant interaction between exit condition and treatment sequence ($p < .001$). The rate of cooperation in the elective exit condition was about the same, regardless of sequence. However, the rate of cooperation in the forced-exit condition was significantly greater when this condition occurred first rather than second. Prior exposure to the game may have taught subjects the futility of tacit collusion with a partner who was constantly changing. We anticipated the possibility of an exposure effect and therefore controlled for this with a fully counterbalanced design.

REFERENCES

Axelrod, R. 1984. *The Evolution of Cooperation.* New York: Basic Books.

Bienenstock, E., and P. Bonacich. 1993. "Game-Theory Models for Exchange Networks: Experimental Results." *Sociological Perspectives* 36: 117-135.

Bonacich, P. 1995. "Four Kinds of Social Dilemmas within Exchange Networks." *Current Research in Social Psychology* 1: 1-9.

Burgess, R. L., and D. Buschell, Jr. 1969. *Behavioral Sociology: The Experimental Analysis of Social Process.* New York: Columbia University Press.

Carnevale, P., D. Pruitt, and P. Carrington. 1982. "Effects of Future Dependence, Liking, and Repeated Requests for Help on Helping Behavior." *Social Psychology Quarterly* 45: 9-14.

Christie, R., and F. Geis. 1970. *Studies in Machiavellianism.* New York: Academic Press.

Cook, K., R. Emerson, M. Gillmore, and T. Yamagishi. 1983. "The Distribution of Power in Exchange Networks: Theory and Experimental Evidence." *American Journal of Sociology* 89: 275-305.

Durkheim, E. 1933. *The Division of Labor in Society.* New York: Free Press.

Hechter, M. 1987. *Principles of Group Solidarity.* Berkeley: University of California Press.

Macy, M. 1995. "PAVLOV and the Evolution of Cooperation: An Experimental Test." *Social Psychology Quarterly* 58: 74-87.

Markovsky, B., D. Willer, and T. Patton. 1988. "Power Relations in Exchange Networks." *American Sociological Review* 53: 220-236.

Michaels, J. W., and J. A. Wiggins. 1976. "Effects of Mutual Dependency and Dependency Asymmetry on Social Exchange." *Sociometry* 39: 368-373.

Molm, L. 1980. "The Effects of Structural Variations in Social Reinforcement Contingencies on Exchange and Cooperation." *Social Psychology Quarterly* 43: 269-282.

Molm, L. 1994. "Dependence and Risk: Transforming the Structure of Social Exchange. Special Issue: Conceptualizing Structure in Social Psychology." *Social Psychology Quarterly* 57: 163-176.

Nowak, M., and K. Sigmund. 1993. "A Strategy of Win-Stay, Lose-Shift that Outperforms Tit-for-Tat in the Prisoner's Dilemma Game." *Nature* 364: 56-58.

Orbell, J., and R. Dawes. 1993. "Social Welfare, Cooperators' Advantage, and the Option of Not Playing the Game." *American Sociological Review* 58: 787-800.

Pruitt D., and M. Kimmel. 1977. "Twenty Years of Experimental Gaming: Critique, Synthesis, and suggestions for the Future." *Annual Review of Psychology* 28: 363-392.

Rabbie, J. 1991. "Determinants of Intra-Group Cooperation." Pp. 238-262 in *Cooperation and Prosocial Behavior,* edited by R. Hinde and J. Groebel. Cambridge, UK: Cambridge University Press.

Rapoport, A., and A. Chammah. 1965. *Prisoner's Dilemma: A Study in Conflict and Cooperation.* Ann Arbor, MI: University of Michigan Press.

Snijders, C., and W. Raub. 1996. "Does 'The Motivating Power of Loss' Exist? An Experimental Test of the Effect of Losses on Cooperation." Pp. 205-214 in *Frontiers in Social Dilemmas Research*, edited by W. Liebrand and D. Messick. Berlin: Springer.

Skvoretz J., and D. Willer. 1993. "Exclusion and Power: A Test of Four Theories of Power in Exchange Networks." *American Sociological Review* 58: 801-818.

Stevens, J. 1992. *Applied Multivariate Statistics for the Social Sciences,* 2nd edition. Hillsdale, NJ: Lawrence Earbaum.

Tallman, I., L. Gray, and R. Leik. 1991. "Decisions, Dependency, and Commitment: An Exchange Based Theory of Group Formation." *Advances in Group Processes* 8: 227-257.

Willer, D. , and J. Skvoretz. 1997. "Games and Structures." *Rationality and Society* 9: 383-385.

Van Lange, P., and D. Kuhlman. 1994. "Social Value Orientations and Impressions of Partner's Honesty and Intelligence: A Test of the Might Versus Morality Effect. *Journal of Personality and Social Psychology* 67: 126-41.

POWER DISTRIBUTION IN CONFLICT NETWORKS:
AN EXTENSION OF ELEMENTARY THEORY TO CONFLICT NETWORKS*

Jacek Szmatka and Joanna Mazur

ABSTRACT

This research offers a theoretical model for study of conflict networks within the framework of Willer's elementary theory. Although this theory proposes three fundamental relations between actors, that is, exchange, coercion, and conflict, only research on exchange and coercion has been fruitful, generating much theory and empirical analysis. Therefore, there are several empirical studies uncovering basic structural principles of power distribution in exchange and coercion networks but no studies of conflict relations in networks. In this paper the new definition of the conflict relation is proposed that facilitates the experimental study of such relations in networks. As a part of a conflict network theory the model of different types of connection within conflict networks, such as exclusion, inclusion, and null, is developed and analyzed. Resistance theory is used to analyze power distribution in differently

Advances in Group Processes, Volume 15, pages 187-211.
Copyright © 1998 by JAI Press Inc.
All rights of reproduction in any form reserved.
ISBN: 0-7623-0362-X

connected conflict networks to prove that these conflict networks behave like their exchange versions. Also, the proposed network conflict theory is compared with the only existing studies on conflict in networks, that is, the theory and research on punishment by Linda Molm to show profound differences between the two. Finally, showing that resistance theory has direct application to conflict relations we demonstrate that network conflict theory is consistent with other aspects of Willer's elementary theory and can be considered as its extension.

INTRODUCTION

Elementary theory (hereafter, ET) is a theory of actors in positions in relationships in structures (Willer and Szmatka 1998, p. 276). ET has a cumulative research program (Szmatka and Lovaglia 1996), the branches of which are related to different types of social relationships between actors and different types of connections between positions (nodes) within the network (Willer 1987; Willer 1992; Willer, Markovsky and Patton 1989; Markovsky, Skvoretz, Willer, Lovaglia, and Erger 1993; Willer and Markovsky, 1993; Skvoretz and Willer 1991; Skvoretz and Willer 1993; Markovsky, Willer, and Patton 1988; Szmatka and Willer 1995; Szmatka 1998). For more than 20 years the theory has undergone intensive revision and development the range of structures to which the theory applies has been extended and new procedures for locating power, such as The Graph-Theoretic Power Index, have been developed (Willer, Simpson, and Pennell 1997). Recent developments have led to the discovery of weak power structures (Lovaglia, Skvoretz, Willer, and Markovsky 1995; Willer and Skvoretz 1997). Further, theoretical bridges have been formed which unite the theory with Status Characteristics and Expectation States Theory (Willer, Lovaglia, and Markovsky 1997) to explain how power produces influence.

In this paper we extend Elementary Theory to conflict networks. As originally formulated, the theory defines three types of social relations: exchange, coercion, and conflict (Willer 1987). Exchange is conceptualized as a mutual flow of positive sanctions, coercion as an asymmetric flow of positive sanctions in one direction and negative sanctions in the other, and conflict is originally (Willer 1987; Willer and Markovsky 1993) defined as a symmetric flow of negative sanctions. Most research related to the theory has dealt with exchange and coercive relations, thus leading to the advent of "Network Exchange Theory" (NET) and "Network Coercion Theory" (NCT) (Willer 1987; Willer and Szmatka 1993). The developments mentioned above in particular, were made in Network Exchange Theory which makes it one of the fastest growing theories in the field. There are also several interesting and important developments in Network Coercion Theory including promising empirical applications (Willer, Simpson, Szmatka, and Mazur 1996; Szmatka, Mazur and Simpson 1996). However, the abundance of work done

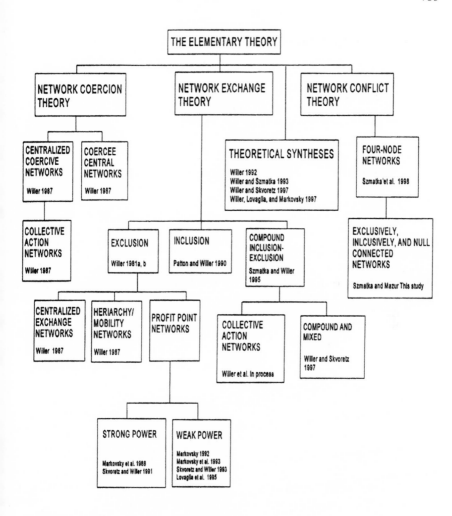

Figure 1. A Schematic for the Elementary Theoretic Research Program

in NET and NCT has resulted in a lack of theoretical or empirical work dealing with conflict relations in networks (see Figure 1).

A possible reason that no research has been done on conflict within the scope of Elementary Theory is how the theory models the conflict relationship. According to ET, no rational actor will ever enter a conflict relationship and start any negotiation with his/her partner. As we will show below, according to this formulation the only outcome of any negotiation is a negative sanction for both actors in a dyad. Therefore, we propose a new abstract model of conflict that, (1) better gen-

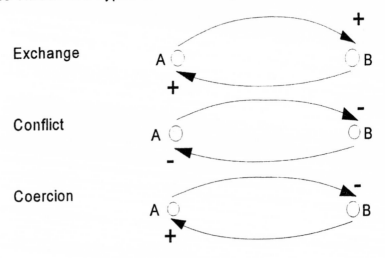

a) The Two Sanction Types

Positive

Negative

b) The Three Pure Types of Relationship

Exchange

Conflict

Coercion

Source: Willer (1987).

Figure 2.   Sanction and Relationship Types

eralizes to real-life conflict situations and, (2) makes the relationship rational for actors to enter and negotiate. We begin with an analysis of the various types of relations within the scope of ET. Next, we compare and contrast the model offered by Willer and the model proposed here. We then elaborate our model by applying three types of connections to conflict relations: null, exclusion, and inclusion.

Finally we apply the theory of resistance to make predictions for some networks. Also, we offer a comparison of Molm's punishment model (Molm 1997a) with the model proposed here.

THREE TYPES OF SOCIAL RELATIONSHIP

In Elementary Theory, three social relationships can be constructed using two actors and two sanction types: exchange, coercion, and conflict. The two sanction types and the three pure types of relations are shown in Figure 2.

A *positive sanction* is a social act that increases the payoff state of the actor receiving the sanction flow whereas a *negative sanction* is a social act that reduces the payoff state of the actor receiving the sanction flow. Elementary Theoretic actors can be individuals, small groups, large organizations and even nation states and are assumed to be rational. For example, the theory states that for any A-B flow, if B is rational, B prefers any positive sanction flow to no sanction flow, and no sanction flow to any negative sanction flow. The above holds true under Principle 1 of the Elementary Theory which asserts that *all social actors act to maximize their expected payoff state.* Furthermore, the above holds true for all three social relations.

THE MEANING OF CONFLICT IN ELEMENTARY THEORY

Remember that in Elementary Theory dyadic conflict relationship is modeled as two actors transmitting only negative sanctions. Certainly, the concepts are consistent with the exchange and coercion concepts, as they are described in the section above. The problem arises when one tries to figure out (or calculate) the results of negotiation between both actors—there are no results because no negotiation in this kind of relation is possible. This problem has even been recognized by Willer and his associates. In a recently published overview of Elementary Theory Willer and Markovsky wrote:

> In conflict [...] neither actor benefits. Applying Principle 1 to the conflict relation implies that no informed actor will exchange in this relation. This follows because only negative payoffs are possible in a relation containing only negative sanctions. Therefore conflict can occur only when the relation is not isolated—when it is a means to an end—or when actors have false beliefs (Willer and Markovsky 1993, pp. 331-332).

For this reason, we think the modification of the original concept of conflict is necessary for further development of this branch of ET.

The principles and laws of a theory, and assumptions we make in a given model, tell us what is theoretically possible, and what is not. But the above analysis suggests that the original model of conflict produces internal contradictions within the theory. To remove these discrepancies one should either modify or remove Principle 1 from the theory (which, in consequence, would change the scope conditions of the theory because actors would no longer be assumed to be rational) or modify the model of conflict itself. The second option means extending the scope of the theory which is the standard procedure of theory growth.

All three prototypes of relationship in Elementary Theory, that is, exchange, coercion, and conflict are to be based on Edgeworth negotiation and bargaining model (Edgeworth 1881; Willer 1987) if the theory is to be internally consistent and elegant. An Edgeworth contract curve is based on the assumption that actors have opposed but complementary interests. For example, *exchange* can now be referred to as any mutually beneficial *agreement* between A and B who play any *two-person mixed-motive (cooperative-competitive) game.* In a game with such an outcome structure, *any* agreement between the two parties is jointly preferred by both actors to nonagreement; hence, both are motivated to cooperate. At the same time, however, the interests of the parties are opposite, because the more one benefits from a transaction the less the other party benefits.

The prototypes of exchange and coercion relationships—and larger structures composed of them—are based on the assumption that concessions may either converge on a mutually acceptable outcome (agreement), or fail to converge, resulting in disagreement and nonexchange. Even in a coercion relationship, agreements between two actors must fall within a contract curve since *coercive relations share the quality of exchange relations* (Willer, personal communication). However, the prototype of conflict relationship as originally theorized by Willer does not meet the above conditions. Willer's conflict is not a *two-person mixed-motive (cooperative-competitive) game*, but actors in the original model of conflict are not motivated to cooperate. What Willer admits overtly (see the quotation above), is that actors do not have any motivation to negotiate and agree in this relationship. What is more, it seems that actors in conflict relationship, as originally formulated, do not have opposed interests. Their interests are complementary: both have an interest in not entering into conflict.

In an effort to save his model, Willer tries to incorporate additional scope conditions that do not apply to exchange or coercion. He argues that conflict can occur only "when the relation is not isolated—when it is a means to an end—or when actors have false beliefs." (Willer and Markovsky 1993, p. 332). Moreover, he argues that conflict is impossible in full information systems of rational actors. Whether it is the rescue for the original model of conflict or not, that proposition alters the scope conditions specific to exchange and coercion. Willer writes:

> But the constantly shifting alliances and consequent conflicts of feudal structures can only be understood if informational conditions are specified. For example, if all actors in a structure of this kind had full information, threats would occur, but, because all would know the outcome of the threatened conflict, no conflict would actually occur (Willer 1987, p. 234).

If conflict is possible only when the relation is not isolated, then the dyadic prototype of conflict is not possible. But could the argument related to an actor's false beliefs have some merit and thus rescue the original model?

First, actor's beliefs are not part of the scope conditions of the theory (Markovsky, Skvoretz, Willer, Lovaglia, and Erger 1993). Informational conditions of the structure were subject to theoretical analysis and experimental tests, but only in respect to subjects' knowledge about the network structures and their positions within them (Skvoretz and Burkett 1994; Lovaglia, Skvoretz, Willer, and Markovsky 1995). But it is actors' false or true beliefs in threat or in actual meaning of negative sanctions that are at stake, not knowledge about the shape of the network. Exactly because in Elementary Theory we relate to forward-looking, rational actors that have full information about network, they would never exchange in conflict relations containing only negative sanctions. We conclude then, that the original prototype of conflict is not realistic because it cannot depict any possible negotiation situation in which rational actors are involved. Thus, for Elementary Theory the original prototype of conflict relationship is characterized by the following:

1. Conflict contains only negative sanctions;
2. In conflict only negative payoffs are possible;
3. Conflict can occur only when actors have false beliefs and/or in systems with no full information; and
4. If it occurs in a full information system it is because conflict is only a precondition for coercion (Willer 1987, p. 234; Willer and Markovsky 1993, p. 332).

We know, however, that conflicts involving rational actors occur very often in social structure. The question is how to model such relations theoretically, using ET concepts. We know now that the modification of the original model of conflict in ET is unavoidable if one wants to proceed with fully featured network conflict theory being a branch of ET. Before we offer our modified model of conflict, we will define a precise distinction between two crucial conditions within networks: confrontation and conflict.

CONFLICT AND CONFRONTATION—MAKING THE DISTINCTION BETWEEN THE TWO

Let us now discuss the second major issue, the problem of conflict vs. confrontation, before we finally present the proposed revision of Willer's model of conflict. One of the major problems in theorizing conflict within the framework of Elementary Theory is relating it to confrontation.

In conflict, similarly as in exchange, we see actors negotiating and reaching agreements. Bargaining and negotiation is being used here by actors to resolve differences in interests between negotiating parties. Explicit bargaining (Bacharach and Lawler 1981; Chertkoff and Esser 1976; Ford 1994, p. 234) presupposes that two actors have divergent interests, that they can communicate with one another, and that mutual compromise is possible. Thus, the whole of the bargaining process is a sequence of offers between actors in a dyad (or larger network) at the conclusion of which both must agree to a given exchange rate for any exchange to occur (Willer 1987, p. 57).

All three prototypes of relationship, that is, exchange, coercion, and conflict, are based on the assumption that concessions may either converge on a mutually acceptable outcome (agreement), or fail to converge, resulting in confrontation, but not in conflict. Conflict is a type of relation between two actors, whereas confrontation is a condition that may occur when two actors in any of the three types of relation fail to agree. The fundamental assumption we made about actors (see Principle 1 of the ET) is that in each type of relationship actors have an interest in making the fewest possible concessions while simultaneously avoiding confrontation. Thus, the confrontation is a specific condition in any of the three types of relationship and by no means should be conflated with conflict. However, this kind of confusion is common. Heckathorn's considerations are a good example of how conflict and confrontation can be conflated.

> If bargainers were jointly rational, they would never confront, for conflicts are jointly irrational. But, as is well known, confrontations are frequent, even when they are mutually destructive. Furthermore, a perfectly jointly rational bargainer could not even (truthfully) threaten confrontation, for to do so would violate the conditions of joint rationality. He would therefore accept any concessions he was asked to make, so long as they were at least equally preferable to conflict (Heckathorn 1980, p. 265).

Heckathorn is apparently identifying one of the possible outcomes of negotiation between actors in relationships, namely confrontation, as "conflict." We think, therefore, that before we propose the modification of the prototype of conflict relationship a careful explication of the meaning of different types of outcomes in exchange and other types of relations must be done.

STATUS QUO AND CONFRONTATION OUTCOMES

Careful analysis of the types of outcomes possible in all three types of relationships will allow us to better define the confrontation condition in order to distinguish it from conflict. Moreover, we expect to receive a better, more formal method to discriminate between exchange, coercion, and conflict (see also Szmatka, Skvoretz, Sozanski, and Mazur 1998). Let us assume that we have two actors A and B and a given pool of positively valued resources $p > 0$. Following the Principle 1, we assume that actors will prefer larger amounts of positive resources to smaller amounts. Allocation of resources between actors before the interaction is given as x_0 and y_0 which stands for the amount of resources owned by A and B respectively. Let us call the pair (x_0, y_0) and the first outcome the *status quo outcome* and let us assume that $x_0 + y_0 \leq p$, allowing several different possible situations. For example, $x_0 + y_0 = 0$ (before initial negotiations actors have nothing), or $x_0 + y_0 = p$ (before initial negotiations the pool of resources is distributed between actors).

Next, let us have the second outcome (x_c, y_c) called *confrontation outcome*. Values x_c and y_c will be interpreted as A's and B's assets when both cannot reach mutual agreement. We assume that the confrontation outcome, for either actor, is worse than status quo outcome; that is, $x_c \leq x_0$ and $y_c \leq y_0$. We do not exclude cases in which x_c or y_c have a negative value, but this case will not be considered here.

If $x_c \leq x_0$ and $y_c \leq y_0$, then we can differentiate between three types of conditions:

1. symmetric relation, when $x_c = x_0$ and $y_c = y_0$ which is specific for exchange relation. Let us recall, that in exchange, no actors have negative sanctions;
2. asymmetric relation of coercion, when $x_c < x_0$ and $y_c = y_0$ or $x_c = x_0$ and $y_c < y_0$ which is specific for coercion relation. One actor can destroy resources of the other without personal losses. Coercion fit these inequalities, since it would be possible to set up an abstract game which satisfied these inequalities but did not require that one actor actually do something to take over some resources held by the other;
3. the symmetric relation, when $x_c < x_0$ and $y_c < y_0$, that is, confrontation for both actors has negative outcomes compared to the status quo. This situation is specific for the conflict relation and fits these inequalities since at confrontation, both actors will for sure transmit negative neutralizing sanctions.

Remember that in conflict both actors have negative sanction that can be used against the other. We now see the difference between conflict relationships and confrontation outcomes in exchange, coercion, and conflict. It should also be clear that the original model of conflict cannot be used here because, in that model, both actors do not have positive resources, hence neither condition (when $x_c \leq x_0$ nor condition when $y_c \leq y_0$) would be possible. In other words the lowering of positive resources from x_0 to x_c and from y_0 to y_c is not possible under the original model of conflict. Let this idea be our guideline in designing the new model of conflict for Elementary Theory.

THE CONCEPT OF CONFLICT FOR NETWORK CONFLICT MODEL

In attempting to design the model of conflict in a dyad, let us remember that the model must meet some important conditions. First, the model is expected to be fully connected with Elementary Theoretic principles and laws. This means, among other things, that Principle 1 of the theory should not be contradicted or become mute when employed in conjunction with the model. Second, the model is expected to meet conventional experimental conditions. Third, although it is not a condition *sine qua non*, we hope the model will be applicable to real-world situations. Following our recent work (Szmatka, Skvoretz, Sozanski, and Mazur 1998) and the above analysis, we know that modeling conflict in terms of negative sanctions alone makes not only the definition of conflict too narrow, but in most cases, the model itself cannot be implemented theoretically or practically. Thus, we propose the following modifications to the original model of conflict relationship.

First, it is proposed that actors A and B have both positive and negative resources. Second, the model assumes that the resources of an actor, A, can be traded and transmitted to an actor, B, through mutual agreement enforced by the threat of application by actor B a negative sanction on actor A and vice versa. Third, both actors are motivated to trade through mutual agreement to avoid the cost of confrontation which, at best, equals the elimination of all their positive resources. Fourth, according to Principle 1 (that remains unchanged), all social actors act to maximize their expected payoff state.

The proposed model departs from the original model of conflict in several ways. Here we list the most important discrepancies. Contrary to the original Elementary Theoretic model of conflict we claim that the conflict relationship does not contain only negative sanctions. Second, we point out that in conflict not only negative payoffs are possible but positive, as well. Third, we claim that actors' false beliefs are not a condition for conflict to occur. Fourth, we also claim that system's incomplete information is not a condition for conflict to occur. Therefore, fifth, in our conception conflict may or may not be a precondition for coercion.

THE DEFINITION OF RESISTANCE

Let us remind that in the conflict relationship the actors can't keep the status quo payoffs when confrontation occurs. Having set all parameters we may ask the following question: what earnings differentials will emerge in conflict networks between actors who try to avoid a confrontation outcome? Our immediate goal is to determine the final results of the negotiation process by means of the resistance theory. This theory which stems from the Kalai and Smorodinsky theory offering a new solution to the Nash bargaining problem has already been used in the study of exchange networks to determine the compromise solution.

The resistance theory postulates that actors settle at the point of equiresistance. The compromise division of the pool of positive resources is derived from the equation $R_i=R_j$ and the condition $x + y = M$.

Let (x, y) be any solution considered by the actors as a possible outcome of their negotiations. The resistance of actor i against (x, y) as defined by Heckathorn takes the form of a quotient of two expressions. The first expression is the difference between i's maximum possible profit and i's profit when the (x, y) solution is accepted. Actor i who initially holds x_0 units of resources can have at best the entire pool of M units at the end of negotiations, so that i's maximum possible profit is $M-x_0$. When actor i accepts the division (x, y) i's profit will be $x-x_0$ (this number can be negative when i is forced to give up part of her resources). Therefore, the numerator in the resistance equation of i will be:

$$(M - x_0) - (x - x_0) = M - x$$

The second expression, that is, the denominator in the resistance equation, is the difference of i's maximum profit and i's profit at confrontation. Since the latter is equal to $x_c - x_0$, the denominator in the resistance equation of i will be:

$$(M - x_0) - (x_c - x_0) = M - x_c$$

Similarly we get the equation for the resistance of j. Hence, we arrive at two following formulas for the resistance of i and j:

$$R_i = \frac{M-x}{M-x_c}, R_j = \frac{M-y}{M-y_c}$$

Note that in the above equation we no longer have the status quo outcome that we needed to speak about "profit" or "preference state alteration" of an actor. The latter term was used by Willer (Willer 1987) and was later replaced by "payoff." Payoffs of actors i and j, symbolically noted by him P_i and P_j are written here as x and y, respectively, and referred to as possible final results of the negotiation process. Moreover, in calculating resistance Willer assumes that maximum payoff to one actor cannot result in a zero payoff to the other actor, that is, $(M,0)$ and $(0,M)$ are not allowed as possible outcomes. As a consequence, the pool must be treated as a discrete set of points. This approach is mathematically inconvenient because the solution of the equation having i's and j's resistance values as its left and right hand side can be a fraction of the pool size M. Therefore, we assume here the continuity of the pool of resources, that is, any two numbers x and y such that $x + y = M$ are allowed as a solution.

THE SOLUTION OF THE CONFLICT RELATION IN A DYAD

In our prototype of conflict dyad (see Figure 3) both partners have 1 neutralizing negative sanction. In the case of confrontation, i's resources (x_0) are eliminated because j sends the negative sanction, which implies that the denominator becomes now $0 - x_0 = -x_0$. In consequence, the resistance formula has now the form of the fraction:

$$R_i = \frac{M - x}{(M - x_0) - (-x_o)} = \frac{M - x}{M}$$

and analogously for j. In consequence the equiresistance equation takes the form:

or simply

$$M - x = M - y$$

Since $x + y = M$, we get the following solution:

$$x = \frac{M}{2}, \qquad y = \frac{M}{2}$$

In our special case where one of the actors was initially endowed with ten units of positive resources and the other actor with one, we have $x_0 = 10$ and $y_0 = 1$, so that $M = 11$ and $M/2 = 5.5$. The conclusion is that the equiresistance equation predicts an even distribution of power in a dyadic relationship. The conflict relation is illustrated in Figure 3.

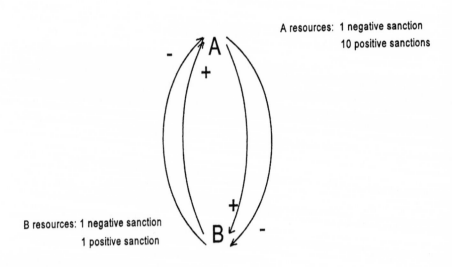

A resources: 1 negative sanction
10 positive sanctions

B resources: 1 negative sanction
1 positive sanction

Negative = neutralizing negative sanction

Figure 3. Conflict Relationship

THE DESIGN OF EXPERIMENT OF CONFLICT IN THE DYAD AND LARGER NETWORKS

In order to implement the experimental design for conflict in the dyad and larger networks we must set initial conditions for this structure. Initial conditions will also be necessary to solve the resistance equation for conflict in the dyad. Consider a conflict relation for which an actor A and actor B negotiate the division of the pool of 24 units of positive resources that are valueless to A and B before negotiation. An actor can gain points by concluding transactions with his partner in the dyad. A transaction consists in splitting the pool of 24 points between the two partners; when a split is bilaterally approved, the actors get their shares which are added to their accounts. Also, A holds 1 negative sanction that is valueless to A and to B, and B holds 1 negative sanction that is valueless to B and to A.

According to Principle 1 of Elementary Theory, both actors are motivated to maximize their payoff state. Payoff state is the total number of positive resources gained in this relationship. Now consider each negative sanction to be a *neutralizing negative sanction*. When transmitted, neutralizing negative sanction reduces positive resources of a recipient to zero. Assume now that, to avoid negative sanction and loss of all resources, actors in such a relationship will trade their own positive resources through bargain or mutual agreement. Both opponents have the "right of protection." The right of protection is the rule which asserts that the negative sanction transmission to reduce positive resources to zero is not allowed when opponents come to an agreement. This right is an analogue to the right of reciprocity in exchange or the right of protection in coercion (Willer 1987). The above conflict dyad is predicted to be balanced with no substantial power advantage on either side. It is predicted that the maximum rate of conflict exploitation on either side of the dyad should be 12.

The experimental implementation of networks larger than dyad consists of the following additional conditions. The pool of 24 points in a relationship is created by the two actors who "put at risk" 12 points each (half of the stake), taken from each's account. No split of the pool except 12 + 12 is mutually beneficial. For instance, a split 13 + 11 means that the first actor gains 1 point and the second actor loses 1 point. The case 12 + 12 means that the players' accounts remain unchanged. Nevertheless, such a compromise allows them, at the least, to avoid being punished for not reaching an agreement. The next assumption introduces the status quo outcome into the model and operationalizes a negative sanction as a deduction from an actor's account. Each actor is initially endowed with a certain number of points, stored in her "personal bank account," so that she is in a position to pay fines for failing to complete transactions with her partners; a fine is deducted from an actor's account. The sanctioning regime makes the dyadic relationships interdependent within the network conflict system. The "regime of sanctioning" is the combination of the following two conditions: (i) an actor may be punished by any partner with whom she does not make a deal; (ii) an actor has the option to punish a partner if she and her partner did not make a deal. Therefore, the possibility of sanctions occurs in all relations where no agreement was reached even if one of the partners made an agreement with someone else. For example, in the three-branch network where A is a central actor, and B, C, and D are peripherals, if A is allowed to make only one agreement, then A should be able to maximize her share of the positive resources by a 23/1 agreement, say with B. The outcome now is that A adds 23 points to her account (the true gain is 11 points) but then gets 24 points deducted, B adds 1 point to her account (as a matter of fact B loses 11 points), and C and D each get 12 points deducted. Partners in each relation not completing an agreement have option to sanction each other. In the three-branch network, A has the option to sanction C and D, and if she did, C and D loses 12 points each, while C and D each have an option to sanction A and if they did, A loses 24 points total. Depending on the type of connection, each actor can conclude precisely defined number of transactions per "round" (the unit of analysis of the system's behavior).

Scope conditions for conflict structures which delimit an actor's behavior are thus: (1) all actors use identical strategies in negotiating compromise; (2) both actors more frequently use negative sanctions as threats rather than transmitting them;[1] (3) both actors will trade the positive resources they put at risk through bargain or mutual agreement to avoid a negative sanction and loss of all resources of a recipient to zero; (4) actors accept the best offer they receive. Scope conditions for conflict structure which delimit positions and their relations are the following ones: (5) each position is connected to, and seeks exchange with, one or more other positions; (6) at the start of a negotiation round, a pool of positively valued resource units is available in every relation; (6a) in every relation both positions will have negative sanction which eliminate all resources of the other when received. The target actor cannot escape the domain of conflict, which means that if one of the actors transmits a negative sanction, the other will receive it. Condition (6b) states, that all actors have the right to protection. Any mutually agreed on positive sanction transmission by one actor cannot be followed by a negative sanction transmission by the other. Condition (7) asserts that compromise can be reached if and only if both actors in the relationship use negative sanctions only as a threat, and that the threat is believed. Finally, condition (8) states that each position completes a deal with at least one other position per round (Szmatka and Mazur 1996a).

RESISTANCE IN NULL CONNECTED CONFLICT NETWORK

We define connection at a position by distinguishing the potential network (N), maximum possible network (P), and minimum necessary network (Q) and by specifying relations between them. i's *potential network* is the set of all relations connected at i (i.e., all current relations for the position i) and its size is Ni. i's *max-*

imum possible network is the largest network in which i can benefit from negotiating and making an agreement (i.e., the largest number of relations for which i can profit in each) and its size is Pi. The typology uses a third kind of network, i's *minimum necessary* network. This network is the smallest number of relations in which i must complete all exchanges to benefit and its size is Qi. By stipulation, $Ni \geq Pi \geq Qi$. Then

> i is null connected if $Ni = Pi > Qi = 1$ and
>
> i is exclusively connected if $Ni > Pi \geq Qi = 1$.
>
> i is inclusively connected if $Ni = Pi = Qi > 1$. (Willer 1992, p. 206; Szmatka and Willer 1995).

Our previous analysis shows that an actor's resistance to a given outcome is the function of the earnings from that outcome, the earnings from the "best hope" outcome, and the earnings from the "confrontation" outcome (Szmatka, Skvoretz, Sozanski, and Mazur 1998). In the experimental task of dividing a pool of M points, each actor's best hope outcome is to receive all M points while the partner earns 0 points. This outcome and its exact opposite define the extremes of the contract zone. In null connected network, negotiation in each dyad is unrelated to negotiation in any other dyad and so the previous results for a simple dyad apply to each of the dyads null connected in a position. As Willer and Markovsky (1993) noted, when i is null connected, i's resistance is unchanged from the dyad. Therefore, let us once again consider two actors i and j in a dyad. The resistances of i and j to a division in which i receives x_i points and j receives $M - x_i$ points and where failure to agree results in a loss of $M/2$ points (a payoff of $-M/2$) are:

$$R_i = \frac{M - x_i}{M - \left(-\dfrac{M}{2}\right)} \qquad R_j = \frac{M - (M - x_i)}{M - \left(-\dfrac{M}{2}\right)}$$

Resistance theory assumes that agreement occurs at a division of the pool to which i and j are equally resistant which is the Equiresistance Principle. The division can be found by equating R_i and R_j and solving for x_i. In the absence of other considerations, the solution for the dyad described above is an equal division of the pool which means that null connected network is equipower throughout.

RESISTANCE IN EXCLUSIVELY CONNECTED CONFLICT NETWORK

In an exclusively connected network the condition $N > P$ has especially powerful effect in branches—it makes the central actor overwhelmingly advantageous over peripheral actors. We apply here what we call *iterative resistance theory for exclusionary conflict branch* which is not new in Elementary Theory for exchange branches (Willer 1987; Fararo and Skvoretz 1993; Szmatka and Willer 1995). In this paper we apply it to conflict branches. It is based on the assumption that the central actor in the branch is powerful because is always included in any agreement and thus escapes negative sanction in at least one conflict tie and a loss of $M/2$ points, that is a payoff of $-M/2$. Peripheral actors are less powerful because all of them face equal probability to be excluded and receive the negative sanction. Therefore peripherals bid to be included and to avoid the negative sanction by sending increasingly better offers to the center (Fararo and Skvoretz 1993, p. 439).

Let us consider a branch with a central actor i and three peripheral actors j. After negotiations with first two peripherals, the third peripheral actor is for the central actor i the exclusive alternative to the first two. The effect of i's exclusive alternatives and the j's prospective exclusion is to change the conditions of i's and j's resistance from those of the dyad. After the first round i has an agreement to exchange at x_I with some actor j who earns $M-x_I$. The others face exclusion and a payoff of $-M/2$. In the second round peripheral actors cannot expect to do better than in the first round, so each peripheral's best hope is no longer M but $M-x_I$. For the central actor the crucial factor that changes after iterating to each next round is the payoff at confrontation with any one peripheral actor. For example, if the central actor made an agreement in the first round for x_1 then that amount less $M/2$ becomes the confrontation payoff with other peripheral. The resistances for a given current cycle of negotiations in exclusively connected conflict branch become

$$R_i = \frac{M - x_t}{M - \left(x_{t-1} - \frac{M}{2}\right)} \qquad R_j = \frac{(M - x_{t-1}) - (M - x_t)}{\left(M - x_{t-1}\right) - \left(-\frac{M}{2}\right)}$$

and the equiresistance equation $R_i = R_j$ solves as

$$x_t = \frac{(M + x_{t-1})}{2}$$

and goes to a limit of $x_t = M$ where the central actor exercises maximal power over peripherals.

RESISTANCE IN INCLUSIVELY CONNECTED CONFLICT NETWORK

The effect of inclusion for a sequence of settlements in $N = Q$ branch is to successively *reduce* resistance of the central position while leaving the resistance of peripherals *unaffected* (Patton and Willer 1990; Willer 1992; Szmatka and Willer 1995; Willer and Szmatka 1993; Willer and Skvoretz 1997). Because the resistance of the central actor decreases with each transaction, all peripherals will attempt to wait until others will make agreements. We assume that all peripherals attempt to exchange last. As a result all settlements become effectively simultaneous. The cost of not making an agreement in any relation is the loss of benefit from *all other* agreements. In addition, because in the case of confrontation with one of j's, no agreement can be made, i loses 12 points in *every* relation. In other words, if one of the agreements is not completed, the results of all previous agreements will be lost and all actors will face the loss of the points they put at risk.

For simultaneous agreements in inclusively connected branch, which theoretically is the simplest case, payoff at confrontation for i completing agreements with each of Q j's, is:

$$x_c = -\frac{M}{2}Q + [-x(Q-1)]$$

The resistance of an inclusively connected i, when making agreements simultaneously with Q js, is:

$$R_i = \frac{M - x_i}{M - \left[-\frac{M}{2}Q - x_i(Q-1)\right]}$$

The resistance of any peripheral actor j is

$$R_j = \frac{M - (M - x_i)}{M - \left(-\frac{M}{2}\right)}$$

The equiresistance equation $R_i = R_j$ has the form of a quadratic equation in x_i. The positive root given by the formula

$$x_i = \frac{-(Q+5)M + M\sqrt{Q + 5^2 24(Q-1)}}{4(Q-1)}$$

is the solution of the problem. The greater the size of inclusively connected branch, the lesser the relative power of i, as the point of equiresistance is shifted in favor of peripherals.

Computed values of x_i in inclusively connected conflict and exchange networks where $M = 24$ and $Q = 10$ are given in Table 1. We see that conflict networks exhibit the same pattern of power development as exchange networks, although the structural effect is greater than their counterparts in the exchange networks. At this point we have no explanation for these differences.

CONFLICT VS. PUNISHMENT—THE MEANING OF CONFLICT IN LINDA MOLM'S THEORY

As shown above, our model of conflict is based on the idea that conflict is a relation in which each actor has positive and negative resources (sanctions) simultaneously. In recent years there have been attempts to analyze the relation in which

Table 1. Earnings of the Central Position in an Inclusively Connected
Branch Structure: Exchange Relations vs. Conflict Relations

	Points Earned by the Center from the 24 Point Pool	
Number of Peripherals	Conflict Relations	Exchange Relations
2	9.26	9.94
3	7.75	8.78
4	6.74	8.00
5	6.00	7.42
6	5.43	6.96
7	4.97	6.58
8	4.59	6.27
9	4.27	6.00
10	4.00	5.77

actors have both positives and negatives. Linda Molm calls it a coercive (not a "conflict") relation and claims that in such a relation both "rewarding" and "punishing" are possible (Molm 1994; Molm 1996). We will show below that her model is different from the proposed here model of conflict.

Scope conditions are a set of universal statements which define the class of circumstances in which a knowledge claim is (or set of knowledge claims are) applicable (Cohen 1989, p. 83; Cohen 1980, p. 92; Walker and Cohen 1985). "Theory of punishment" developed by Molm has elaborated explicit scope conditions. The scope of her theory is restricted to the following four conditions:

1. Actors seek to increase outcomes they positively value and decrease outcomes they negatively value.
2. Outcomes obey a principle of satiation or declining marginal utility.
3. Relations are characterized by mutual dependence in which rewards obtained from others are contingent on rewards given in exchange.
4. Exchanges occur over time between the same actors or sets of actors (Molm 1997a, 1997b; Emerson 1981; Molm and Cook 1995).

Additionally, there are six conditions further describing the scope of this research program:

1. Coercive power is studied in the context of relations in which actors have the capacity both to reward and to punish each other.
2. Actors' resources are capacities to perform behaviors that produce valued outcomes for others—not to provide tangible goods.
3. Exchange transactions are reciprocal, not negotiated.

4. All actors have alternative partners with whom they can exchange. They also have alternative behavioral choices.
5. Actors cannot "leave the field" of influence, nor can they change the structure of the network.
6. Actors have full information about the values governing the relative dependencies in their own relation, but not in distal relations in the network (Molm 1994, p. 77, Molm 1997a, pp. 72-73, Molm 1997b, p. 116).

Scope conditions of network conflict theory are different in all regards. They were discussed in the previous sections. If scope conditions of these theories are different, then different avenues should be taken in the theories' development. Thus, essential differences in scope will make any crucial test between them impossible.[2]

When the scope of one theory overlaps the scope of another, there are opportunities for both to develop in tandem, competing in predictions and explanations. This is one of the ways knowledge accumulates (Szmatka and Lovaglia 1996). If, however, the scope conditions of two theories do not intersect, then there are no empirical situations that may serve as sites for critical tests between them (Walker and Cohen 1985).

There are two forms of social exchange—negotiated and nonnegotiated—and these represent the main difference between the scopes of the two theories. Negotiated exchange involves a joint decision process such as bargaining. The benefits enjoyed by both exchange partners are easily identified as paired events, called transactions. Most economic exchanges and many social exchanges fit this category. In reciprocal, nonnegotiated exchanges the contributions to the exchange are separately performed and nonnegotiated. Actors act without knowing if/when the other will reciprocate, and the relation takes the form of a series of sequentially dependent acts. Actors individually provide benefit for each other without negotiation and without knowing whether, when, or to what degree the other will reciprocate. While reciprocity and contingency characterize the relation, there is difficulty in identifying the transaction (Molm and Cook 1995, p. 212). "A 'free gift,' or altruistic act might initiate the process. It is "free" in the sense that it is performed in a noncontingent context (with or without an underlying expectation of return). The other's contribution might or might not occur. If it does occur, and if it is contingent upon (prompted by) the initiating contribution, a *reciprocal transaction* has occurred" (Emerson 1981, p. 33. Italics in original). At present, the scope of network exchange theory requires negotiated exchanges. In contrast, Molm uses nonnegotiated exchanges in her experiments.

Molm's analysis of power encompasses both reward and punishment. In the relation, actors control varying amounts of reward and punishment outcomes for one another. Following Emerson (Emerson 1972), Molm defines rewards and punishments as resources, which are not an attribute or a possession of an actor, but rather, attributes of his relation to another. "...social exchange theory reminds us that resources depend on their value to others and, therefore, they are attributes of *relations*, not actors." (Molm 1997a, p. 15, italics in original). Resources, in turn, are capacities to perform behaviors that produce valued outcomes for others, rather than tangible goods. They are not physically transferred and resource supplies are not depleted—the actions of one actor produce some kind of outcome for an exchange partner (Molm 1996, 1997a).

As opposed to the "theory of punishment" research program as theorized by Molm, negative and positive sanctions in network conflict theory are not "punishments" and "rewards." "A sanction is a social action transmitted by one actor and received by another, which alters the preference state of the actor receiving the sanction" (Willer 1981, p. 32). A negative sanction then is a social act that reduces the payoff state of the actor receiving the sanction flow. Conversely, a punishment in a "theory of punishment" program can be defined as a negative outcome of some act such as terminating an ongoing positive reinforcement. In nonnegotiated reciprocal exchange, the reinforcement process is the one through which the power advantage is converted to successful power use. Rewards and punishments affect behavior in opposite directions: rewards increase and punishments decrease the frequency of behaviors on which they are contingent (Cook, Molm, and Yamagishi 1993). This leads to the conclusion that, as opposed to network conflict theory, Molm's predictions derive from the learning model and operant psychology that underlies classical exchange theory.

David Wagner claims that there are certain features that related theories must have in common. Each relation between theories can be described in terms of the degree of similarity in structure, problem focus, and character of predictions (Wagner 1984). We have already shown that the theoretical structure of the "theory of punishment" is essentially dissimilar to the network conflict theory in such structural elements as concepts, definitions, propositions, derivations and scope conditions. Now let us consider the domain of explanation of these two theories. Following Wagner we claim that competing theories must have the social phenomena or processes they try to explain in common (Wagner 1984; Wagner and Berger 1985, 1986; Berger and Zelditch 1998).

We claim that, at this point, Molm's theory of punishment and network conflict theory differ in regard to the social phenomena they try to explain. The explanatory domain of network conflict theory concerns how the structure of relationships affects social interaction and how structural change emerges out of patterns of interaction. The explanatory domain of the "theory of punishment" is created by questions addressed to nonstructural processes in social exchange, like the effects of power use, strategy to increase rewards and the way actors' strategies can affect exchange outcome independent of structure (Molm 1994; Molm and Cook 1995). The main research question that Molm's program addresses is an effect (in terms of influence, for example) of punishing power on social exchange. She tries to explain "the use and effects of coercive power in social exchange" (Molm 1996, p. 149). The theory of punishment is focused on two aims: (a) theoretical—"to determine whether the scope of exchange theory can be extended to incorporate coercive power, and, if so, what modifications of the theory might be necessary;" and (b) empirical—"to investigate the similarities and differences between the effects of the two bases of power on behavior" (Molm 1994, p. 77).

To the contrary, the theoretical aim of network conflict theory is to uncover basic structural principles of power distribution in conflict networks. The empirical aim is also defined as an application of the network conflict theory to the explanation and interpretation of historical and institutional cases (Willer, Simpson, Szmatka, and Mazur 1996; Szmatka, Mazur, and Simpson 1996; Willer and Szmatka 1998). Network conflict theory's basic theoretical questions are "how is the power in the form of exploitation and domination structurally produced in a conflict relation?" and "how does a configuration of conflict structure determine the rate of conflicting exploitation that will occur?" The theoretical model of conflict proposed here remains within the scope of elementary theory and addresses the same structural processes. Network conflict theory is a theory of social interaction and social structures, and like elementary theory, seeks to relate structure to activity.

The explanatory domain of "punishment theory" is also constrained by the unit of analysis—the dyadic exchange relation. That theory addresses the problem of power relations within the dyad, not in the network as the whole. Conversely, network conflict theory is based on a basic dyadic model of conflict, but accounts for larger structures composed of conflict relationships. Therefore, we claim that, because the theory of punishment and network conflict theory differ not only in scope and character of predictions, but also in domains of explanations, they are not related in terms of competition.

We also believe that relations which produce theory growth can occur only when related theories share similar scope. If they are not, it is impossible to determine which theory is better, and comparisons of competing theories would be nothing more than metatheoretical disputes. Therefore, let us return to the issue of competition as a relation between theories which provides theory growth.

Critical tests between theories are impossible if scope conditions are different. No theory can be reliably tested beyond its limits. A theory tested beyond its limits will yield inconsistent evidence which neither falsifies nor supports the theory (Walker and Cohen 1985). As presented above, Molm's theory of punishment in exchange and network conflict theory have different scope conditions and thus scope. As a result, they cannot be accurately tested against one another.

CONCLUSIONS

We have offered a theory to explain how power develops in conflict networks. Our theory is based on the revised model of conflict found in Willer's Elementary Theory. However, it should not be treated as a simple extension of that theory. Our model of conflict is fundamentally different from the original model of conflict offered in ET and eliminates flaws of that model.

From all theories being developed in the area of exchange networks only one was focused on conflict related phenomena, and that was Linda Molm's theory of punishment. Our analysis of that theory shows, however, that it has different scope conditions and hence cannot be competitive with our network conflict theory. Our theory, being different from Willer's original formula is, nevertheless, consistent with several important aspects of elementary theory, in particular, the use of resistance theory to analyze and calculate earnings from agreements.

Although our preliminary empirical test of the theory (Szmatka, Skvoretz, Sozanski, and Mazur 1998) shows that structural effects in exchange networks are greater than their counterparts in conflict networks, this theoretical analysis demonstrates that conflict networks behave like their exchange versions, with one exception. We found that inclusively connected conflict branches should develop stronger power advantages at the periphery than their exchange counterparts. We cannot offer any speculations about this effect at this time, as it requires, first, an empirical confirmation.

Two important limitations were imposed on the theory in this analysis. First, we analyze power processes in conflict networks in which only neutralizing negative sanctions are possible. Second, there are at least two sanctioning protocols possible: automatic and manual. The automatic protocol eliminates any intentionality in the issuing of negative sanctions, as any sanctions for failure to agree are certain to be applied. We assumed this sanctioning protocol because it fits the formal definition of a conflict relation (Szmatka, Skvoretz, Sozanski, and Mazur 1998). However, a variety of further theoretical options opens up when this scope restrictions are lifted. Thus, we think that besides testing this model, which seems to be an obvious next step in developing the theory, a further theoretical work should be focused on conflict networks with confiscatory sanctions. We also think that more empirical studies should be pursued with the application of manual sanctioning protocol.

ACKNOWLEDGMENTS

Authors acknowledge research grant No. 1 H02E00114 from the Polish Committee for Scientific Research (KBN) and the first author acknowledges support from the Research Support Scheme of the Open Society Institute grant no: 746/94. The authors thank John Skvoretz, Tad Sozanski, Brent Simpson, and David Willer for helpful comments on earlier drafts of this paper. Direct all correspondence to Jacek Szmatka, Institute of Sociology,

Jagiellonian University, 52 Grodzka Street, 31-044 Krakow, Poland. (E-mail: usszmatk@cyf-kr.edu.pl; FAX: +48-12- 422-2129).

NOTES

1. There is one exception to this rule. In our first experimental test (Szmatka, Skvoretz, Sozanski, and Mazur 1988) we compare different protocols. In the first protocol, the ConNet software that we use for managing subject negotiations in a system of networked personal computers automatically transmits the negative sanction when agreement fails. As we see this protocol does not exactly meet scope conditions of the theory. In the second protocol, subjects control the transmission of the negative sanction when agreement is not reached. The second protocoal is, as we see, in accordance with scope conditions of the theory.

2. Another issue is whether there are crucual experiments in science. According to Popper crucial experiments require only a *reproductible effect* to falsify a theory, however, he also noted that a crucial experiment should be designed to decide between two theories. Subsequently, the "historical school" has questioned Popper: some assert that crucial experiments are logically impossible (Feyerabend) and others assert their practical impossibility (Lakatos). As a possible solution to this controversy, Such has proposed that the appropriate unit of analysis be a series of tests between theories, which he calls a *crucial situation* (Such 1975). While the views of the historical school have gained some currency in sociology, recently Laudan have criticized the studies of the school as antidotal and based on secondary and tertiary sources.

REFERENCES

Bacharach, S., and E.J. Lawler. 1981. *Bargaining: Power, Tactics, and Outcomes*. San Francisco: Jossey-Bass.

Berger, J., and M. Zelditch Jr. 1998. "Theoretical Research Programs: A Reformulation." Pp. 29-46 in *Status, Network, and Structure. Theory Development in Group Processes*, edited by J. Szmatka, J. Skvoretz and J. Berger. Stanford: Stanford University Press.

Chertkoff, JM., and J.K. Esser. 1976. "A Review of Experiments in Explicit Bargaining." *Journal of Experimental Social Psychology* 12: 464-486.

Cohen, B.P. 1980. "The Conditional Nature of Scientific Knowledge." Pp. 71-110 in *Theoretical Methods in Sociology*, edited by L. Freese. Pittsburgh, PA: University of Pittsburgh Press.

_____. 1989. *Developing Sociological Knowledge*. Chicago: Nelson-Hall.

Cook, K.S., L.D. Molm, and T. Yamagishi. 1993. "Exchange Relations and Exchange Networks: Recent Developments in Social Exchange Theory." Pp. 296-322 in *Theoretical Research Programs: Studies in Theory Growth*, edited by J. Berger and Morris Jr. Zelditch. Stanford: Stanford University Press.

Edgeworth, F.Y. 1881. *Mathematical Physics*. London: Kegan Paul.

Emerson, R.M. 1972. "Exchange Theory, Part 1: A Psychological Basis for Social Exchange." Pp. 38-57 in *Sociological Theories in Progress*, Vol. 2, edited by J. Berger, M. Zelditch Jr, and B. Anderson. Boston: Houghton Mifflin.

_____. 1981. "Social Exchange Theory." Pp. 30-65 in *Social Psychology: Sociological Perspectives*, edited by M. Rosenberg and R.H. Turner. New York: Basic Books.

Fararo, T.J., and J. Skvoretz. 1993. "Methods and Problems of Theoretical Integration and the Principle of Adaptively Rational Action." Pp. 416-50 in *Theoretical Research Programs. Studies in the Growth of Theory*, edited by J. Berger and M. Zelditch. Stanford: Stanford University Press.

Ford, R. 1994. "Conflict and Bargaining." Pp. 231-56 in *Group Processes. Sociological Analyses*, edited by M. Foschi and E.J. Lawler. Chicago: Nelson-Hall.

Lovaglia, M., J. Skvoretz, D. Willer, and B. Markovsky. 1995. "Negotiated Exchanges in Social Net-
    works" *Social Forces* 74: 123-55.

Markovsky, B., D. Willer, and T. Patton. 1988. "Power Relations in Exchange Networks." *American
    Sociological Review* 53: 220-236.

Markovsky, B., J. Skvoretz, D. Willer, M.J. Lovaglia, and J. Erger. 1993. "The Seeds of Weak Power:
    An Extension of Network Exchange Theory." *American Sociological Review* 58: 197-209.

Molm, L.D. 1994. "Is Punishment Effective? Coercive Strategies in Social Exchange." *Social Psychol-
    ogy Quarterly* 57: 75-94.

_____. 1996. "Punishment and Coercion in Social Exchange." Pp. 149-88 in *Advances in Group
    Processes*, Vol. 13, edited by E. Lawler and B. Markovsky. Stamford, CT: JAI Press.

_____. 1997a. *Coercive Power in Social Exchange*. New York: Cambridge University Press.

_____. 1997b. "Risk and Power Use: Constraints on the Use of Coercion in Exchange." *American
    Sociological Review* 62: 113-33.

Molm, L.D., and K.S. Cook. 1995. "Social Exchange and Exchange Networks." Pp. 209-35 in *Socio-
    logical Perspectives on Social Psychology*, edited by K.S. Cook, G.A. Fine, and J.S. House.
    Boston: Allyn and Bacon.

Patton, T., and D. Willer. 1990. "Connection and Power in Centralized Exchange Networks." *Journal
    of Mathematical Sociology* 16: 31-49.

Skvoretz, J., and D. Willer. 1991. "Power in Exchange Networks: Setting and Structural Variations."
    Social Psychology Quarterly 54: 224-238.

_____. 1993. "Exclusion and Power: A Test of Four Theories of Power in Exchange Networks."
    American Sociological Review 58: 801-818.

Skvoretz, J., and T. Burkett. 1994. "Information and the Distribution of Power in Exchange Networks."
    Journal of Mathematical Sociology 19: 263-278.

Such, J. 1975. *Czy Istnieje Experimentum Crucis? [Is There a Crucial Experiment?]*. Warsaw: PWN -
    Polish Scientific Publishers.

Szmatka, J. 1998. "Testing Elementary Theory for Universality." Pp. 87-109 in *Status, Network, and
    Structure. Theory Development in Group Processes.*, edited by J. Szmatka, J. Skvoretz and J.
    Berger. Stanford: Stanford University Press.

Szmatka, J., and D. Willer. 1995. "Exclusion, Inclusion, and Compound Connection in Exchange Net-
    works." *Social Psychology Quarterly* 58: 123-32.

Szmatka, J., and J. Mazur. 1996a. "Orienting Strategies, Working Strategies, and Theoretical Research
    Programs in Social Exchange Theory." *Polish Sociological Review* 115: 265-288.

Szmatka, J., and M.J. Lovaglia. 1996. "The Significance of Method." *Sociological Perspectives* 39:
    393-415.

Szmatka, J., J. Mazur, and B. Simpson. 1996. "Networks, Structures, and Explanation: Historical and
    Institutional Applications of Elementary Theory." Paper presented at the American Sociologi-
    cal Association Meetings. New York, 16-20 August.

Szmatka, J., J. Skvoretz, T. Sozanski, and J. Mazur. 1998. "Conflict in Networks." *Sociological Per-
    spectives* 41: 49-66.

Wagner, D.G. 1984. *The Growth of Sociological Theories*. Beverly Hills, CA: Sage.

Wagner, D.G., and J. Berger. 1985. "Do Sociological Theories Grow?" *American Journal of Sociology*
    90: 697-727.

_____. 1986. "Programs, Theory, and Metatheory." *American Journal of Sociology* 92: 168-82.

Walker, H.A., and B.P. Cohen. 1985. "Scope Statements: Imperatives for Evaluating Theory." *Ameri-
    can Sociological Review* 50: 288-301.

Willer, D. 1981. "The Basic Concepts of Elementary Theory." Pp. 25-53 in *Networks, Exchange and
    Coercion*, edited by D. Willer and B. Anderson. New York: Elsevier.

_____. 1987. *Theory and Experimental Investigation of Social Structures*. New York: Gordon and
    Breach.

_____. 1992. "Predicting Power in Exchange Networks: A Brief History and Introduction to the Issues." *Social Networks* 14: 187-211.

Willer, D., M.J. Lovaglia, and B. Markovsky. 1997. "Power and Influence: A Theoretical Bridge." *Social Forces* 76: 571-603.

Willer, D., and B. Markovsky. 1993. "The Theory of Elementary Relations: Its Development and Research Program." Pp. 323-363 in *Theoretical Research Programs: Studies in Theory Growth*, edited by J. Berger and M. Zelditch Jr. Stanford, CA: Stanford University Press.

Willer, D., and J. Skvoretz. 1997. "Games and Structures." *Rationality and Society* 9: 5-35.

Willer, D., and J. Szmatka. 1993. "Cross-National Experimental Investigations of Elementary Theory: Implications for the Generality of the Theory and the Autonomy of Structure.." Pp. 37-81 in *Advances in Group Processes*, Vol. 10, edited by E.J. Lawler, B. Markovsky, K. Heimer, and J. O'Brien. Stamford, CT: JAI Press.

_____. 1998. "Structural Formulations and Elementary Theory." Pp. 273-92 in *Status, Network, and Structure. Theory Development in Group Processes*, edited by Jacek Szmatka, John Skvoretz and Joseph Berger. Stanford: Stanford University Press.

Willer, D., B. Markovsky, and T. Patton. 1989. "Power Structures: Derivations and Applications of Elementary Theory." Pp. 313-353 in *Sociological Theories in Progress: New Formulations*, edited by J. Berger and M. Zelditch Jr. Newbury Park, CA: Sage.

Willer, D., B. Simpson, and K. Pennell. 1997. "Breaking Networks and Finding Power Structures." Paper presented at the XII Sunbelt Network Conference. San Diego, California, 13-16 February.

Willer, D., B. Simpson, J. Szmatka, and J. Mazur. 1996. "Social Theory and Historical Explanation." *Humbolt Journal of Social Relations* 22: 63-84.

UNDERSTANDING THE NATURE OF SCOPE CONDITIONS:
SOME CONSIDERATIONS AND CONSEQUENCES, INCLUDING HYBRID THEORIES AS A STEP FORWARD

Geoffrey Tootell, Alison Bianchi, and Paul T. Munroe

ABSTRACT

Scope conditions provide a way to describe the circumstances in which a theory can be claimed to be valid. They also state the conditions under which the theory should be tested. Careful use of scope conditions in research improves the quality of designs and the likelihood of creating credible research traditions. Their absence can lead to testing the theory beyond its proper range, which can lead to its premature falsification. We define the characteristics of these restrictions in such terms as abstraction, existential reference, and logical form, and by restricting the domains of a particular set of relevant causal relationships or associations. A variety of logical operations and set theory can be used to simplify a theory's assumptions and to help generate hybrid theories. If these hybrids are evaluated carefully, and survive, they can help us

Advances in Group Processes, Volume 15, pages 213-235.
ISBN: 0-7623-0362-X

understand cross-results of two distinct processes explained by separate theories but potentially operating in the same situations.

This paper takes another look at the nature of scope conditions. In gist, they are the conditions which suffice to warrant that a given theory can be evaluated properly in specific kinds of situations. Using scope conditions to guide theory development and evaluation is a conscious strategy which, though still relatively rare, offers some very useful consequences: It directs theorists to design theories to apply to specific domains, thus to create special or middle range theories. This reduces the demands on both theory and theorist, as it addresses the theory to a domain in which it is most likely to be valid. By the same token, scope conditions inform researchers and readers of existential conditions which should be incorporated in the research design to obtain an appropriate test of the theory.

The character, usages, and consequences of scope conditions have been considered carefully by Berger (1974, pp. 13-16; also see Lakatos 1970), Walker and Cohen (1985), Cohen (1989, pp. 82-85 et passim) and Foschi (1997). We try to convert their discussions into a wider understanding, to push them a little farther to see what we get.

The logical conditions under which a theory can be evaluated are suggested by a simple truth table in which we look at variations of "if, then" statements. An "if, then" statement is a compound proposition; it is true under all variations of truth or falsity of either antecedent or consequent except a true antecedent and a false consequent. Testing a sufficient condition offers a good example; if the presumed sufficient condition (the antecedent) is (found to be) true, but the predicted consequence is (observed to be) false, the compound (theory) must be false. Scope conditions claim that if the scope conditions are specified and are met, then a test of the theory will be valid (the theory can be said to apply). Thus if we know the scope conditions are true (exist as specified), as are all other conditions of the theory, and results disagree with predictions, then the test result signals that the theory is false. When there exists a credible history of successful tests of a theory using particular scope conditions, they may be said to guarantee a valid test of the theory, although negative findings remain possible.

Foschi (1997, pp. 545-549) discusses the kinds of testing needed to be sure that experimental manipulations work. Tests of this sort can spare a rash researcher from claiming to have rejected the theory when what really happened followed from failure of a scope condition. By defining test situations carefully, scope conditions also help us to rid ourselves of weak tests.

In other words, using scope conditions should help reduce confusion and assist in accumulation of consistent, precisely described research results. Accumulation of knowledge may also be increased by an interesting consequence: the chance to develop hybrid theories which are otherwise distinct but share scope conditions.

They may be used to supplement our abilities to explain processes or outcomes which appear in situations where both theories apply.

OVERVIEW

Types of Assumptions

All theories begin with assumptions, even if they are unstated (implicit premises/enthymemes). These assumptions can be divided into several categories: First are existential propositions from which the theorist deduces other propositions (derived knowledge claims), including the theory's significant predictions which are to be (have been) tested empirically. The original propositions, or the theory's premises, may be believed to be empirically valid, or they may be treated as if they are true. Some may refer to theoretical constructs or to concepts concerning processes or phenomena, existence or properties of which can only be inferred (e.g., norms, see Festinger, Schachter, and Back 1950; Tootell, Mason, Taraldson, Barnhill, and Prather 1986).

Second, theorists depend on technical or formal statements of logical, mathematical, or other rules to deduce consequences from the assumptions in the first set. These assumptions set the foundations of the intellectual apparatus scientists will use (e.g., real numbers, etc.). Assumptions of this kind are commonly implicit in the social sciences.

Third are scope conditions. They are existential propositions which are stated independently of the theory's premises. Finally there are descriptions (or assignments) of initial conditions.

In sum, a scientific theory's assumptions include descriptions of the conditions under which the theory operates. To interpret a model, theorists make substantive assumptions about existential conditions to which the theory applies. Technically speaking, the theorist is vesting abstract variables with substantive meaning. Conceivably, where a theory has a formal model, the same formal structure can be assigned distinctly different interpretations, providing two or more applications of the same abstract theoretical structure. The theory is enhanced if several distinct interpretations can be constructed. An interpretation directs attention of researchers and audiences; it is fitted to substantive problems; it guides the choice of data; it shapes measures. In more mature sciences, a theory may apply to two or more very different sets of phenomena (that is, the same metaphor may help explain each, though they appear to have little else in common). While the theory has only one set of formal assumptions and of formal consequences, it could be assigned distinct sets of existential assumptions. Different applications might require different sets of scope conditions. We know of no good example in the social sciences yet, but we can imagine, say, a model which shows how certain characteristics of exchange relations could be used to sort these early exchanges into a set of ranked categories, where properties associated with the ranking criterion affect the results of subsequent exchanges. This model could easily become the structure of a theory of stratification, but it might need different scope conditions for its macrosociological and microsociological applications.

Assumptions may be phrased with universal quantifiers. Others specify the particular conditions under which a theory applies. Scope conditions are of the latter kind; they include qualifications which restrict the domains of chosen variables, viz., they are the substantive assumptions which propose that the theory will apply if specific constraints exist on the variation of given variables.

Though most theories in the social sciences are presented without scope or technical conditions, sometimes applicability of a theory appears to be improved dramatically by adding a scope condition. This can often be done by replacing a universal quantifier by an existential quantifier or by specifying exactly how to restrict the domain of an independent variable. These changes appear to be supplied relatively easily. Examples occur in some branches of coalition formation research, especially those which developed from ideas of Simmel by way of Caplow (1956) and from work on bargaining, such as, Miller (1980), or Komorita, Aquino, and Ellis (1989). Here some assumptions are offered as if they are universal characterizations, such as the degree to which actors govern their behaviors by both logic and self-interest. Yet some research results show that claims of rationality are not universally true; results of some studies might have been more persuasive had researchers dropped any claims of universal applicability in their theories and altered their designs to include task orientations and attractive rewards as scope conditions (see Nydegger and Owen 1977; below).

Establishing a practice of using scope conditions is consistent with a step by step cumulative strategy. It carries out the dictum of working on middle range theories (Merton 1949) rather than assuming the validity of unproved generalizations. In the past special theories have commonly been defined by subject matter or domain, as, say, a theory of stratification or of organizational behavior. An intelligent alternative is to limit a theory's application to a constant or to a restricted set of values of one or more relevant independent variables (Foschi 1997).

Some Existing Uses of Scope Conditions

Possible uses of scope conditions have appeared with other names, or no names, in existing works. Consider the role of a test factor in uses of elaboration (Kendall and Lazarsfeld 1950, pp. 147-167). On the whole, Kendall and Lazarsfeld were looking for better ways to identify and explain (interpret) spurious findings. They suggested various techniques. In particular, in the P type (for partial relationships, or "specification"), researchers looked for a condition which strengthens a relationship, like the effect of time in service on increasing the relationship between education and rank of enlisted men (Stouffer, Suchman, Devinney, Star and Williams 1949, p. 249ff.). This was certainly analogous to the reasoning underlying the conception of a scope condition, though the earlier focus was on finding the conditions under which an empirical relationship is strong, rather than those under which a theory may be warranted to explain a result.

One of the clearest delineations of differences among axioms, universal substantive assumptions, and scope conditions occurred in von Neumann and Morgenstern (1944, pp. 6-45). The technical axioms used to guide theorists' mathematical reasoning were stated simply (1944, pp. 24-27). Concepts of a social exchange economy and of utility theory were incorporated as general background (pp. 7-24). Scope conditions were not labeled, but they were distinguished: for example, rationality (combining dimensions of logic and of self-interest) (1944, pp. 8-9, 31-43), availability of complete information (pp. 29-30), or use of a single monetary commodity (pp. 8-9). Possible scope conditions from older thought (e.g., exclusion of coalitions, by the Lausanne School; 1944, p. 15) were removed, extending the theory.

Status characteristics theory (SCT) is probably the first and most familiar example in which scope conditions are specified explicitly: (SCT1) Only groups which are task oriented (SCT2) and collectively oriented are covered by the theory (see Berger, Fisek, Norman, and Zelditch 1977, pp. 93-96,104-105; note that scope conditions are initialed by theory and numbered henceforth). Another appears in Zelditch, Harris, Thomas, and Walker's reexamination (1983) of Bacharach's and Baratz' papers concerning the framing and study of decisions, nondecisions and metadecisions within community power theory (CPT; 1962, 1963). Zelditch and colleagues added four scope decisions to be used in their study: (CPT1) The groups engage in collective interdependent tasks and can make authoritative collective decisions (1983, pp. 15-16). (CPT2) Study focuses on the agenda stage of policy processes. (CPT3) All agenda are member-initiated. (CPT4) Conflicts are n-person mixed motive, rather than dyadic (as Bacharach and Baratz had assumed).

Network exchange theory (NET) is a third example with explicitly specified scope conditions (Markovsky, Skvoretz, Willer, Lovaglia, and Erger 1993, p. 198; Markovsky, Willer, and Patton 1988, p. 223). Scope conditions of power predictions are (from Markovsky et al. 1988): (NET1) Actors use identical strategies when negotiating. (NET2) Actors who are consistently excluded from exchanges will raise their offers. (NET3) Actors who are regularly included will lower their offers. (NET4) Actors accept the best offer available or choose randomly among ties. (NET5) Each position is related to at least one other position. (NET6) At the beginning of each cycle of exchanges, equal pools of resources are available for every potential relation. (NET7) Two positions receive resources from their common pool if and only if they complete an exchange.

Michener (1992), showing how central-union theory clarified some anomalies in coalition formation (game) theory, included some scope conditions (1992, p. 72). These were that the games involved must be cooperative n-person games, with transfer payments and superadditivity, in which players are motivated to maximize utility (i.e., rationality).

Some Problems of not Specifying Scope Conditions

One of the most common errors in specifying a theory's application is the assumption that some human trait is pervasive, for example, rational thinking, especially in uncritical use of game theory constructs (e.g., some examples of coalition formation research). Use of rationality in these contexts usually involves at least two or more dimensions (logic, self-interest). It obviously masks other issues: if one is trying to maximize return, one disregards other considerations (kith or kin), therefore discipline and emotional and moral commitments are involved. By the same token, one must avoid interpersonal comparisons. Though game theory can be applied aptly to describe or explain behavior, it has normative or prescriptive aspects which cannot be ignored in making game theoretic analyses. In assuming that people will use the most powerful intellectual, political or physical tools available to get their goals, it is clear that absence of overriding commitments or passions is a scope condition for theories of rational behavior (Munroe and Cohn 1996). In applying rationality to help explain ordinary behavior, optimization is a more realistic concept than maximization.

Other issues concern the level of cognitive difficulty associated with rationality and standards of behavior (von Neumann and Morgenstern 1944, pp. 30, 40-44 et passim). Rationality, as used by subjects in an experiment, might be defined in terms of different standards, such as the knowledge of the subjects, of an experimenter, or of a logician or mathematician who specialized in relevant topics. This requires us to specify the standards of a referential community. An obvious remark is that good arguments can be made for choosing either the first or third standards, which can be loosely associated with behavioral and normative theories, respectively. Experimenters may unwittingly substitute the second for the third, however, committing their evaluations to a (deficient) normative measure, when the first choice might be more realistic. Any such choice is a scope condition of sorts, even if it is an unintentional one.

It is interesting to see Michener (1992) apply scope conditions explicitly to game theory, clearly certifying the domain of central-union theory. Von Neumann and Morgenstern (1944) were astute enough to use the strategy before the concept was salient. Many social scientists who have tried to use game theory, however, have suffered from several problems. For one, they have sometimes confused where game theory can be treated as a tool to explain behavior with where it is more wisely considered as normative theory. In a study comparing three models of coalition formation, Miller (1980) used the Shapley value theorem (see Owen 1982, pp. 193-198) as a solution concept which might be used by freshmen psychology students. This does not necessarily raise the issue of whether the students would use this function consciously as an exercise in rationality. At best, probably very few of them could have had any idea it existed or the skill or desire to apply it. Yet without knowing of its existence, relying on years of trial, error, and accumulated sophistication, senior legislators might be able to approximate its effects as a way to solve difficult problems in practical coalition formation, especially where political stakes are high. Second, social scientists have sometimes treated game theory as a general theory, when in fact, there are many and various applications of this theory which (a) are contradictory and (b) are designed to fit entirely distinct situations. Third, there is an important difference between theorists assuming that people behave as if they were rational under conditions x or y (e.g., relatives of victims weeping loudly during a trial vs. grieving alone at night) and observers imputing rationality to subjects under a large variety of conditions (e.g., voters).

This issue was brought to a head nicely in a study by Nydegger and Owen (1977) which should have figured prominently in subsequent literature but unfortunately has not. These researchers examined what subjects might do when no clear solution technique existed. In brief, they created a situation in which two members of a triad might maximize their returns by dealing with each other. On the other hand, they permitted side payments, so that while dealing with the third member would cost each something, it would be possible for bargaining to occur, so that this problem could be overcome. While they expected that most players might not use this option, they thought that choice would cause some inner discomfort (imbalance) which could be offset by recognizing some fault in the third, expensive member. In fact, 13 of 20 groups formed three way coalitions and split the returns evenly.

In looking at previous coalition formation research, Nydegger and Owen conjectured a variety of factors which could have explained the deviation of findings from their expectations (1977, pp. 32-34). They recognized that subjects' behaviors sometimes violated investigators' assumptions. Subjects have multidimensional utility schema, so researchers should expect them to optimize rather than maximize. They recognized many specific issues which can be converted into scope conditions. Relative cognitive complexity is important. Subjects are sometimes given so much information that they cannot manage it. Even people who try to behave rationally must be limited by their understanding of logic, mathematics, mechanics or whatever skills are germane. To explain their problematic results, Nydegger and Owen (1977, p. 36) suggested that the reward must be large enough to be appealing. It may help if the problem challenges, or at least interests, subjects. People also live within a normative context, and they may import or invent norms (e.g., of fairness) which members accept to fit the situation. These can differ from group to group (while 13 groups split three ways, two used a chance procedure to exclude a member). Where social scientists apply game theory behaviorally, a deft use of scope conditions promises to be very helpful.

This study not only emphasizes the importance of recognizing scope conditions explicitly but also the critical role they play in research design. Of course, this issue must be anticipated properly. This is evident in the development of status characteristics theory (Berger et al. 1977; Webster and Driskell 1978; Wagner and Berger 1993). A sage agenda is outlined by Foschi (1997), where she shows how to design studies to anticipate potential problems from easily made assumptions, changing social or cultural conditions, or other possible sources of error, and also how to check whether the design succeeded.

Logical Analyses of Assumptions

A propositional logic can be used to glean truth (falsity) of specific sentences, to reduce any redundancies, to identify contradictions or certify independence, or to demonstrate existence of logical relations and to help derive theoretically true testable predictions (assuming the assumptions are valid). An alternative is to use mathematics, especially when that tool is available. Recently Bonacich (1996) has shown that it may be possible to reduce the set of NET's scope conditions by eliminating NET3 and at least part of NET4. Perhaps others could be combined or cut without damage by using more powerful mathematical theory, namely game theory, as a background and resource. Simplifying statements and making conditions more abstract can increase their generality and make them more interesting theoretically.

Logical analyses may be useful to examine if, and if so, how a theory's scope conditions are related to its premises. [This is a controversial issue with critical consequences, which we shall discuss below.] A reasonable way to start is to recognize that the theory may only apply within parts of the domains of certain independent variables. This might be indicated by theoretical conjecture, previous findings or pilot studies. When theorists start work, they should distinguish these variables from others in their initial variable list. Scope conditions are the assumptions constructed to propose when and how the theory will apply, with reference to specific parts of the domains of these scope variables. For example, in network exchange theory (NET; see Markovsky et al. 1988; Willer and Skvoretz 1997; below) the scope conditions are not deduced from the axioms. In particular, one scope condition requires that, in case of duplicate offers, actors choose randomly. It is a sensible way to explain what happens in an experiment, which researchers need to resolve for practical reasons. But NET's axioms do not introduce probabilistic concepts and are consistent with a deterministic model. That is not the theorists' intent, as they use probability concepts with respect to weak power outcomes.

An excellent reason exists to distinguish scope conditions from the theory's premises. Suppose that the scope conditions are implied by the premises. Then if any criterion, such as a test, shows that a statement of a scope condition is falsified, the correct conclusion would be that the theory has failed. That would be true either if the cause was that the condition was not met or that the condition was met but failed, in fact, as a scope condition. Its falsification would imply that the theory is false. This is contrary to the nature and conception of scope conditions as well as to the theorist's intent in introducing the specific scope condition. If the scope condition is independent of the premises, failure of the test may imply that the scope condition was either poorly chosen or poorly operationalized. It would not necessarily imply that the theory is false. Thus theorists must take care not to choose scope conditions which can be inferred directly from the theory's premises.

Yet it may be reasonable to claim that theorists should use theoretical, not just methodological, grounds to justify their selection of a particular set of scope conditions. For example, looking at SCT (Berger et al. 1977; see Cohen 1989, pp. 245, 315), it is clear that if a group is committed to achieve some goal, it seems reasonable that its members may place a premium, temporarily at least, on the competence needed to complete the task. They need to estimate the relative relevant abilities of each member with regard to task completion, especially concerning decisions about to whom to listen and whom they might better expect to ignore or instruct. This requires that they pay some minimal attention, at least, to each member's ideas. Yet they are likely to listen more carefully to those whom they believe to be more competent than they, and they may expect those whom they think are less able to listen to them. Furthermore, in the absence of telling information, it is reasonable to infer this assignment of relative ability from common beliefs about the competence of people who have specific states of characteristics on which the group is differentiated. When a group is differentiated by several characteristics, it increases the chance that the combination of its more valuable states may be scarce. This reduces the likelihood of disagreement and may yield a more efficient communication process (Munroe, Tootell, and Kuhn 1995). In contrast, if there exists no important task of common interest, members' beliefs about, or inferences of, each other's competence seem less consequential. Violation of task orientation may mean there is insufficient motive to form a power and prestige hierarchy based on imputed degrees of competence. Nor will the process work effectively if members completely ignore each other. Hence task and collective orientation are reasonable choices as scope conditions for SCT. These scope conditions are independent of SCT's premises. Either could occur without the other. This suggests an interesting conclusion, that any theory may have more than one set of scope conditions (see below).

This points to a way to clarify this issue. It depends on the independence of the scope conditions from the premises the theory and the choice of logical forms used to phrase the test of the theory. The argument used by Cohen implies that the theory's predictions can be observed under conditions which are contingent on the truth values of its component premises, expressed in a compound statement in which a conjunction is used to join the scope conditions and the premises. This compound describes the coincidence of independent events (as stated in the premises of SCT and the definitions of task and collective orientation). The premises and the scope conditions, joined by the conjunction (represented by "and"), are then used as an antecedent in a conditional statement of which the consequent is a prediction of the theory. This states a condition under which it is sufficient to evaluate the theory.

The truth of the consequent depends on the truth of each of the components in its antecedent. As long as these parts are independent, the truth of the conclusion (the entire statement) is contingent on the truth of each component, as well as that of the consequent. This argument imitates the (logical) form of contingent schemata (Pospesel 1984). It also corresponds to the way in which most experimenters use scope conditions while testing theories.

This statement creates an interesting opportunity, for which we need set theory to explore relations among sets of substantive assumptions, and in particular among statements of scope conditions. This can be used to help sociologists grow a new sort of theory, useful hybrids, in which distinct theories may share some or all scope conditions (below). As a result, subject to restrictions mentioned below, theorists may be able to identify clusters of theories which, even if otherwise unrelated, can be tested jointly to see whether both theories can be applied in a complementary manner to help explain broader ranges of properties of the units being studied. When useful, this step can be applied backward to distinguish theories which apply to common sorts of situations.

Applications and Benefits

Walker and Cohen (1985) pointed out that the debate over the falsifiability of sociological theories can be ameliorated by providing a set of explicit scope conditions. Cohen (1989, p. 248) acknowledged the argument of Popper (1959) that the criterion of falsifiability separates science from other intellectual realms. This works if and only if a theory can be falsified when its conclusions (predictions) are falsified. But there are several problems implicit in this statement. For example, in most theories there are several premises. If only one is false, it could lead to a result by which the theory is falsified. Further, that state might not be discovered immediately. Next, many statements may link a prediction to its premises. By inspection of truth tables it is easy to see that logical relations of the "if, then" or "only if, then" require careful interpretation. Some linking statements may be false when the premises are true, thereby weakening an appeal to an hypothetical syllogism to justify the conclusion. Misrepresenting an initial condition can mislead researchers. A test may consider but one instantiation of a theory. That is slim evidence on which to reject it, especially if other tests support the theory, or if there are possible flaws in the test procedure. Researchers are reluctant to abandon a theory until they are convinced that another theory is better, or unless the preponderance of evidence clearly refutes it.

One way of ameliorating this situation is to edit a theory's assumptions very carefully. Some may be converted to scope conditions by restricting the domain(s) of one or more variables, providing derivation of predictions does not depend on the "new" scope conditions. Analysis may suggest that others may not hold unless another condition is added (which may or may not be a scope condition). This procedure may account for many of the exceptions to theories which attempt universal application.

When the practice of stating relevant scope conditions is conducted systematically, it may reveal overlaps among various sets of scope conditions. These may foretell occasions when distinctly different theories help explain why otherwise independent processes may operate side by side or in sequence. Finally, by specifying scope conditions under a formal discipline, we can increase the rigor of the intellectual structure with which we address our understanding of the phenomena we investigate.

Formal theories use mathematics or logic to derive a variety of consequences from a few assumptions. Nonformal theories refer to no explicit rigorous device to relate one set of sentences to another. As a result, it is usually problematic whether one sentence follows from another, contradicts the other or whether they are independent. This condition can be relieved if the natural language cloaks a logical structure. As an example, Cohen showed how analysis could reveal the underlying logical structure of SCT (1989, pp. 230-236). (SCT had been formalized, which does not diminish Cohen's demonstration [Berger et al. 1977]).

Theories can also be divided between those whose authors believe that their initial assumptions are generally true (general or "grand" theories) and those who think they hold only under certain, specific conditions (special theories). Members of the first group often think their initial assumptions are based on "observations" which hold generally. [From here on "generally" will mean "always" rather than "usually."] An example might be that people act in their own self-interest. Careful, objective scrutiny of cases indicates that substantial exceptions exist, for example, soldiers who have thrown themselves on grenades to protect their fellows or the anonymous neighbors of the Cypress Expressway who risked effects of aftershocks, as well as arrest, to free people from their cars after the earthquake in the San Francisco Bay area in 1989.

Sometimes it is possible to show that there is a relation between a pair of theories such that one theory incorporates another, as some (if not all) physicists say celestial mechanics is a special case of relativity theory. In this example, the second is usually said to be a special case of the first. Such relationships are more clear in the case of formal theories, where relations can be spelled out unambiguously. Here we shall look for a way to determine sets of approximate relations among theories which may be empirically associated but which we cannot prove to be formally related, at least not now.

DEFINING SCOPE CONDITIONS

The nature of scope conditions is not completely clear yet. As defined by Cohen (1989, p. 83), "Scope conditions are a set of universal statements that define the class of circumstances in which a knowledge claim (or a set of knowledge claims) is applicable." We shall qualify this somewhat; for example, scope conditions must be expressed by existential quantifiers. We can define a set of scope conditions now and explicate our ideas below. A theory's scope conditions are defined by a set of propositions, containing specified scope variables, which have the following properties:

1. They are either true or false.
2. They are abstract.
3. They cannot be inferred from the theory's premises, nor vice versa.
4. They are applied as components of conditional statements of antecedent conditions, in which they are joined by a conjunction ("and") to one or more or the theory's premises; taken together they state conditions sufficient for the theory to apply.
5. They restrict the domains of specified knowledge claims, to identified subsets or intervals, that is, the values of the scope variables are either constant or greater than, less than, or in intervals defined by specified bounds.
6. They are existential statements associated with a theory, in which the specified scope variables bear existential referents. The theory asserts knowledge claims with empirical applications, such that these statements document conditions under which it is reasonable to believe the theory's assumptions are satisfied and that its predictions can be verified. Therefore the theory can be properly evaluated empirically, that is, refuted under conditions that are convincing if it is not true.
7. Scope statements are those propositions which form the intersection of properties (1-6).

Scope statements indicate social conditions within which a given theory is thought to be valid; these conditions are assumed to be fixed unless specifically changed by processes covered by the theory (Berger 1974, p. 15; Cohen 1989, p. 84). Note that they do not specify initial states of variables needed to make predictions. Collectively, they are sufficient conditions needed to test the theory in a way which reasonable and knowledgeable scientists would consider to be fair and convincing. Thus they should be considered as a set. When all of them are true, the authors should be ready to guarantee formally that if one tests the theory empirically, its mechanisms will satisfy appropriate evaluation criteria. Hopefully, theorists offer the guarantee with fear and trembling until researchers can embolden them with evidence. Of course, predictions may be true even if not all the conditions hold. But no one warrants that this will happen regularly.

This definition implies several consequences. A particularly important one is that by using a truth table or other logical devices, a theorist can show clearly that these sets of conditions state exactly circumstances under which the theory can be falsified.

As scope statements are abstract specifications of the substantive conditions under which the predictions of the theory can be shown to be accurate (or not), they can have varieties of specific existential referents (instantiations). This allows the theory to have a potentially wide range of applications, while each distinct interpretation of a formal model may have its own set of scope conditions.

Clearly scope conditions should play an important part in the design of tests of the theory (Cohen 1989, pp. 85-113). A classic example is the formulation of scope conditions by Zelditch and colleagues to circumnavigate the methodological issues (and controversies) aroused by Bacharach and Baratz (see Zelditch et al. 1983; above, below). As tests of theories are not valid if their scope conditions are violated, researchers must carefully design each condition into each test. This requirement gives a researcher guidelines which, in the long run, ease his/her task and improve quality. For example, the effort by Lee and Ofshe (1981) to show shortcomings of SCT was weakened by, among other things, their failure to test the theory within its scope conditions (e.g., collective orientation was violated by an inability of subjects to respond to confederates shown on a videotape).

APPLICATION OF FORMAL METHODS

After the elements are defined in a theory of scope conditions, the operations can be specified. Typical operations are negation, alternation, and conjunction. Using them we can apply the rules of inference and axioms of a propositional logic (see Pospesel 1984; also Carlsen-Jones 1983; Copi 1982; Suppes 1957; Rescher 1964; Stoll 1963). This approach is particularly useful for examining a theory's consistency or the extension of its image (range). We might use set theory or a Boolean algebra (Birkhoff and Mac Lane 1953; Pinter 1971) to look at potentially supplementary relations among theories. We can use such methods to prove the validity, or invalidity (see Cohen 1989, p. 236), of (new) combinations of statements or even of new operations, such as implication. Before worrying about such adventures, let us consider some simple examples of practical issues.

Scope statements should consist of independent propositions which contain one or more logical connectives. There may be occasions when a theorist or researcher wants or needs to use these connectives to join two or more statements (e.g., see discussion of task orientation and competence above).

We should note the use of universal and existential quantifiers, for one or more members x of set X: The universal quantifier, $(\forall x)$, means for all x, each x has some property P. The existential quantifier, $(\exists x)$, means there exists some x, at least one, which has property P.

SOME SIMPLE APPLICATIONS

Testing Consistency

Cohen (1989, pp. 236-238) used a logical analysis to show that Homans' (1964) argument about punishment of criminals does not follow from its premises. Researchers who founded the human relations hypothesis (HRH) provided evidence that the most productive work groups were cohesive (Roethlisberger and Dickson 1939 [1964]; Mayo 1943; also Guest 1962). But Stogdill (1972) discovered a number of studies which showed that cohesive groups were often unproductive (see also Homans 1950). It is obvious that cohesiveness may be a necessary condition of high performance (cf. below), but it is not sufficient. On both counts, a proposition which represents such a condition would provide an inadequate basis for stating scope conditions of a productivity model.

In a revised model of the HRH, Tootell and Munroe (1997) suggest that appropriate scope conditions include (HRH1) task and (HRH2) collective orientations for group members, plus (HRH3) adequate training and (HRH4) a provision of rewards sufficient to motivate members. Yet further thought indicates that HRH4 is implied by HRH1: if task commitment, including extrinsic motivation, is too weak to activate members, it is not possible to maintain task orientation.

By adding an independent condition applicability is usually narrowed. Dropping an independent scope condition always extends the theory's range (image). Adding or dropping a scope condition which depends on another scope condition should not. Suppose set $S_{net1} \supset S_{net2}$. Thus $(\exists\ x)\ (S_{net1}(x) \Rightarrow S_{net2}(x))$. If S_{net1} is regarded as this cluster's universal set (which includes all of its possible scope conditions), and x and y are specific scope conditions, then for any set $S_{net\ i}$ of its scope conditions $(\exists\ x)\ (S_{net1}\ (x) \cap S_{net\ i}\ (x))$. It is also true that for $(\exists\ y)\ (S_{net1}\ (y) \cap S_{net\ j}\ (\sim y))$, which implies that since these assumptions are restrictions, S_{netj} has a more extended application than S_{net1}. In comparing two theories, one may have a set of scope conditions which is implied by the second theory's scope conditions, but the converse is untrue.

In Markovsky's work on distributive justice, he lists three scope conditions plus a requirement that they hold from the actor's perspective (1985, pp. 826-827). He also stresses the importance of a difference between his theory and the status value theory proposed by Berger, Zelditch, Anderson, and Cohen (1972). In his theory the group may either develop its own unique standards or import ones which are generally recognized externally (as required by Berger et al). Thus he claims its domain of applicability is extended. [Other evidence favors his claim that group norms can be either invented or imported (Tootell et al. 1986). If norms can emerge through a variety of processes, it helps explain why groups can develop either "appropriate" or "inappropriate" norms so easily.]

Does this necessarily extend the range of application of a theory which includes norms as a term? To be extended, a theory must be made more general in one or more of several ways. For example, in a semantic sense, someone can reinterpret its terms in new ways which are sound, meaningful, and useful without costing the loss of the former meanings (this includes raising the level of abstraction to cover more meanings). Second, a theory can be made more potent in a syntactic sense if its structure is modified to enable theorists to derive new useful predictions while saving existing derivations. Or in a pragmatic sense, someone may show that it is possible to eliminate a scope condition without doing any damage to the theory's credibility. [Per above, the first theory can be used under a wider variety of conditions.] Markovsky's interpretation fits the first strategy mentioned above.

Coordination of Social Theories to Form Hybrids

Here we want to look for clusters of theories which share scope conditions but which are not related by logic, mathematics or by common premises (original knowledge claims) or perhaps even common terms. Obviously, significant overlaps among either premises or technical assumptions should invite attention from theorists and researchers. The goal here is to find theories which explain distinct processes which may be operating simultaneously in the same situations. If these coincidences occur frequently, these hybrid theories could help explain some anomalies, add breadth to what we know, and provide interesting insights into processes about which we know something but not enough.

An example of such a theoretical cluster associates SCT with CPT (community power theory), at least with that part of it examined by Zelditch, Harris, Thomas, and Walker (1983). As noted, the recognized scope conditions of SCT are that the group is (SCT1) task oriented and (SCT2) collectively oriented (Berger et al. 1977, pp. 93-96). The first is clear; members of the group must be motivated to solve a problem or achieve a group goal. The second means that it is legitimate and necessary for each member of the group to consider the contribution of every other member as a way to accomplish the group task. Zelditch and colleagues used four scope conditions (1983, pp. 15-16). We have broken down their scope conditions differently here: (CPTz1) Groups are task oriented and (CPTz2) collectively oriented. (CPTz3) Group tasks are interdependent, and the groups have procedures for making authoritative collective decisions. (CPTz4) Agenda are member initiated n-person, mixed motive conflicts which afford a focus of attention for members (and researchers). SCT has been supported by results of many studies. CPT has not been supported as prolifically, but we assume that researchers believe (quite reasonably) that existing studies are convincing.

It is clear that the CPTz1 and CPTz2 are equivalent to SCT1 and SCT2. Let SCT1 and SCT2 compose set S_1. Now let CPTz1, ... , CPTz4 be the members of S_2. Then $S_2 \supset S_1$. This suggests that in this situation, researchers have grounds to search for signs of status generalization processes. If they find these processes, this might help explain other effects which accompany community decisions (perhaps certain features of the power and prestige hierarchy or larger than expected influence of some members due to impacts of their imported status differences). From what we know, coincidence does not imply that community power processes generate status generalization processes (obviously the converse is untrue). It does not even mean we should claim without further inquiry that status generalization processes are operating where this type of community power process appears.

Identifying these clusters, and forming hybrids of them, is problematic. One problem is the limited use of explicit scope conditions. The greater difficulty is logical. If theories X and Y have the same scope conditions, either of them can be tested under these conditions, but they would not be assumed to apply unless their premises were also realized in the pertinent circumstances. Even then, however, that if both are evaluated under these conditions in the same test, we cannot be sure that either will be supported (see below; we have not derived joint predictions and conceivably they could cancel each other's consequents). Clearly, before we can trust that they do operate simultaneously in the same situation, we must test the validity of the hybrid.

Even the amount of evidence known to favor a theory does not affect the probability of its performance under its next test. For the "paradox" of probability theory indicates that while past occurrences in similar circumstances provide the best information on which to base expectations, what happens next is not determined by the past. Nor is this contrary to the epistemological assumption that what scientists observe under carefully specified conditions should also be expected to occur with the same probability when no scientist is looking, as long as the same conditions hold.

Suppose theoretical coincidence is indicated by intersecting scope conditions of theories X and Y, the researchers should begin with a logical analysis of the assumptions the theories involved (X, Y, ...). They should examine the premises and technical assumptions in particular. The issues are (1) whether or not there are contradictions, (2) whether there are other identical assumptions or any cases of dependence of a premise of one theory on an assumption of another (or whether the assumptions of one independent are of those of another), and (3) whether premises of both theories hold in the conditions being observed. If (1), there is a contradiction, it should be clear that these theories are incompatible, and researchers should be able to show that one applies better than the other (one should be refutable). If the theories are compatible, and their scope conditions intersect, they may be suitable partners in a hybrid theory. If they share premises (2), the theories may be related. Finally, (3) if their premises often coincide empirically, we should investigate effects of the hybrid.

If premises are similar, but technical assumptions differ, formal theorists should examine the latter carefully to seek ways to strengthen or extend one or both. An interesting case occurs if the technical assumptions are the same, but the substantive ones are distinct. What results is the case under which a formal theory has two different interpretations.

A potential example in the social sciences raises the possibility that a theory can have several distinct sets of scope conditions, as long as none is both necessary and sufficient with respect to its applicability. This can occur if there are alternative sets of conditions under which it can be applied. As an approximation of this, Johnston (1985) has expanded expectation states research to a new domain, the activation of "personality attributions" to ambiguous social settings. The scope conditions for this research are that the situation of action involves socioemotional orientation toward the meeting of the needs of the group members under a set of agreed upon rules. These differ from the scope conditions for SCT, another branch of expectation states research.

Given disparate theories X and Y which share scope conditions, how likely is it that each of their predictions will be observed whenever those conditions apply? For convenience, suppose each theory has five original premises which differ and five scope conditions which coincide. These sets are clearly distinct. Consider the sets separately, for they present different problems. If the technical assumptions of the two theories are not contradictory, they should pose no problems. Then, looking at the premises of each theory, we can separate those which make universal claims from those which are conditional. Comparing the sets of the two theories, if any assumptions are contradictory, we would not expect to see them apply simultaneously. Suppose two assumptions are universally true (e.g., in triadic coalition formation theory, labels may be permuted so that the power distribution is always $A \geq B \geq C$); consider the three conditional assumptions to see if each is met. Some of them may not pose an overall problem; others might surprise us. For example, in SCT a variable which differentiates the group members will become salient unless its task relevance has been dissociated. Suppose the variable chosen for experimental manipulation has been dissociated previously, and its dissociation is unknown to the experimenter (i.e., an initial condition fails). A misleading result will occur even if every other condition is met (including the usual scope conditions). Yet the process underlying the theory will be working according to theory, though it will produce a different power and prestige hierarchy than expected.

Suppose theories X and Y have been well supported previously by data in well designed studies, our analyses of them show no contradictions among their premises, and at least one study shows that both sets of premises apply simultaneously in situation T under shared scope conditions. We should expect that, in the field, if one is known to apply, there is a reasonable probability that the process explained by the other also will be operating. This probability takes account of the possibility that the theory's predictions would fail. Failure might occur because they are refutable or because the processes were suppressed somehow. Overlapping scope conditions do not mean different processes work in concert. Their effects are presumably theoretically independent of each other; yet we may find that they may enhance, dampen or squelch each other for reasons unknown. The possibility that they interact is worth investigating.

Although he did not use scope conditions, Fligstein (1985) completed theoretical and empirical analyses analogous to those we advocate to examine how five theories of organizational change might explain emergence of multidivisional organizations among large business firms in the United States between 1919 and 1979. His data (1985, pp. 387-388) were inconsistent with the structural inertia hypothesis of Hannan and Freeman (1984) and did not support Williamson's argument (1975, ch. 8) that unitary functional forms in organizations outgrow their capacities to contain transaction costs and thus multidivisional forms are the necessary adaptation. Data did support the other theories: (1) Chandler's strategy-structure thesis (1962), (2) the power perspective, based on an assumption that since grounds for decisions are usually murky, outcomes are decided by power based on structural claims for resource allocation (e.g. Pfeffer 1981; Perrow 1970), and (3) Dimaggio's and Powell's argument (1983) that cultural expectations, dependence on professional managers, and uncertainty produce organizational mimics and homogeneity. Finally, and most significantly, rather than identifying other tests to distinguish which remaining theory is most valid, Fligstein (1985, pp. 387-389) indicated that since the processes of organizational change are complex, more than one theory should be used to explain them. In the absence of a unified theory, this suggests a policy of using a hybrid, complementing the surviving theories with others, as needed, to help explain changes.

The relationship of two or more theories in a hybrid begins as an empirical generalization. Subsequent logical and empirical studies can reveal whether these theories can be unified in some stronger way. If so, then joint or common predictions will be possible, including the effects of these processes on each other.

Given these warnings, from here on we shall consider the inclusion of theory X's scope conditions by those of theory Y as a signal to perform such analyses and research, and we shall not repeat the appropriate disclaimers. Theorists must be meticulous when they speculate whether two or more theories might form a reasonable hybrid, while researchers must do the same when they test the proposition that two or more theories can behave in harness. Yet when all disclaimers are made, a researcher who is trying to explain the processes operating in situation T would be foolish to close his/her mind to the possibility that both theories apply and that both sets of processes are operating. Researchers in the field trying to explain some anomaly should be imaginative enough so that if the scope conditions of X and of Y are met in the field in T, and if researchers find that theory X helps explain what is happening in T, the possibility that theory Y might apply there as well should be noted, and thus the processes explained by theory Y might be operating there as well.

A similar pattern applies to SCT and HRH. The notion of a group developing its own standards (Markovsky 1985; Tootell et al. 1986) is basic to the interactionist approach to HRH (see Arensberg and Tootell 1957; Guest 1962), which anticipated Stogdill's findings (1972). In the current model of HRH (Tootell and Munroe 1997), the scope conditions include (1) task and (2) collective orientation, and also (HRH3) adequate training. Let p = (HRH1), q = (HRH2), r = (HRH3). Then S_1 = $\{p, q\}$ is the set of scope conditions of SCT, and S_3 = $\{p, q, r\}$ are the scope conditions of HRH.

It is obvious that $S_3 \supset S_1$. Whenever S_3 applies, S_1 applies too. In practice, this proposes that in any situation in which the HRH is found to be true, that SCT may apply too. While this does not imply that SCT's predictions will be true, it does suggest that we should be aware that status generalization processes might be operating in these situations. This simple result is certainly not obvious from a reading of the premises of each theory. Formally, the two are compatible, but one does not imply the other. A researcher is only alerted after reading their scope conditions. A (delicious but perhaps unhappy) irony is that under these conditions status generalizing processes may often interfere with group effectiveness (for evidence of this, see Troyer, Silver, and Watkins 1994). We note that without HRH3 the reservations in the newer model of HRH do not apply, and status generalization processes could advance productivity growth (see Marglin 1974). This is consistent with the conclusion that status generalization processes increase the probability of attaining collective decisions (Munroe et al. 1995).

If more theorists specified their theories' scope conditions, it would be interesting to develop propositions about their relationships with each other. And we can comment about research already reported, for example, coalition formation (see Caplow 1956; Burhans 1973; Nydegger and Owen 1977; Komorita et al. 1989). It is intriguing that this tradition has often foundered on data which approach the authors' claims, but generalizations fall short of conviction. Conditional versions of these premises may be adequate as scope conditions. Had they been treated as such in the research processes, more careful designs might have produced data which supported the predictions more securely. Indeed, where (SCT1) and (SCT2) apply, it is reasonable to interpret the results of status generalization processes as a coalition formation process; the power and prestige hierarchy generates an influence process which helps to form collective decisions (Munroe et al. 1995). To the extent that coalition formation theories do not apply outside those conditions (see Nydegger and Owen 1977), SCT may be one of the better ways to explain how coalitions form. These conditions apply to legislative coalition formation, though other conditions also may be necessary.

COMMENTS

At this point, theorizing and research about scope conditions need more raw material, especially interesting cases. Suggestions about strategies, rules or the like would also advance these endeavors.

The usefulness of logical analyses of existing theories is theoretically unassailable. At times they confirm that a logical structure exists (e.g., Cohen 1989; Merton's presentation of a syllogism to represent Durkheim's use of egoistic suicide to help explain differences of suicide rates in Protestant England and Catholic France (1949)). Yet they seem to serve little purpose when they appear to be an unnecessary and tedious confirmation of the structure of an underlying logically coherent argument.

The underlying problem is that one never can be sure if a theory written in a natural language is logically coherent until someone tries to formalize it. No matter how well a theory reads in English (German, etc.), if its predictions do not follow from its assumptions, we can substitute any set of predictions which neither depend on these assumptions nor contradict them, and we shall not change the meaning of the theory as a whole (it is meaningless). Validity of its "predictions" is contingent on unknown conditions.

Formalization is the "inverse" of interpretation. A formal model may be elegant, but we do not know what it means until it is given substantive flesh: it must be described in a natural language and assigned a set of specific measures with a prescribed organization. Only then can it be translated into a good research design to be tested.

The value of logical analysis is clear when an author is uncertain or makes one or more logical errors (see Cohen on Homans, Cohen 1989), or when an author is planning to make an argument, prior to drafting theory or designing research. After all, it is in the early stages of work that logical analysis is most profitable. Logical coherence, coupled with scope conditions, aid in creation of retesting schemes to validate or refute a theory's applicability after the argument is made.

When and if scope conditions are used more widely, hybrid theories may provide media for some very interesting discoveries. This may lead to deeper analyses and reconstruction of these theories, yielding fresher, stronger, more sophisticated, more abstract, and more extensive theories. A strategy of relying on composite or hybrid theories may not only help us find more powerful explanations among middle range theories; it can provide practice fields for surveying and studying the kinds of mathematics that are most workable in sociology. These advances will probably be phrased in more powerful mathematics eventually, considering the increasing interest in mathematics and formal theory in sociology and the increasing success of several formalized models. Yet given the need for conditional substantive assumptions, which include scope conditions, it appears that no matter how sophisticated our formal theories get, hybrid theories may be here for some time.

ACKNOWLEDGMENTS

Debts are due to Robert K. Merton, Joseph Berger, Bernard P. Cohen, Morris Zelditch Jr., Martha Foschi, and two anonymous reviewers. This essay revises a paper presented at the International Group Processes Conference, Cracow, Poland, 1996. An early version was presented at the West Coast Group Processes Conference, San Jose, CA, 1996. Please address all correspondence to Geoffrey Tootell, Department of Sociology, San Jose State University, San Jose, CA 95192-0122.

REFERENCES

Arensberg, C.M., and G. Tootell. 1957. "Plant Sociology: Real Discoveries and New Problems." In *Common Frontiers of the Social Sciences,* edited by M. Komarovski. Glencoe, IL: Free Press.

Bacharach, P., and M.S. Baratz. 1962. "Two Faces of Power." *American Political Science Review* 56: 947-952.

Bacharach, P., and M.S. Baratz. 1963. "Decisions and Nondecisions: An Analytical Framework." *American Political Science Review* 57: 632-642.

Berger, J. 1974. "Expectation States Theory: A Theoretical Research Program." In *Expectation States Theory: A Theoretical Research Program,* edited by J. Berger, T.L. Conner, and M.H. Fisek. Cambridge, MA: Winthrop Publishers.

Berger, J., M.H. Fisek, R.Z. Norman, and M. Zelditch Jr. 1977. *Status Characteristics and Interaction: Expectation States Approach.* New York: Elsevier.

Berger, J., M. Zelditch, Jr., B. Anderson and B. P. Cohen. 1972. "Structural Aspects of Distributive Justice: A Status-Value Formulation." In *Sociological Theories in Progress,* Vol. 2, edited by J. Berger, M. Zelditch Jr., and B. Anderson. Boston: Houghton Mifflin.

Birkoff, G., and S. Mac Lane. 1953. *A Survey of Modern Algebra.* New York: The Macmillan Company.

Bonacich, P. 1996. "Macro and Micro Process in Exchange Networks: Finding the Missing Link." Paper presented at the International Group Processes Conference, Cracow, Poland.

Burhans, D.T. 1973. "Coalition Game Research: A Reexamination." *American Journal of Sociology* 79: 389-407.

Caplow, T. 1956. "Theory of Coalitions in the Triad." *American Sociological Review* 21: 489-493.

Carlsen-Jones, M.T. 1983. *Introduction to Logic.* New York: McGraw-Hill.

Chandler, A. 1962 *Strategy and Structure.* Cambridge: MIT Press.

Cohen, B.P. 1989. *Developing Sociological Knowledge, Theory and Method,* 2nd edition. Chicago, IL: Nelson-Hall.

Copi, I.M. 1982. *Symbolic Logic.* 6th edition. New York: Macmillan.

DiMaggio, P., and W. Powell.1983. "Institutional Isomorphism." *American Sociological Review* 48: 147-160.

Festinger, L., S. Schachter, and K. Back. 1950. *Social Pressures in Informal Groups.* New York: Harper.

Fligstein, N. 1985. "The Spread of the Multidivisional Form Among Large Firms, 1919-1979." *American Sociological Review* 50: 377-391.

Foschi, M. 1997. "On Scope Conditions." *Small Group Research* 28(4): 535-555.

Guest, R.H. 1962. *Organizational Change: The Effect of Successful Leadership.* Homewood, IL: Dorsey Press and Richard D. Irwin.

Hannan, M., and J. Freeman. 1984. "Structural Inertia and Organizational Change." *American Sociological Review* 49: 149-64.

Homans, G.C. 1950. *The Human Group.* New York: Harcourt Brace Jovanovich.

Homans, G.C. 1964. "Contemporary Theory in Sociology." In *Handbook of Modern Sociology,* edited by R.E.L. Faris. New York: Rand McNally.

Johnston, J.R. 1985. "How Personality Attributes Structure Interpersonal Relations." Pp. 317-349 in *Status, Rewards, and Influence: How Expectations Organize Behavior,* edited by J. Berger and M. Zelditch Jr. San Francisco: Jossey-Bass.

Kendall, P.L., and P.F. Lazarsfeld. 1950. "Problems in Survey Analysis." In *Continuities in Social Research,* edited by R.K. Merton and P.F. Lazarsfeld. New York: Free Press.

Komorita, S.S., K.F. Aquino, and A.L. Ellis. 1989. "Coalition Bargaining: A Comparison of Theories Based on Allocation Norms and Theories Based on Bargaining Strength." *Social Psychological Quarterly* 52: 183-196.

Lakatos, I. 1970. "Falsification and the Methodology of Scientific Research Programmes." In *Criticism and the Growth of Knowledge,* edited by I. Lakatos and A. Musgrave. Cambridge: Cambridge University Press.

Lee, M.T., and R. Ofshe. 1981. "The Impact of Behavioral Style and Status Characteristics on Social Reference: A Test of Two Competing Theories." *Social Psychology Quarterly* 44: 73-82.

Marglin, S.A. 1974. "What Do Bosses Do? The Origins and Functions of Hierarchy in Capitalist Production." *The Review of Radical Political Economics* 6: 33-60; 7: 120-137.

Markovsky, B. 1985. "Toward a Multilevel Distributive Justice Theory." *American Sociological Review* 50: 822-839.

Markovsky, B., D. Willer, and T. Patton. 1988. "Power Relations in Exchange Networks." *American Sociological Review,* 53: 220-236.

Markovsky, B., J. Skvoretz, D. Willer, M.J. Lovaglia, and J. Erger. 1993. "The Seeds of Weak Power: An Extension of Network Exchange Theory." *American Sociological Review,* 58: 197-209.

Mayo, E. 1946. *The Human Problems of Industrial Civilization.* Boston: Division of Research, Graduate School of Business Administration, Harvard University.

Merton, R.K. 1949. *Social Theory and Social Structure.* Glencoe, IL: Free Press.

Michener, H.A. 1992. "Coalition Anomalies in Light of the Central-Union Theory." In *Advances in Group Processes,* Vol. 9, edited by E.J. Lawler. Greenwich, CT: JAI Press.

Miller, C.E. 1980. "Effects of Payoffs and Resources on Coalition Formation: A Test of Three Theories." *Social Psychology Quarterly* 43: 154-164.

Munroe, P.T., and S. Cohn. 1996. "Exploring the Conditions Under Which People Behave Rationally." Paper presented at the Annual Meeting of the West Coast Group Processes Conference, San Jose, CA.

Munroe, P.T., G. Tootell, and T. Kuhn. 1995. "Agreements as a Function of Initial Choice and Stay Response Probabilities in Status Characteristics Research." *Small Group Research* 26: 427-441.

Nydegger, R.V., and G. Owen. 1977. "The Norm of Equity in a Three-Person Majority Game." *Behavioral Science* 22: 32-37.

Owen, G. 1982. *Game Theory.* 2nd edition New York: Academic Press.

Perrow, C. 1970. "Departmental Power and Perspectives in Industrial Firms." In *Power in Organizations,* edited by M. Zald, Nashville, TN: Vanderbuilt University Press.

Pfeffer, J. 1981. *Power in Organizations.* Marshfield, MA: Pitman.

Pinter, C.C. 1971. *Set Theory.* Reading, MA: Addison-Wesley.

Popper, K.R. 1959. *The Logic of Scientific Discovery.* New York: Basic Books.

Pospesel, H. 1984. *Introduction to Logic: Propositional Logic.* 2nd edition, Englewood Cliffs, NJ: Prentice-Hall.

Rescher, N. 1964. *Introduction to Logic.* New York: St. Martin's Press.

Roethlisberger, F., and W.J. Dickson. 1939 [1964]. *Management and the Worker.* New York: John Wiley and Sons.

Stogdill, R.M. 1972. "Group Productivity, Drive, and Cohesiveness." *Organizational Behavior and Human Performance,* 8: 26-43.

Stoll, R.R. 1963. *Introduction to Set Theory and Logic.* San Francisco: W.H. Freeman and Company.

Suppes, P. 1957. *Introduction to Logic.* New York: Van Nostrand Reinhold Company.

Stouffer, S.A., E.A. Suchman, L.C. Devinney, S.A. Star, and R.M. Williams Jr. 1949. *The American Soldier (Studies in Social Psychology in World War II, Vol. I).* Princeton, NJ: Princeton University Press.

Tootell, G., L. Mason, J. Taraldson, M. Barnhill, and P. Prather. 1986. "The Independence of Norms in Small Groups." *International Journal of Small Group Research,* 2(1): 43-59.

Tootell, G., and P.T. Munroe. 1997. "Social Network Theory and Labor Productivity: Some Consequences of Nonnegative Solutions of Problems Involving Square Matrices." Technical report, Department of Sociology, San Jose State University, San Jose, CA.

Troyer, L., S. Silver, and G. Watkins. 1994. "Investigating the Process of Social Influence in Group Decision Making: An Event History Analysis of Status and Information Exchange on Organizational Teams." Paper presented at the annual meeting of the American Sociological Association, Los Angeles, CA.

von Neumann, J., and O. Morgenstern. 1944. *Theory of Games and Economic Behavior.* New York: Wiley.

Wagner, D.G., and J. Berger. 1993. "Status Characteristics Theory: The Growth of a Program." In *Theoretical Research Programs, Studies in the Growth of a Theory,* edited by J. Berger and M. Zelditch Jr. Stanford, CA: Stanford University Press.

Walker, H.A., and B.P. Cohen. 1985. "Scope Statements: Imperatives for Evaluating Theory." *American Sociological Review,* 50: 288-301.

Webster, M. Jr. and J. Driskell. 1978. "Status Generalization: A Review and Some New Data." *American Sociological Review,* 43: 220-236.

Willer, D., and J. Skvoretz. 1997. "Games and Structures." *Rationality and Society* 9(1): 5-35.

Williamson, O. 1975. *Markets and Hierarchies.* New York: Free Press.

Zelditch, M., Jr., W. Harris, G. M. Thomas, and H. A. Walker. 1983. "Decisions, Nondecisions, and Metadecisions." In *Research in Social Movements, Conflicts, and Change,* edited by L. Kreisberg. Stamford, CT: JAI Press.

J A I   P R E S S

Advances in Group Processes

Edited by **Edward J. Lawler**, *Department of Organizational Behavior, Cornell University*

Advances in Group Processes publishes theoretical, review, and empirically-based papers on group phenomena. The series adopts a broad conception of "group processes" consistent with prevailing ones in the social psychological literature. In addition to topics such as status processes, group structure, and decision making, the series considers work on interpersonal behavior in dyads (i.e., the smallest group), individual group relations. Contributors to the series include not only sociologists but also scholars from other disciplines, such as psychology and organizational behavior.

Volume 14, 1997, 331 pp. $73.25/£47.00
ISBN 0-7623-0172-4

CONTENTS: Preface, *Barry Markovsky, Michael J. Lovaglia and Lisa Troyer.* Performance Under Different Contingent Reward Systems: A Reconceptualization of the Cooperative-Competitive-Individualistic Literature, *Jerome M. Chertkoff and Debra J. Mesch.* A Reformulated Social Identity Theory, *Christopher Barnum.* Decision Making in a Dyad's Response to a Fire Alarm: A Computer Simulation Investigation, *William E. Feinberg and Norris R. Johnson.* A Solidaristic Theory of Social Order, *Satoshi Kanazawa.* Comfort Regulation as a Morphogenetic Principle: Local Dynamics of Dominance, Competition, and Attachment, *Thomas S. Smith and Gregory T. Stevens.* Transitions in Teamwork in New Organizational Forms, *Gerardine DeSanctis and Marshall Scott Poole.* "I Think We Can, I Think We Can . . .": The Role of Efficacy Beliefs in Group and Team Effectiveness, *Leann J. Mischel and Gregory Northcraft.* Network Connection and Exchange Ratios: Theory, Predictions and Experimental Tests, *David Willer and John Skvoretz.* Who Benefits from Being Bold: The Interactive Effects of Task Cues and Status Characteristics on Influence in Mock Jury Groups, *Lisa Slattery Rashotte and Lynn Smith-Lovin.* The Theory of Structural Ritualization, *J. David Knottnerus.* Grounding Groups in Theory: Functional, Cognitive, and Structural Interdependencies, *Siegwart Lindenberg.*

Also Available:
Volumes 1-13 (1984-1996) $73.25/£47.00 each

Research in the Sociology of Organizations

Edited by **Samuel B. Bacharach,**
New York State School of Industrial and
Labor Relations, Cornell University

Volume 15, 1998, 262 pp. $78.50/£49.95
ISBN 0-7623-0180-5

CONTENTS: Introduction: Research on Organizations and Deviance—Some Basic Concerns, *Peter A. Bamberger and William J. Sonnenstuhl.* PART I. BRIDGING THE MICRO-MACRO GAP IN THEORY AND PRACTICE. Subcultures and Deviant Behavior in the Organizational Context, *James W. Coleman and Linda L. Ramos.* Exploring the Micro-Macro Link in Corporate Crime Research, *Sally S. Simpson, Raymond Paternoster, and Nicole Leeper Piquero.* PART II. MULTILEVEL ANALYSES OF DEVIANCE OF ORGANIZA-TIONS. Antitrust and Organizational Deviance, *Gilbert Geis and Lawrence S. Salinger.* Embeddedness of Interorganiza-tional Corporate Crime in the 1980s: Securities Fraud of Banks and Investment Banks, *Mary Zey.* PART III. MULTI-LEVEL ANALYSES OF DEVIANCE IN ORGANIZATIONS. Understanding Organizational Insider-Perpetrated Work-place Aggression: An Integrative Model, *Constant D. Beugré.* Organizations as Targets and Triggers of Aggres-sion and Violence: Framing Rational Explanations for Dra-matic Organizational Deviance, *Christine M. Pearson.* Everyday Struggles at the Workplace: The Nature and Impli-cations of Routine Resistance in Contemporary Organiza-tions, *Anshuman Prasad and Pushkala Prasad.*

Also Available:

Volumes 1-14 (1982-1996) $78.50/£49.95 each

JAI PRESS INC.
100 Prospect Street, P. O. Box 811
Stamford, Connecticut 06904-0811

Studies in Symbolic Interaction

Edited by **Norman K. Denzin,** *Institute of Communications Research, University of Illinois*

Volume 21, 1997, 282 pp. $78.50/£49.95
ISBN 0-7623-0380-8

CONTENTS: PART I. REMEMBERING ANSELM STRAUSS. Memorial Session for Anselm Strauss, Toronto, 1997. A Collective Tribute to Anselm Strauss, *Kathy Charmaz, Virginia Oleson.* Introductory Remarks, *Virginia Oleson.* Anselm Strauss (a tribute): Contributions to Symbolic Interactionism, *Robert Prus.* Anselm Strauss: A British Memoir, *Robert Dingwall.* Professions, Work and Organizations: Comments on the Contributions of Anselm Strauss, *Mayer N. Zald.* Anselm Strauss and the Generic Importance of His Work in Structuring My Research, *Jacqueline P. Wiseman.* Remembering Anselm, *Norman K. Denzin.* The Sociologists as Author: A Homage to Anselm Strauss, *Richard Koffler.* Anselm's Festschrift, *David Maines.* Another Remembrance: Anselm Strauss: An Appreciation, *Susan Leigh Star.* PART II. THE PRAGMATIC HERITAGE. Me(a)diating the Past: Reflections on the Problem-Solving Potential of Disciplinary Histories, *Regina Hewitt.* The Reemergence of John Dewey and American Pragmatism, *Gideon Sjoberg, Elizabeth Gill, Boyd Littrell, Norma Williams.* PART III. READING SELF, MEDIA, AND CULTURE. Natural-Born Oranges: From Modern Anti-Hero to Postmodern Media Stars, *Andrea Fontana and Simon Gottschalk.* The Pains of Everyday Life: Between DSM1 and the Postmodern, *Simon Gottschalk.* Using a Nonsociological Text to Understand Sociological Classics: Godot and the Postmodern Challenge to Sociology, *William Reese II and Michael Katovich.* Video Games: Analyzing Gender Identity and Violence in this New Virtual Reality, *Sean Gilmore and Alicia Crissman.* The Slanted Smile Factory: Emotion Management in Tokyo Disneyland, *Aviad Raz.* Riding the Black Ship, *Aviad Raz.* The Social Creation of Deviant Status: Gender, Race, and Criminality in Antebellum Louisiana, *Daniel Dotter and Marianne Fishert-Giorlando.*

Also Available:

Volumes 1-6, 8, 9-20 (1978-1996)
  + Supplements 1, 3 (1985-1997) $78.50/£49.95 each
Volumes 7, 10
  + Supplement 2 (2 part sets) $157.00/£99.90 each

Current Research on Occupations and Professions

Edited by **Helena Z. Lopata,**
Department of Sociology and Anthropology,
Loyola University, Chicago

Volume 10, Jobs in Context:
Circles and Settings
1998, 272 pp. $78.50/£49.95
ISBN 0-7623-0034-5

Also Available:
Volumes 1-9 (1980-1996) $78.50/£49.95 each

JAI PRESS INC.
100 Prospect Street, P. O. Box 811
Stamford, Connecticut 06904-0811

J A I

P R E S S

Religion and the Social Order

Edited by **David G. Bromley,** *Department of Sociology and Anthropology, Virginia Commonwealth University*

Volume 7, Leaving Religion and Religious Life: Patterns and Dynamics
1997, 329 pp. $73.25/£47.00
ISBN 0-7623-0251-1

Edited by **Mordecai Bar-Lev,** *Bar-Ilan University* and **William Shaffir,** *Department of Sociology, McMaster University*

The internationally renowned group of contributors to this volume focus on the patterns and processes connected with leaving religion. The papers range from theoretical analyses of the dynamics underlying religious exiting to case studies examining specific instances of distancing from and departing a religious lifestyle. Leaving Religion and Religious Life provides a much needed investigation of the problem and its effect on formal religious institutions as well as the individuals who elect to dramatically alter their religious way of life.

CONTENTS: Preface. Introduction. Leaving Religions: An Inventory of Some Elementary Concepts, *J. Simpson.* Falling from the New Faiths: Toward an Integrated Model of Religious Affiliation/Disaffiliation, *D. Bromley.* Organized Humanism in Canada: An Expression of Secular Reaffiliation, *J. McTaggart.* Defection, Disengagement and Dissent: The Dynamics of Religious Change in the United States, *W.C. Roof and S. Landres.* Patterns of Religious Separation and Adherence in Contemporary Australia, *T. Lovat.* Atheism, Religion, and Indifference in the Two Pars of Germany: Before and After 1989, *J. Henkys and F. Schweitzer.* Leaving the Distant Church: The Danish Experience, *H. Iverson.* The Changing Face of the British Churches: 1975-1995, *L.J. Francis.* Culture-Specific Factors which Cause Jews in Israel to Abandon Religious Practice, *M. Bar-Lev, A. Leslau, and N. Ne'eman.* Disaffiliation: The Experience of Haredi Jews, *W. Shaffir.*

Also Available:
Volumes 1-2, 4-6 (1991-1996) $73.25/£47.00 each
    Volume 3 (2 part set) $146.50/£94.00